LOST
IN THE
MIDDLE

LOST
IN THE
MIDDLE

Midlife and the Grace of God

PAUL DAVID TRIPP

Shepherd Press
Wapwallopen, PA

ISBN 0-9723046-8-1

Shepherd Press
PO Box 24
Wapwallopen, PA 18660
www.shepherdpress.com
(800) 338-1445

Graphic Layout and Design by Tobias' Outerwear for Books
Interior Design and Typesetting by Lakeside Design Plus

Manufactured in the United States of America

To Dave and Ed

You have been my teachers, friends, and partners in ministry for 20 years. I am grateful for all the ways you have helped me to see, to think, and to hear. Most of all I am thankful for how you have helped me grow in love and appreciation for my Lord.

Contents

Preface: A New Awareness

I don't believe one grows older. I think that what happens early on in life is that at a certain age one stands still and stagnates. —T. S. Eliot

There is still no cure for the common birthday.
—John Glenn

I like to be busy. I don't like to analyze everything, because it gets in the way of doing. For me, one day of frenetic activity layers over another, day after day, until days have become weeks, weeks have become months, and months have become years. I try to spend most of my time looking forward, living expectantly. But recently, in one powerful moment, life thundered in on me with a power I was unprepared for. It wasn't a dramatic moment. No one in the room even noticed.

It was Christmas, a time of year I love. We had decorated the house, wrapped many gifts, and prepared more food than any one family should eat (though we tried). We had just finished our wonderful Christmas day feast and were all sitting around the table engaged in a gaggle of random, interweaving conversations, when for no reason I got quiet and looked across the table. To my surprise I saw two men sitting across from me discussing their careers, one in marketing and the other in design. My immediate thought was, *Where did these men come from? What right do they have intruding on our family Christmas?* As I listened further I realized these men weren't interlopers; they were my sons! Men, not boys! Why weren't they discussing skateboarding or arguing over who gets to do his wash first?

It didn't seem possible that they could be my sons. *I'm not that old! There simply haven't been enough years. There are things I wanted to do with them. This whole thing just is not possible,* I said to myself. I was alone in my head, and no one around me had a clue that all of a sudden my eyes had been opened. Things would never again be the same.

I now have to look up to speak to my youngest child, who is in college. The old proverbial nest is, in fact, empty. I am no longer a newly married man. I am no longer a young pastor. I am no longer the father of four young children, or even a bunch of teenagers. I am not about to celebrate my tenth anniversary or the purchase of our first home. I am not facing the excitement and fear of a new place of ministry. I am not embarking on the first grand family vacation. I am not in the midst of studying for an advanced degree.

Most of my family firsts are behind me. I am not making the first breakfast in bed for my wife. Our children have all spoken their first words, taken their first steps, had their first day at school, finished their first music lesson, and survived their first overnight stay with a friend. They have all attempted their first sport, graduated from their first school, had their first job, and survived their first romance.

There have been scores of report cards and progress reports. There have been countless teacher's conferences, athletic events, camps, and proms. There have been more day-trips, weekends away, and vacations than I am able to recount. There have been endless moments of discipline, correction, and instruction. We have purchased mountains of clothes, truckloads of food, and enough notebook paper to reforest the Amazon!

Luella and I have talked and prayed, discussed and wept. We have escaped to an endless number of restaurants just to be together. We have gone on many weekend mini-vacations to catch our breath and renew our love. We have left behind a parking lot of used-up vehicles, a warehouse of out-grown clothes, and mounds of broken glasses, dishes, and decorations—the artifacts of a family civilization gone by.

Yet, it all passed by with blinding speed and went largely unnoticed—until that watershed Christmas day. It was a moment of profound personal awareness. I finally saw it: I am not young anymore! I have a huge chunk of my life behind me. I have more life behind me than ahead of me, and if you are reading this book, there is a good possibility you do, too.

The next day, things were different. As I got out of bed, I was more aware of aches and pains than I had been before. The face I shaved seemed older, and I had more gray hair than I had noticed before. I found myself, in the quiet moments, musing about the past more than I ever had before. My eyes were open, and I couldn't shut them anymore.

It is hard to make sense out of your own story while you're living in the middle of it. But God hasn't left us to wander through the hallways of our own dramas. He has given us a bigger story, the story of redemption that fills Scripture's pages. This grand story enables us not only to exegete the internal and external realities of our own stories, but more importantly, to come to know him in new and glorious ways.

The Bible never discusses midlife, just like it never discusses teenagers. Yet the Bible is able to unpack any of life's experiences because it was written by the One who made them all. You do not have to be lost in the middle of your own story. You do not have to be paralyzed by regret, defeated by aging, and discouraged by the passing of your dreams. You do not have to make greater trouble out of the trouble you are already experiencing. This time of life, which can seem like the end of many things, can actually welcome you to a brand new way of living. As is so often the case in your walk with the Lord, this moment of pain is also a moment of grace. Because of him, there is hope for you on the other side.

Life on this side of glory is hard. This world *is* a broken place. You will face things that beat at the borders of your faith. Because of this, all of us need to occasionally step back, slow down, and stop, look, and listen. My hope is that *Lost in the Middle* will help you to do just that.

One final word: Although this book is targeted at those who are struggling with the issues of midlife, it has a much broader net than that. *Lost in the Middle* can help all who are struggling with life in this broken world and have lost their way. The Bible speaks with power and practicality to everything you are facing, thinking, and feeling. The God who seems so distant to you in this moment is actually near and active. *Lost in the Middle* is written to give you eyes to see him, to see yourself more clearly, and to find the functional hope you need to carry on.

Paul David Tripp
March 2004

Introduction: The Bible and Midlife

Why do you say, O Jacob,
and complain, O Israel,
"My way is hidden from the LORD*;*
my cause is disregarded by my God"?
Do you not know?
Have you not heard?
The LORD *is the everlasting God,*
the Creator of the ends of the earth.
He will not grow tired or weary,
and his understanding no one can fathom.
He gives strength to the weary
and increases the power of the weak.
Even youths grow tired and weary,
and young men stumble and fall;
but those who hope in the LORD
will renew their strength.
They will soar on wings like eagles;
they will run and not grow weary,
they will walk and not be faint.

—ISAIAH

Let me present you with two seemingly contradictory statements and then connect them for you:

- The Bible has nothing whatsoever to say about midlife crisis.
- The Bible tells you everything you need to know about midlife crisis.

Let's consider the first statement. If you go to Scripture looking for midlife crisis as a topic, you will not find anything. Of course, this is true with many topics. As a result, many Christians unwittingly adopt a "Bible-for-the-religious-part-of-my-life" perspective on Scripture. They tend to seek the Bible's help only where it has spoken clearly about certain topics. As a result they will tend to look elsewhere for the wisdom they need in the vast areas of life that are not *directly* addressed within the pages of Scripture.

Or they may fall into another subtle error. If they are Christians, they know that the Bible is a book filled with stunning wisdom revealed by the God who is the source of all wisdom. They will be hungry to know his mind in every area of their lives. Driven by this zeal, they may bend, twist, and stretch Scripture to provide the information that they are seeking.

Now, both groups of people have made the same mistake. Both view the Bible as God's great encyclopedia, a topical index of human problems and divine solutions. The one person is a bit sad that the Bible doesn't speak to more of life. The other person is growingly convinced that the Bible speaks to more topics than he first thought. Both have missed the genius, the core of what the Bible is really about.

Because the Bible is not an encyclopedia, it is right to say that the Bible has nothing whatsoever to say about midlife crisis. In this book we are not going to cull through the history, poetry, prophecy, and teachings of Scripture hunting for the embedded midlife material. We're not going to wonder if David's sin with Bathsheba was a midlife crisis, or if Moses was having a midlife moment when he wrongly whacked the rock for water. We won't look at the Gospels for any evidence that Jesus struggled with midlife temptation. This is simply not what the Bible is, or how it has been organized. Yet we will not go elsewhere for the truth and wisdom that we need.

The Bible is a narrative, and because it is a narrative, it tells us everything we need to know about midlife concerns. The Bible is the great story of redemption that encompasses the stories of every human life. It is *the* overarching "everything" story. It is comprehensive in scope without being exhaustive in content. It gives us wisdom for everything without directly discussing every particular thing.

The great narrative of the Word of God gives me everything I need to know about God, about myself, about the purpose and meaning of life, and about what is true, good, and beautiful. The Bible is the lens through which I look at all of life. In it I find the truths, values, goals, and hopes that are meant to give shape and direction to my life. All of these things are cords woven into the fabric of one grand and amazing story. It is God's story. He is the principal actor and the grand hero. Without his story, the doctrines, principles, commands, and promises make no sense whatsoever.

In light of this story, every passage of Scripture reveals things about God, about people, about life in this fallen world, about redemption and eternity, which helps me understand whatever I am considering at the moment. For example, most of what the Bible has to say about marriage is not found in the passages that explicitly discuss marriage. Psalm 73 is a passage on marriage because it exegetes one kind of struggle that every person living in the fallen world will experience. 1 Peter 1 is a passage on marriage because it lays out what God is doing in the period of time between our salvation and his coming—the period of time in which every marriage exists. Revelation 5 is a passage on marriage because it allows us to eavesdrop on eternity and thus to clarify the values that must structure every Christian marriage.

So, even though the Bible never directly discusses the experience of midlife crisis, it is a rich resource for understanding it and for learning how to respond to it. But before we examine the particular experiences of midlife, it is important to examine how four biblical perspectives exegete or interpret the deepest issues of every human experience.

The Bible Presents Us with a Real World

You cannot read very long before encountering the shocking honesty of the Bible. Living in the fallen world isn't minimized or sugar coated. As early as the fourth chapter of Genesis, you encounter a sibling homicide—the kind of account that would cause you to shiver if you read it in your morning newspaper. From domestic violence to war, plagues, and diseases; from vicious animals and sexual perversity to corrupt government; Scripture unflinchingly depicts the daily drama of real life. It is a world of broken promises, failed expectations, and dashed dreams. It is a world where bad people seem to prosper and good people find themselves suffering. It is a world where good things go bad, where fresh things decay, where young things grow old, and strong things grow weak. It is a familiar world because it is the same world we live in.

The Bible is also honest about *why* the world is the way it is. Why does Cain kill Abel? Why is a global flood necessary? Why are spouses ever unfaithful? Why does David need to run from his own son Absalom? Why do people tell lies? Why does Judas betray the Messiah? Why do children rebel against their parents? Why is debauchery ever attractive? Why is there any philosophy that competes with the truth? The Bible rises boldly to answer these questions that capture the experience of every person.

The explanation Scripture gives may seem simple, yet it is the only perspective that is extensive enough to span the vast range of what is wrong, from dark inner personal motivations to wide cultural, historical, and environmental maladies. We live in a world that has been bent and twisted by a force so fundamental, so powerful, that it literally impacts every human thought, every human intention, every situation, every experience of society and every moment of history. This force is the inescapable pathology of the created universe. It is sin. One syllable, three letters in English, yet a concept without which it is impossible to ever understand your life or mine.

This foundational issue is powerfully unfolded in Romans 8:20–22:

> *For the creation was subjected to frustration, not by its own choice, but by the will of the one who subjected it, in hope that the creation itself will be liberated from its bondage to decay and brought into the glorious freedom of the children of God. We know that the whole creation has been groaning as in the pains of childbirth right up to the present time.*

What a powerful description! Three phrases in this short passage capture real life in the fallen world. First, the creation was *subjected to frustration*. Things simply don't work the way that they were ordained to work. Next, Paul says that the world is in *bondage to decay*. The mournful fact is that everything is in the process of dying. Finally, he says that the creation *groans as in pains of childbirth*. The world we live in writhes in pain so acute that it cannot be ignored.

All of these realities find concrete expression in the pages of Scripture. From the drama of wars between nations (Joshua) to the dark tunnel of personal despair (Psalm 88), from the joys of a long-awaited infant's birth (Luke 1) to the mourners at a dead man's tomb (John 11), the Bible captures what real life is about with a profound familiarity and clarity.

So how does the Bible help us deal with a topic like midlife? By providing us with *context*—an honest and expansive portrayal of the real world. Many people are lost simply because they do not understand the context in which they live, work, play, and worship. They are constantly surprised and unprepared because they have not benefited from the functional wisdom that the Bible affords.

The Bible Introduces Us to Real People

The characters of the Bible are not wax figures in a museum of human nobility. Nor are they cartoon characters with saccharine smiles and melodic voices. We recognize the people of the Bible because they are just like us. Adam and Eve are skillful blame-shifters. King Saul is paranoid and duplicitous. Peter is inexplicably proud. When we gaze into the pages of Scripture we encounter people in familiar relationships: they're sons and daughters, husbands and wives, preachers and poets. We see crowds of onlookers, needy beggars on the street, political leaders caught between two agendas, people of diverse ethnicities and social classes, teachers and students, craftsmen and artisans, lawyers and judges, the elderly and the very young. A rich display of the variegated colors of humanity dyes almost every page of Scripture.

God's Word also carefully displays the full range of human passion. We see joy and rejoicing, grief and mourning, fear and timidity, contentment and delight, jealousy and greed, faith and doubt, patience and perseverance. We see rage, discouragement, hatred, self-sacrificing love, lust, obsession, and selfishness. We are able to witness how human beings respond to the situations and people around them. And we are ushered into the hallways of human hearts to examine their thoughts, inspect their desires, and understand their choices. In the process we ourselves are exposed and confronted.

Even the Bible's commands and principles depict real flesh-and-blood humanity, addressing the same mundane issues that every human being experiences. These commands speak to the eyes, the tongue, the hands, and the mind. They tell you how to respond to mistreatment, how to plan for the future, how to view your government, how to reconcile a relationship, how to instruct and correct a child, how to lead a church, how to love your husband or wife, how to treat the elderly, and how to live with your neighbor.

There is no better means of self-knowledge and self-exposure than the mirror of Scripture. As I examine myself in its light, I learn fundamental things about myself that have practical implications for everything I encounter in this broken world. The Bible exposes us for who we really are.

Scripture never allows us to believe in a neutral, undirected, or unmotivated humanity. It requires us to admit that behind everything we do or say, we are pursuing *something*—some hope or dream or thing that we refuse to live without. There are things we value so much that we will willingly sacrifice other good things to get them. We will debase our humanity in order to deify the creation. The very things we seek to possess begin to possess us. We live for shadow glories and forget the only Glory that is worth living for.

In its masterful portraiture of humanity, the Bible requires us to make one painfully humbling admission—the one confession we work so hard to avoid: *that our deepest, most pervasive, and most abiding problem is us!* If you can humbly make this admission, your life will never be the same.

Once again, see how this connects to midlife. Why is it that so many people in Western culture tend to lose their way during this time of life? Because all the labyrinthine pathways of human existence on which Scripture takes us lead to one place. They lead to *us*. Only here will we ever understand the true nature of our need and the true magnitude of God's provision.

The Bible Calls Us to the Worship of a Real God

The God of Scripture is not the hero of myth. He is not the projection of weak minds who simply need something more to depend on than themselves. He, the creator, sustainer, and ruler of all that is, is the only being in the universe worthy of worship. The light of his glory shines on every page of Scripture. His voice is heard first, he scripts the end of the drama, and every scene in between is dominated by his presence.

He exists without a beginning and has no need of sustenance. He is the ultimate in wisdom yet has never had a single teacher. He made everything that exists but had no raw materials with which to work. He has never failed and has no personal flaw. Every word he has spoken is true, and every promise he has ever made comes true. He is never confused, dismayed, or overwhelmed. He is never wrongfully jealous, demanding, or enraged. He is present everywhere all at once. There is no circumstance that is not under his control. All things continue to work because he holds everything together by the power of his will.

He has the power to damn but delights to forgive. He can move mountains but is tender, gentle, and kind. His wisdom and knowledge are beyond our imagination, yet he speaks in simple words that anyone can understand. He is the source of all true justice, yet he is abundant in mercy. He is distant in his glory yet ever present and ever near. He demands our allegiance but gives us the power to obey. He calls us to follow but patiently allows us to learn and grow. Every day he gives us what we have not achieved and could not earn.

Yet this grand and glorious God, for the purpose of redemption, becomes a man. The untraversable line between Creator and creature is crossed. The Word becomes flesh. The feet of God touch earth! The voice of God is heard on earth! The LORD comes as the Second Adam, the Word of Life, the Final Priest, and the Sacrificial Lamb. He satisfies God's requirements, he atones for God's anger, and he defeats death.

This meeting of glory and humanity reveals all other gods to be the counterfeits that they actually are, figments of man's imagination and images made by man's hand. It is only the God of ultimate glory and incarnating grace who offers what is needed in the face of the horrible personal and environmental ravages of sin. He who created it all has faced what we have faced. He who is pure and holy paid the ultimate price for sin. He who is the creator of life walked away from death. He can help!

How does all of this help us as we approach the experience of midlife? The revelation of God in Scripture is the only place to find real hope. He is the only one who is at once completely above everything that we face yet is intimately familiar with all of it by personal experience. We run to him because he is Lord over it all and has the power to help.

The Bible Welcomes Us to Real Redemption

The world is full of false systems of redemption. Government, education, philosophy, sociology, and psychology all promise redemption, yet none can deliver, because human systems can never redeem. If they could have dealt with the comprehensive and devastating results of sin, Jesus would have never come. He came to earth to suffer and die, because that was precisely what was needed. The Bible invites me to the hope that can only be found in a Redeemer. I need more than help; I need rescue. I need someone to do for me what I could not do for myself. What I grapple with most is not the evil outside of me, but the evil inside of me. If there is no help and hope for what is *inside* of me, there is no way that I will ever properly deal with what is *outside* of me.

Two biblical passages illustrate the need for real redemption. The first passage, Genesis 6:5, is devastating in its portrayal of the comprehensive and internal nature of our struggle with sin. "The LORD saw how great man's wickedness on the earth had become, and that every inclination of the thoughts of his heart was only evil all the time." Wow! Let these words sink in. Sin is about something more foundational than doing what is wrong or failing to do what is right. Sin dyes every cell of the heart and twists everything we do toward evil. We want to believe that we are better than that. We want to hold on to the fantasy of the pure and untainted intention. We want to think that our gossip was really a prayer request. We want to think that it was not ugly self-absorption but physical tiredness that made us irritable. We want to believe that it was zeal for truth not self-righteous impatience that caused us to speak loudly and sharply. Proverbs 16:2 says, "All a man's ways seem innocent to him, but motives are weighed by the LORD."

Genesis 6 rips open our hearts and reveals the sin at the depths of our every thought and every intention. If this is true, then you cannot educate me out of it. You cannot exercise enough power over me to squelch its effects. You cannot provide practical techniques for rising above it. Without divine help I am riddled with the cancer of sin, and my prognosis is death. Anything that cannot eradicate this cancer within is powerless to help me.

But there is a second passage the must be placed alongside of Genesis 6.

> *The Son is the radiance of God's glory and the exact representation of his being, sustaining all things by his powerful word. After he had provided purification for sins,* ***he sat down*** *at the right hand of the Majesty in heaven.*
> (Hebrews 1:3, emphasis mine)

With three words, "*he sat down*," the writer of Hebrews captures the completeness of Christ's work. Jesus did everything that was needed to deal with every one of sin's effects. He was able to do what the Old Testament priests could never do: to stop.

The Old Testament priests were called to sacrifice for the ongoing sins of God's people. Exhausted and knee-deep in blood, they offered sacrifice after sacrifice, day after day. If we viewed the scene, we would find it nauseating. It wasn't just the daily offerings but dozens of daily, weekly, and seasonal sacrifices offered according to the religious calendar. Thousands of animals would be slaughtered every year. Yet it was never enough. Before one layer of blood dried, more was sprinkled. The stench of burning flesh never abated. This sacrificial labor was never permitted to stop, because the power of sin was never broken and the penalty for sin never fully paid for. So it is an amazing thing to read that after Jesus did his work, *he sat down*! The only reason he could have possibly sat down is that he had done everything that needed to be done to deal with every aspect of sin. Full and complete redemption had been provided.

Put the following two Bible phrases together and you will begin to understand the magnitude and practicality of the redemption that could only be supplied by Christ Jesus: "Every inclination of the thoughts of his heart was only evil all the time," and "After he had provided purification for sins, he sat down." In Scripture's redemption story, the sadness of the totality of our depravity kisses the celebration of the totality of Christ's provision. God is satisfied, Christ has sat down, and there is hope for us—a practical hope stretching from now to the ends of eternity. As a result, we come to every topic of our lives as the saddest and the most celebrant people on earth. This functional tension between sadness and celebration results in the kind of practical wisdom that the Bible alone affords. Midlife must be viewed from these two redemptive perspectives.

Boiling It all Down

These four biblical perspectives (Real World, Real People, Real God, Real Redemption) give us essential wisdom for anything we will ever face in human life. Only when we see the world exegeted as it really is, ourselves as we really are, God in all his glory, and the completeness of the Redeemer's work, can we have a balanced and functionally worthwhile perspective on anything.

Let me detail what these four perspectives provide for us as we approach a topic like midlife.

1. ***A comprehensive worldview that addresses everything that is.*** Scripture is not exhaustive in that it directly addresses every subject, but it is comprehensive in that it gives information for understanding all aspects of reality.

2. ***Practical perspectives on every human problem.*** The Bible has something to say about everything that is important for human life. It gives us an essential understanding of these things and how we should respond to them.

3. ***Life before death.*** The Bible doesn't simply promise that some day in distant eternity we will know life. The Bible calls us to embrace a quality of life *now* that would otherwise be impossible without the person and work of the Lord Jesus.

4. ***Real hope of self-knowledge.*** You do not have to be trapped in the prison of personal spiritual blindness. You can see, know, and understand yourself, even to the thoughts and motives of your own heart. This is possible because the Bible functions as the ultimate mirror. When you gaze into it, you see yourself as you really are.

5. ***Practical help for the deepest issues of the human experience.*** In the Bible I find the Creator who made me and therefore knows everything about me. I find a Savior who walked on earth in my shoes and understands everything about my experience. The Bible faces the deepest issues of the human experience head-on, with bright hope and functional wisdom.

6. ***Real hope for lasting personal change.*** Because Christ has come, change is really possible. The Bible, in all of its shocking honesty, is also shockingly positive and hopeful. There is not a cynical page in all of Scripture. There is no hint of giving up. The promise of radical and lasting personal change brightens every dark corner of sin that is found in Scripture.

7. ***Real comfort.*** The more you read the Bible, the more you realize that no human experience is outside of the scope of the Gospel. God understands it all, and his Son has covered it all. Every day we can allow ourselves to be comforted with the amazing biblical reality that provision has been made for everything we will face.

As we begin a journey of biblical and personal discovery, we must recognize the personal challenge that these seven benefits of a biblical perspective lay before us. Too often, even in our celebration of the wisdom of Scripture, we hold it separate from the situations and relationships of our daily lives. Ask yourself, right now, where you have allowed yourself to respond to the push and pull of life in this fallen world in less than biblical ways. Where have you failed to observe scripture's honest depiction of humanity and reserved its wisdom for the "religious" part of your life? Where have you sought insight into particular life challenges from every source *except* the Bible? Where have you ignored the internal source of your problems and relentlessly sought to place blame outside of yourself? Where have you reduced Christ's work to forgiveness of sins and lost hope in the total renovation of your heart, your relationships, and your world?

It is easy to pursue a religion of the mind; it is another thing to surrender your heart, and therefore every aspect of your life, to God. The hope of this book is nothing short of changed hearts leading to radically transformed lives. We cannot settle for expanding knowledge and enhanced understanding. We cannot because God will not. God demands all of us. He will not settle for a portion of who we are. Accordingly, as we begin our examination of the crisis that often breaks out in midlife, I urge you to make the following commitments:

1. I will carefully examine and unpack this important period of my life.
2. I will seek to understand all that I unpack from the vantage point of Scripture.
3. I will look at myself in the always-accurate mirror of the Word of God.
4. I will personally identify and own the areas in which change is needed.
5. I will resolve to act on the basis of the hope and help that is found in the Lord Jesus Christ.

Will you make these commitments as we take this journey?

Chapter 1

Midlife: A Portrait

I think age is a very high price to pay for maturity.
—Tom Stoppard

I suppose real old age begins when one looks backward rather than forward.
—May Sarton

They were in their late forties, yet that first morning they seemed much older. She slumped into my office as if she really did have the weight of the world on her shoulders. He seemed irritated from the get-go. They had come to talk about their marriage, but whatever problems they were experiencing were the result of something bigger, something unexpected, for which neither of them had been prepared.

They had married right out of college. Bill soon landed a very good job and Tammy got pregnant in their first few months of marriage. They were both delighted with how their lives had turned out. The purchase of their one and only house was soon to follow. Tammy thought she was living everyone's dream: a great husband with a good job, the house of her dreams, and a family on the way. They talked much about the years to come, looking forward to building their family, adding on to their house, and the career advancement that was surely in Bill's future. It all seemed too good to be true.

They found a good church to attend and began to meet couples their age. It seemed like the final piece of the puzzle was in place. Tammy's pregnancy flew by quickly until the last month when she began to experience complications and was sent to bed for the remainder of her pregnancy. It was a violent and painful delivery, followed by the devastating news that she could not get pregnant again. Bill and Tammy were surprised and saddened, but it was soon overshadowed by the joy they felt as they held little Lori in their arms. She was perfectly healthy, right down to ten chubby fingers and ten symmetrical little toes.

Tammy decided that if this was all the family she was going to have, she was going to do it right. She threw her heart and soul into her precious little girl. No job was too arduous or no expense too great. From early morning to late at night, Lori was the center of Tammy's attention. She didn't forget that Bill existed, but she saw Lori as the central focus of her job description. Bill didn't mind. He was very thankful for the amazing gift of this little girl, and he doted on her any way he could.

Soon Lori was in school. Tammy was involved in every way she could with Lori's education. She initiated a volunteer mother's program and worked as a classroom aid. Bill and Tammy enrolled Lori in ballet classes, piano lessons, and gymnastics. Each weeknight was dedicated to Lori's homework, with either mom or dad at her side at all times. Bill and Tammy attended a myriad of performances, recitals, sporting events, and award banquets. They took Lori on every kind of vacation a child would love and sent her to all the best camps. They made sure that she was involved with their church's children's program and then with the youth group.

Eventually Lori was ready to graduate from high school. In all the celebration of her accomplishments, Tammy was dread-ing the moment when Lori would be out of the house and no longer at the top of her personal job description. So when Lori was awarded a scholarship to a local university, Tammy was greatly relieved. Although Lori lived in a dorm, she was home every weekend and at least one night per week for supper. And because she was still in town, Bill and Tammy were able to participate in many of her activities.

Then in September of her senior year in college, Lori met the man of her dreams. Tammy knew that she should be delighted for her daughter, but she was not. A sense of dread followed her throughout her days. She joyfully participated in all of the wedding planning, determined that Lori would have the most perfect wedding that she could pull off. Yet she was often sad and tearful during the process. Just before the wedding, Lori's fiancé surprised her with the news that he had been given an unexpected job offer in Seattle. They flew out for the weekend and soon concluded that it was an offer they could not refuse. Three days before the wedding, Lori broke the news to her mom and dad; she would be moving three thousand miles away.

Tammy wanted to be happy for Lori, but it felt like she had been told she had cancer, like something inside of her had died. She cried herself to sleep that night and was teary-eyed right through the wedding. Lori and her husband visited Bill and Tammy for one weekend after their honeymoon and then began the long drive to Seattle.

Bill was concerned for Tammy those first few weeks after Lori and her husband left, but he thought she would rebound. She was constantly emotional and strangely silent. It was bad enough that the empty house and the lack of activity made Bill feel old, but he was frustrated by Tammy. He tried getting her away for the weekend, but they came home early because Tammy "didn't feel well." He tried having people over, but Tammy saw it as more of a duty than a delight. He tried getting them enrolled in activities together as a couple, but she showed little interest.

Things didn't get better. There were days when Tammy would spend hours in bed. She barely cooked and seldom did the kind of cleaning that once kept their house looking immaculate. Bill grew more and more irritated with it all. Although he still worked, he had looked forward to the freedom that they would enjoy once their parenting days were over. He had researched places to go and things to do, but Tammy wasn't even interested in going out to eat. Bill's irritation soon became bitterness. "Is this what I worked for?" he thought. "Is this what I get for doing what is right?"

Soon Bill was feeling like he had missed out, like life had passed him by. He was envious of the young families around him. He couldn't help regretting decisions that he and Tammy had made. He began losing interest in his job, and more importantly, entertained subtle doubts about his faith. He was increasingly bitter, angry, and discouraged. It drove him crazy that the only time Tammy seemed to brighten up was when Lori called or visited. He thought maybe he should get a hobby, like restoring a car or buying a motorcycle. After all, he and Tammy did very little together and seldom had an extended conversation.

It was about three years after Lori's departure that Bill realized something was wrong and that it was time for them to seek help. His eyes were opened by their family physician, who had taken Bill aside and told him that Tammy's problems were not physical and did not require medication. She suggested that they needed to talk to someone who could help. That was when they called me.

Although Bill and Tammy's story is unique in its specific details, their struggle is quite typical. We all tend to fall into believing that what is, will always be. We tend to ignore the fact that everything, this side of God, is always changing and that all of creation is in a state of decay. We get lulled to sleep by our frenetic busyness, one day lapping upon another until huge chunks of time have passed. In the meantime we have not noticed how much we, and the things around us, have changed.

Then suddenly, something shocks us into the startling realization that we are way older than we thought and life has changed much more than we had noticed. This realization and the disorientation that flows from it is what our culture calls a midlife crisis. So many people from 35 to 55 go through this experience that in recent years it has received almost as much press as adolescence.

Does everyone have a midlife crisis? Not necessarily. Just as many teenagers never have a tumultuously rebellious adolescence. Yet attending to the potential difficulties and dangers of the teen years has helped both teenagers and parents to be more prepared for it. My hope is that this book will do the same for the hordes of people who are now in, or approaching, the midyears of their adult lives.

A Problem of Interpretation

One of the most important biblical perspectives about people is that human beings think. There is a way in which we never leave our lives alone. We are always picking up our story in our hands, turning it over, and trying to make sense of it all. When doing menial or repetitive tasks, we quickly descend into the caverns of our own minds. We go to sleep, tossing our lives around in our heads, falling asleep without figuring it all out.

Two things are true of every middle-aged person. First, we are aware that *our lives have not worked according to our plan.* You and I could not have written our own stories. We couldn't even have written the story of last week! Our lives have taken twists and turns that we could have never imagined. Some of those turns have left us amazed and thankful while others caused profound pain and loss. In all of our planning and our careful decision making, we are still caught up short, surprised by the details of our own existence.

Two recent experiences powerfully demonstrated that my life is not working out according to my plan. The first took place at the end of a normal day at The Christian Counseling and Educational Foundation. It was 5:30 pm and I was just about to leave when I got a call from my brother, Tedd. Tedd is a very level person. If plan A doesn't work, he is always able to conceive plan B and C all the way to triple Z. He seldom seems distressed or out of sorts. Yet this call was different. The minute I heard his voice, I knew something was very wrong.

What broke that day would forever change us, our family, and everything about it. One conversation, and life had forever changed. We were all shocked. It was a turn in the story that we did not see coming and were ill-prepared to face. Powerful emotions hit fast and hard. Racing thoughts and intense and searching conversations were the order of the day. In an instant it seemed like I had not only lost my family history, but I had lost my identity as well. I was hurt, angry, and at sea. I had been to seminary, but I had never taken the course to prepare me for this. I could not escape it, because, confusing and distressing as it was, it was *my* story.

My second unforeseen experience came in Seoul, South Korea. I was sitting on the platform of the largest Presbyterian church in the world (35,000 members), getting ready to preach in a Sunday afternoon service. I looked out over that sea of Korean faces while listening to familiar hymns being sung in a foreign tongue. In an instant I was overwhelmed. It seemed impossible that Paul Tripp could possibly be invited to sit on this platform, let alone speak! In that moment I was so amazed by my own story that I began to weep. How could it be that I was here? How could it be that this was my life calling? How could it be that I actually get paid to expound the Gospel day after day? How did I get from 3437 North Detroit Avenue, in Toledo, Ohio, to this massive church in the middle of Seoul, South Korea? The more I took it all in, the greater my sense of gratitude and wonder, and the more I wept. I simply couldn't get control of myself. My translator looked over at me with a look of concern that said, "Paul, I'm quite prepared to function as your interpreter, but I haven't prepared my own sermon. You need to get yourself together or this is never going to work!" By God's grace, my tears abated and I stood to preach in the throes of my own amazement at my own story.

Life never works according to our plan because our individual stories are all part of a greater story. The central character of the STORY is sovereign over each detail of our stories. So we will always live with the recognition that there are twists and turns that were never part of our plan for our lives.

But a second thing is also true of every middle-aged person. *We are always trying to figure our lives out.* From the incessant questions of the all-too-curious toddler to the dying queries of the old man, we all are our own private investigators. We sort through the details of our existence every day. Sometimes we are archeologists, sifting through the pottery shards of personal civilizations gone by. Sometimes we are detectives looking for that one clue that will make it all make sense. Sometimes we are philosophers and theologians, bringing the profound questions of life to the detail of our own stories. Sometimes we are diagnosticians, examining the personal symptoms to discover what is wrong. Sometimes we are historians, examining the past for wisdom as we face today. We play all of these roles at one point or another. Yet, our thinking is so constant and so instinctual that we don't realize how incessant and influential it really is.

These two points—that our lives never work according to our plans and that we are always trying to figure out our lives—effectively define and explain the "crisis" of midlife. The disorientation of midlife is the result of the collision of a *powerful personal awareness* and a *powerful personal interpretation*. Now, that should not surprise us, because we do not live by the facts of our experiences, but by the ways that our interpretations have shaped those facts for us. The difficult disorientation of midlife is not because the passage itself is disorienting. Whatever trouble midlife brings to us is essentially caused by the wrong thinking we bring to it. Suddenly we see things about ourselves that have been developing for years but went by unnoticed. We don't respond to our new awareness based on the facts of our age or place in life but based on the meanings we attach to them. These meanings will form and determine how we respond to midlife.

The two elements of *powerful personal awareness* and *powerful personal interpretation* must always be included in whatever we do to understand and deal with the realities of midlife. Think of Bill and Tammy. Lori's departure suddenly opened their eyes to changes in their age and status that had been developing for years but had gone largely unnoticed. The difficulty they experienced was not created by their situation but by a very important interpretive grid which set an agenda for their response.

Sloppy Categories

One of the ways that we make sense out of life is by organizing it into categories. We say God is a Spirit, Sally is a girl, and Fido is a dog. We talk of things being big or small, important or unimportant, trash or treasure, healthy or unhealthy, true or false, and valuable or cheap. We divide things into categories like biological, mechanical, artistic, philosophical, and emotional. We think of things as being Eastern or Western, feminine or masculine, cultured or barbaric, and legal or illegal. Instinctively, we organize things into the little boxes that we carry around in our brains. Sometimes we are wise enough to see that our boxes are too little or too few, but often we are quite skilled at squeezing our story into whatever boxes we happen to be carrying around in our minds. In doing so, we fail to recognize how important and influential this interpretive function is. Life will always look like the categories that you bring to it, and what you do will always be determined by the way you have organized your understanding of your own story.

One of the interpretive problems that gets us into trouble in midlife is that our typical cultural categories for organizing human life are woefully inadequate. We tend to organize the full range of human development into only four categories: child (0-12), youth (13-20), adult (21-65), elderly (65+). When you examine these categories it doesn't take long to uncover their inadequacy. The categories of child, youth, and elderly are relatively brief spans of time, while the category of adult encompasses forty-five years! Consider for a moment the massive differences between a man twenty-one and a man who is sixty-four. Or, let's narrow the scope. Consider the remarkable difference in maturity between a person who is twenty-two and a person who is thirty-five. Emotionally, physically, spiritually, relationally, economically, and socially these two people are in very different places. To say that a person is an adult is to make an observation of such wide generality that it almost means nothing.

The overgeneralized category of adult tends to ignore the fact that as human beings we are always in some kind of process of change. One of the stark differences between the Creator and the creation is that everything on this side of the line is always in some state of change while God is constant in his unchangeableness. The Bible presents all of life as ever changing. Rulers rise up and are cast down. The grass fades and the flowers wither. People grow and mature. Young men become old men. People spiritually pass from death into life. Generations give way to generations. Fools become wise. All that has been created will be different in some way tomorrow. Anticipating change and committing to change is an essential part of a productive Christian life. But we get caught up short. Parents are continually surprised that their baby has suddenly become a teenager. Sons and daughters seem shocked that mom and dad have suddenly become old. Mom can't believe that somehow she woke up to a new title, grandmother. We seem unwilling to accept the fact that we can't do things that we were once capable of doing—a dynamic that keeps emergency rooms busy on the weekends!

We need more robust ways of thinking about human life, growth, and change than broad, age-oriented categories.

Although the Bible does think of people in terms of their age, it has much richer ways of locating and understanding human beings. Let me suggest just one.

It's All about Relationships

Scripture in a very natural way understands people by locating them in four fundamental relationships. The first and most foundational relationship is *my relationship to God*. Everything I am and everything I do is shaped by the health and vitality of this relationship. No matter where you are (location), what is going on around you (situation), and how you are responding to it (behavior), the most important way of understanding yourself is to examine your relationship with God. For example, Adam and Eve were quite unified as husband and wife when they consumed the prohibited fruit. But they were in rebellion against God. In the same way, like every other period of life, midlife powerfully exposes the true condition of our relationship with God.

The second relationship is *my relationship to others*. The Bible always sees people in some kind of community with one another. Even in his saving grace, God is not just giving spiritual birth to a mass of isolated saved individuals, but as Paul says in Titus, "a people for his own possession" (NASB). I am a child or a parent. I am a husband or a wife. I am a neighbor or a friend. I am a citizen of the kingdom of God. I am a covenant child, a member of the body of Christ and a stone in the temple in which God dwells. From Genesis 2 on, the Bible always looks at people from the vantage point of the communities to which they have been called. Human life is about relationships, and relationships define human life. I am never okay, no matter what I seem to be achieving and no matter how happy and satisfied I am, if I am not living properly in the primary relationships in which God has placed me.

Paul communicates this with thunderous clarity in Galatians 5:14: "The entire law is summed up in a single command."

Wouldn't you now expect him to say, "Love God above all else"? But he doesn't. Instead he says, "Love your neighbor as yourself." Since we were created by God to be social beings and are invested by God with a moral responsibility to our neighbor, our calling to live in community is a primary way of understanding who we are and what we have been called to do. There is help for us here as well as we seek to understand the issues and struggles of midlife. Those struggles do not exist apart from the principal relationships of human life; rather, they are interwoven together with them. The struggles of midlife expose the true health and character of the relationships to which God has called me.

The third relationship is *my relationship to myself*. Now, this may seem odd to you, but there is a real way in which we all are relating to ourselves. The Psalmist records a conversation with himself, "Why are you downcast, O my soul?" (Psa. 42:5). Think about this: there is no voice more influential in your life than your own, because no one talks to you more than you do. You've had regular conversations with yourself today, most of the time not even being aware of it. This relationship has to do with the way we think about our *identity* and our *responsibility*. Everything we do is somehow shaped by who we think we are and what we think we have been called to do. Peter, for example, says that people's lives are "ineffective and unproductive" because they have forgotten who they are (See 2 Peter 1:8–9). We all live with some sense of moral responsibility, whether accurate or misshapen, and we all either hold to our responsibilities or in some way take ourselves off the hook. Once more, there is real help here for understanding the disorientation of the midlife years. Midlife crisis *is* a struggle of identity and responsibility, and it exposes weaknesses in these areas that have existed for a long time but are laid bare during this passage of life.

The fourth relationship is *my relationship to the rest of creation*. As a human being made in the image of God, I am also called to a responsible interaction with the physical world. This relationship gets at two very important dimensions of human life: my life of labor, and the way I view and relate to the world of material things. We live in a culture that tends to view work as the painful price you have to pay to afford the pleasure that you're actually living for. Our culture tends to see one's material body and material possessions as essential to any true happiness and satisfaction. So Western culture tends to be averse to work and obsessed with things.

The Bible, on the other hand, doesn't say that the body and possessions are unimportant but calls me to moral responsibility in each area. How I view and use my body is biblically very important. (See 1 Cor. 6:12–20, for example.) How I relate to the created world and how I view and hold my possessions are also presented in Scripture as being of great importance. (See Luke 12:13-21.) The Bible presents work, not as a curse, but as a principal part of God's ordained plan for all of humanity since it existed before the fall. Living as God ordained is not a matter of begrudgingly working in order to experience the excitement of pleasure but finding pleasure in the various spheres of labor to which God has called me. I am designed to be a laborer, and my labor is part of an agenda much greater than the acquisition of momentary material pleasures. Once again, this final relationship exegetes the struggles of midlife. Those struggles have to do with the physical body, they have to do with where we seek to find pleasure, and they have to do with how we tend to view the world of material things.

So, having these four relationships always in focus provides better preparation for midlife than the typical ways our culture tends to organize and categorize life. (We will examine these categories in future chapters.)

Midlife Crisis: a Portrait

We have said that the struggles of midlife result from a collision of powerful personal awareness and powerful personal interpretations, but what does the actual "crisis" of midlife look like? Here are some characteristics of a person in the throes of midlife confusion and struggle.

1. ***Dissatisfaction with life.*** Suddenly you begin to look around and you don't like your life. You may struggle with your job or your marriage in ways that you never have before. You may look at your life in general and it seems purposeless, routine, and dull. You may experience a rather consistent boredom, restlessness, discontent, or disillusionment. The bottom line is that you are not happy with your story. The lives of others around you seem interesting and attractive in ways that they have not before. This dissatisfaction is not necessarily about a particular thing but a general feeling of discontent.

2. ***Disorientation.*** There are times when each of us loses our way for a moment, when we get lost in our own stories. The disorientation of midlife has to do with identity and function. During this time of life, many of the ways a person has thought about himself don't apply anymore. Many of the principal duties that occupied him are not necessary anymore. When this happens, people often experience a loss of identity. This identity loss is not philosophical in that it results from not being able to answer the profound questions of life; rather, it is functional; *I thought I knew who I was and what I was supposed to be doing, but now I am not so sure.*

3. ***Discouragement.*** At some point you begin to realize that you have lost the expectancy, vibrancy, hopefulness, and courage of your youth. When you are young, it is easy to hold onto your potentials as possibilities, but the older you get, the harder it is. There is an old proverb that says, "The young man if he is not liberal has no heart and the old man if he is not conservative has no brain." Whether you completely agree with the proverb or not, it surely does point to the differences in the way the young person and the older person look at life. Youth is a time of boundless possibility. Young people are visionaries and dreamers. It is crushing to wake up to the fact that you long ago put away your satchel of dreams. It's hard to face the fact that you are more cynical than you are expectant.

4. ***Dread.*** Not many people in Western culture look forward to old age. With the high value we put on physical beauty and physical youth and with the constant emphasis that is placed on physical health, it is hard to be positive about aging. When you are young, you live with functional feelings of invincibility. I happened to be observing my seventeen year old son's diet recently. What he eats would either leave me weighing seven hundred pounds or dead! It became clear that the thought of being careful with what he eats never enters his mind. He doesn't think about his veins, his heart, or his waistline. Death is a remote concept to him. Not so for the person in midlife. Things like tiredness, weight gain, aches and pains, and high cholesterol begin to remind me that I am not young anymore, that my physical clock is ticking every day. Often this results in generalized worry or dread about aging and death.

5. ***Disappointment.*** Two realizations can hit you very powerfully in midlife. The first is regret. You assess your life and realize that there were things you wanted to accomplish that you never seemed able to pull off. Perhaps you look back and say, "I always wanted to have a daily time of worship with my children, but I was never able to do it consistently." Or, "I wanted to have regular date nights with my wife, but things always got in the way." Or, "I wanted to be more involved in the ministries of my church, but it never quite happened." Or, "I had always hoped I could deal with my weight, but I never seemed to be successful over the long run." We all have our own personal regrets.

The second realization has to do with dashed dreams. We all have entertained our personal dreams. Maybe it was to do well in your career so that you could retire early and give yourself to a more active ministry. Maybe it was that you always wanted to buy a small farm or have more children. Perhaps you always dreamed of going back to school and getting out of the occupation that has never really stimulated you. When you are young, you are still able to tell yourself that you have time to realize your dreams, but the older you get the harder it is to do.

6. ***Disinterest.*** Here I begin to realize that I am no longer interested in the things that once excited me. In fact, I find it hard to motivate myself to do the things that I once found stimulating and attractive. I may have once enjoyed certain relationships, but now, if I'm honest, I really don't care if I see those people again. Or maybe it is my job. I find it hard to go to work in the morning and hard to give myself fully when I am there. Or maybe my husband or wife, whom I once found very physically attractive, is no longer attractive to me in that way. Or perhaps it is spiritual disinterest. My pursuit of God becomes joyless, personal devotions basically fade away, and active ministry participation is rare. I have lost interest in my own life.

7. ***Distance.*** In all of my disorientation, lostness, and inability to find motivation for the things that once excited me, it is hard not to withdraw. And I don't want people to pursue me. I don't want people to ask me how I am doing. I don't want to have to explain why I no longer participate the way I once did. I just want to be left alone. I don't feel comfortable with your knowing how lost I actually am and I don't want to try to explain things that I myself don't understand.

8. ***Distraction.*** With all of this swirling around inside of me, I am in a place of real vulnerability to temptation. Every sinner's tendency is to deal with inner struggles by feeding the outer man. Some of us overeat when we are upset. Some of us deal with disappointment by acquiring things that we think will satisfy us. Some of us numb ourselves with excessive pursuit of leisure or pleasure. When I am disappointed with myself and discouraged with my life, it is tempting to give way to the lust of the flesh. It is tempting to deal with the absence of true contentment by pursuing the fleeting, but potentially enslaving, physical pleasures that are all around me. I am always in danger when I am functionally exchanging the glory of walk-

ing with, trusting, and serving God for the shadow glories of the created world.

So What is Really Wrong?

Several themes that subtly run throughout this list must be recognized for what they are. They get at the heart of what the midlife struggle is all about because they get to the heart of our struggle as sinners living in a fallen world. We will be unpacking these themes for the remainder of this book. They are simple, yet profound. They are personal but at the same time the general struggle of every human being. They are deeply theological but live in the most mundane moments of our daily lives. They tend to hide behind the masks of people who on the surface seem like they are doing quite well. They run deeper than our choices and behavior, yet they influence everything we do.

Perhaps the best way to unpack these themes is by examining the lives of three people. Look for these themes as you read.

Phil seemed to have it all; forty years old, a beautiful wife, three healthy children, and a great job. He had started at the bottom of his firm as a draftsman, doing details for engineering projects. Over the years he had slowly advanced through the ranks. Now he was the managing engineer for a 250-person design team with one of the most influential firms in the world. He loved the power and prestige that came along with his position. He loved the dynamic and creative environment that he got to participate in every day. He loved the fact that they designed projects that mattered. He couldn't believe that he was actually getting paid to do what he had always wanted to do, and he loved the many benefits his family enjoyed that resulted from his job. Phil was a happy man, and he was fully engaged in his home and in his church.

It was while listening to the news one evening that Phil first heard that his firm was involved in a massive lawsuit because of injuries that had resulted from one of their designs. He was concerned, but he thought that surely the firm had insurance for that kind of thing. It wasn't long before clients began to back out of their contracts, having lost confidence in the ability of Phil's firm to do their work well. Phil was told that he would have to lay off half of his department. It was hard for him, but Phil was a team player and knew it was necessary. It wasn't until Phil had only five people left working under him that he saw the handwriting on the wall. Phil was laid off a month later.

At first Phil seemed like he was doing quite well. He talked about God's sovereignty and faithfulness. He seemed quite confident that, with his resume and experience, he would soon be back to work. He got his resume out and anticipated quick responses. Phil was shocked when the first batch of mailings didn't even get one response. After a month of the same, his confidence began to flag.

Phil's wife Sarah noticed it first. He was spending hours alone in his office at home. He was increasingly short tempered and irritable. There were outbursts of anger that she had never experienced before. Phil became more sullen and depressed as the months dragged on. Yet he angrily refused to look for any other kind of work. He was getting to the end of his severance pay, and unemployment funds would not fund the needs of his family.

Many mornings Phil would not even attempt to get out of bed. He would wander down to the kitchen sometime in the afternoon and get violently angry at any question about how he was living. Phil had resigned his positions at church and could barely get himself to the services on Sunday. Sarah began to notice that Phil was spending long periods of time away from their home. He had never done this before, and it alarmed her. He would make a variety of excuses, but none really provided a real explanation for his many absences. It wasn't long before Sarah discovered that her husband had been having an affair with another woman for several months. When she confronted Phil, he at first denied his unfaithfulness but eventually admitted what he had done. Sadly, Phil didn't seem repentant. Rather, he began to be more vocal about his doubt of God and his questions about the truths of the Bible.

He couldn't believe that a good God would let this happen to him. He couldn't believe that after years of obeying God, this is what he got. He felt like everything he had ever worked for had been taken away from him. How could he ever compete with guys half his age who would require half his salary? He saw life as unfair and unjust and God as distant and uncaring. Bitter and cynical, Phil not only forsook his family; he forsook his faith as well.

What is going on with Phil? Why did he so completely lose his way? It is not unusual for midlife struggles to be triggered by something like the loss of a job and the inability to find commensurate employment. But there is more going on here. Yes, it's hard to have the career rug pulled out from under you. It's hard to watch the impact it has on your lifestyle and on your family. Yet it is clear that what he subsequently experienced was not the result of his job loss, but the heart that he brought to it.

Dean had always been very physically active. He loved sports and the outdoors. He loved the fact that he could share these interests with his three sons. Reared in a nominally Catholic home, Dean and his wife came to know the Lord soon after they were married and experienced a radical turnaround in their lives. Their relationship with God, the truths of his word, and the work of his kingdom became the central focus of their lives. Whether it was their marriage, their parenting, or Dean's work, he and Emma looked at each area of their lives from the perspective of their identity as children of God.

Dean was also very thankful for his work. He had been promoted to an upper management position and saw it as a golden opportunity to be salt and light in an environment where there was much corruption and darkness. He had regular opportunities to either stand for right or to share his faith at work.

Often the person Dean was discipling was someone who had come to Christ through Dean's witness.

At about forty-six, Dean noticed three things that concerned him, although he did not tell Emma at first. He began to experience an unusual amount of fatigue, nagging pains, and what seemed like a loss of physical coordination on his left side. Dean found himself dropping things or tripping when walking. When he finally went to the doctor, he was given a battery of tests and was shocked to learn that he had had a series of strokes and was at risk for even more. It was the kind of thing you hear, and immediately your life passes before you. He wondered how soon he would be completely incapacitated or even die. When he got over the initial shock, Dean began to do some research and realized he hadn't yet been given a death sentence.

Dean learned that he could do better with a combination of physical therapy and powerful medications. He did do better and was able to return to work but not without difficulty. Yet, despite all the medications, he had another minor stroke, his condition worsened, and it became clear that Dean was going to have to go on permanent disability.

Dean had been a very active man, and not getting up to go to work to support his family was a huge thing for him. He would not be able to go fishing or play catch with his boys. The days of long bike trips with the family were over. He wondered how he was ever going to serve the Lord if he spent most of his time locked up in his own house.

Dean was very discouraged to be on disability at such a young age. He had lost his physical capabilities so early in life that he could not imagine what the years to come were going to bring. It was hard at first for Dean to see the families of his healthy friends. He hated sitting on the sidelines at picnics and family outings. He felt guilty for taking early retirement and was tempted to conclude that he had strayed out of the will of the Lord. But Dean was firm in his belief that God is good, and he was humble enough to recognize that he did not deserve anything that had been taken from him. He also realized that every day he still received from the hand of the Lord everything he needed to do what God had called for him to do.

Dean began to see disability as an opportunity and the fact that he had many years ahead of him as a real benefit. He could do things that many people yearn to do but are never able. Dean had been able to put his job behind him at a very young age and turn his focus to active kingdom ministry. He realized that there were many local ministries that could benefit greatly from his experience and gifts. Dean refused to give in to the discouragement that he so powerfully felt or the doubts that had hit his heart with the force of a sledgehammer. He began to embrace the truth that God's grace is most powerful in our moments of greatest weakness. In the middle of weakness and fear, he experienced the joys of God's kingdom work. Although living with a chronic disease was very hard, Dean lived each day with joy and expectancy, busy at the work that God had given him to do.

What is going on with Dean? How could he face this devastating disease and have his life totally turned upside down without losing his way? Where did Dean and Phil differ? Why is it that Dean seemed more prepared than Phil to face the unwanted and unexpected? Let's consider one more person's story.

Sally had always been a hard worker. She had done very well in school and was awarded a full scholarship to an Ivy League university. In college she did stellar academic work, graduated with honors, and had a host of job offers from major corporations. It wasn't long before she got a great job, found a good church, and purchased a condominium in a downtown high-rise. The church she joined had a wonderful singles ministry which Sally participated in fully and enjoyed very much. It was there that she found a circle of girlfriends that became her primary source of friendship and fellowship.

Sally's job was creative, challenging, demanding, and frenetic—what she as a high achiever loved. There was plenty of room for advancement, and Sally soon advanced. There always seemed to be more responsibility, more authority, and more money coming her way. The years flew by, almost without Sally's notice.

Meanwhile Sally had really bonded with her circle of Christian friends. She loved their informal Chinese takeout and Bible study group on Tuesdays. They shared this powerful commonality of belief coupled with an ability to talk honestly about almost anything. They even took many vacations together, always watching old videos and laughing late into the night.

When she began her job and moved into her condominium, Sally had silently hoped to meet a man she could share her life with, but it wasn't a burning need. She had a very busy and full work life, and with church and friendship activities, her schedule was pretty full. At one point she concluded that her relationship with her cat, Franco, was all she could handle. She did date quite regularly, but none of the relationships went anywhere, and it was hard to pursue a friendship with a man since the demands of work always seemed to get in the way.

Over the years Sally had attended so many weddings that she dreaded it whenever she got an invitation. She had thrown showers for many of her friends and had participated in many bachelorette parties. Still, her life was full.

One Thursday evening Sally came home after a very long day. She dropped her briefcase at the door, threw her trench coat on the couch and called for Franco. She thought that it was strange that he hadn't run down the entrance hallway and hopped up on the bench, like he had done for years. Sally found him lying on her bed. She stood at the door and looked at him and thought, "He must be the most beautiful Angora God ever made." He looked regal lying there. Sally walked over, extended her hand to caress him and was shocked as she touched his cold body. She burst into tears and cried frequently over the next few days.

It was Monday of the following week when it all came thundering down upon her. She opened the door after a long and challenging day, but there was no feline friend on the bench to greet her. She dropped some things in the bedroom and went to the bathroom. Standing in front of the mirror, it hit her that she was thirty-nine! The person she saw seemed too old to be her. Where had the time gone? Why hadn't she paid more attention? Could it be that life had passed her by, and she was simply too busy to see it?

That night Sally's condo seemed unbelievably empty and claustrophobic, so much so that Sally had to get out. She spent much of that evening walking the downtown streets. She felt old and alone. Her Tuesday group had long since disbanded. Most of its members had moved on or gotten married. Her job was more demanding than ever, and often Sally felt like they simply wanted too much from her. She still loved the Sunday service at her church, but she couldn't take the singles gatherings. She just didn't feel that she had anything in common with those people anymore.

As the days passed, Sally drew more and more inward. Her life consisted of work and the Sunday morning worship service. She spent hours in her condo alone, curled up on the couch, numbing her heart with the remote. The TV was simply background noise, electronic company that made the empty condo a bit more bearable. Each night Sally replayed the video of her life, scene after scene, decision after decision. Every replaying filled her with more remorse and regret. Why had she let her job so control her? Why hadn't she made more time for other things? How could she watch so many friends move on and get married and not "get it"? Why would God say he loved her and yet leave her so completely alone? She felt tired, but it was a kind of exhaustion that was more than physical.

On Mondays, Sally found it increasingly difficult to work up enough internal motivation to go to her job. There were many days when she rehearsed her resignation speech as she walked to work, never getting around to giving it when she arrived. She found less and less joy in those Sunday worship services that once delighted her, and it had been a long time since she'd had her evening personal times of worship. She increasingly found it hard to give herself to anything (church, work, her appearance, her condo) because none of them seemed to make any difference. She had no life, and there seemed to be nothing that could change that.

What would you say to Sally? How would you help her unweave the fabric of her cynicism and discouragement? What is wrong with her? How should Sally deal with the things that she is now facing?

Recognizing the Themes

To properly understand Phil, Dean, and Sally, you have to see the themes that run through each of their experiences. These powerful, life-altering themes can create a struggle so unsettling that our culture has coined the term "midlife crisis" to capture it. If we are going to bring the stunning wisdom of Scripture to this troubling time, it is important to understand the dynamics of what is actually going on and to identify these universal themes.

1. ***An unexpected event.*** There is a way in which we don't live our life, but our life lives us. We just get carried along by its locations, relationships, situations, responsibilities, opportunities and activities without stopping very long to look, listen, and consider. Huge chunks of time can pass virtually unnoticed. Clearly this is what happened with Phil, Dean, and Sally. Then each of them hit the same thing. They all experience some unexpected event that suddenly opens their eyes. People who study these things call them *trigger event*s. For Phil it was the loss of his job, for Dean it was a physical disease, and for Sally it was the death of Franco, her cat. For each of them, the event provided a window into their life that they had not looked through before.

2. ***A new awareness.*** Because the trigger event opens their eyes, Phil, Dean, and Sally begin to see and feel things that were probably already there but in the busyness of life got no

attention. They suddenly realize how much time has passed and how much they have failed to accomplish. They become aware of their physical health and the realities of aging. They recognize how several important decisions along the way have set the course of their lives. They perceive great differences between their lives and the lives of others around them.

3. ***Powerful personal interpretations.*** Midlife crisis is about more than an unexpected event followed by powerful new awareness. The crisis is really rooted in the way people interpret the things that they see. In fact, it is more powerful than that. Their interpretations actually *determine* what they see and how they see it. As sinners, the problem with our interpretations is that they tend to be narrow and selective. Remember, sin not only affects what we do; it also affects what we think and how we see. In ways that we often don't notice, sin reduces all of us to fools. The way that seems right to us can lead to death, and the way that makes no sense to us is often the way of life and wisdom.

That is why we all need the wise perspectives of God's Word. Midlife crisis is powerfully theological. It all balances on the fundamental ways we make sense out of life. It is all about how our functional systems of belief shape the way we respond to whatever God puts on our plate. This explains why Dean responds to his diagnosis very differently than Phil does after he loses his job and Sally does after the death of Franco.

4. ***Exposed ruling desires.*** Midlife struggles very pointedly reveal the heart. The interpretations a person brings to the events and new awareness of midlife are not the result of objectively held abstract theology. No, the functional theology that shapes the way a person responds during this period is rooted in the values, treasures, and cravings of the person's heart. Midlife crisis in its most basic form is not an event crisis, an awareness crisis, or a crisis of aging. It is a crisis of the heart. Midlife exposes what a person has really been living for and where a person has tried to find meaning and purpose. It has the power to reveal the significant gap between a person's con-

fessional theology and their functional theology. What we say we are living for on Sunday may not, in fact, be the thing that has actually taken daily rulership over our hearts. And when these things that rule us are taken out of our hands, we tend to become angry, fearful, bitter, or discouraged. We will experience a loss of identity and a flagging of meaning and purpose. We will look at this area much more extensively in chapters to come, but it is important to understand that midlife crisis is a crisis of desire.

5. ***Reflexive responses.*** This is where the person in midlife gets himself into trouble. Reflex responses may seem logical, but they are only the twisted logic of desire. The person is actually trapped in the cul-de-sac of the thoughts and motives of his heart. His responses to his new awareness will only change to the degree that he addresses the underlying issues of his heart. Phil's regrettable actions are propelled by the distorted thoughts and inordinate desires of his heart. Sally ends up as a depressed recluse not as a result of Franco's death, but because of the thoughts and motives that she brought to it. Dean faces devastating things, but he doesn't throw his life away because he brought a different heart to this scary and painful moment in his life. Like Phil and Sally, Dean's true treasures are revealed in this moment, and like them, his actions are not forced by the circumstances, but formed by the thought and motives of his heart.

These five themes tend to run like cords through the fabric of the typical midlife crisis. They need to be unpacked and understood biblically. In doing so, we will not only come to know ourselves better but also come to know our Lord more fully. Only in such moments of humble, honest self-examination are we able to grasp how wide, how deep, how full, and how complete the love of God is for us. It is here that we will really begin to understand that Scripture not only lays before us the wonderful promise of eternity, but it also understands the deepest issues we experience before we get there. In the narrative of God's Word we find an eloquent and practical wisdom that speaks directly to these pressing issues.

So we need constantly to carry two commitments with us wherever we go. First, we need to commit to be persistent and teachable students of God's Word. We were never designed to figure out life on our own. Only as we submit to the wisdom of the Wonderful Counselor will we escape the hold of our own foolishness. Second, we need to be committed to a habit of ongoing self-examination. You and I need to get used to standing before the mirror of the Word of God, so that we can see ourselves as we really are. Healthy Christianity is found at the intersection of accurate self-knowledge and the true knowledge of God.

What about you? Perhaps you are reading this book because you have lost your way. Or maybe you're reading it because you are in a relationship with, or minister to, someone who is in the throes of some kind of midlife struggle. Or maybe you are simply interested in how the Gospel practically applies to the daily issues of human life. Whatever your reason for picking up this book, I invite you to examine your own heart, so that you too, will not lose your way.

What keeps you going?
What makes your life worthwhile?
What dreams have tended to capture your heart?
Right now, how are you making sense of your life?
What are you convinced you cannot live without?
Where do you seek to find identity?
Why do you call one day good and another bad?
What, in life, do you crave most?
Be honest—Why do you really do the things you do?
As you make choices and decisions, what are you hoping to get out of them?

May God expose our hearts, so that in really seeing ourselves, we may hunger all the more deeply for him!

Chapter 2

Two Midlife Psalms

The darkest day, if you live tomorrow, will have passed away. —William Cowper

We must accept finite disappointment, but never lose infinite hope. —Martin Luther King, Jr.

Sam's day started out like any other. He had followed his usual morning routine: shower and shave, touch-up iron his clothes, drink a cup of coffee while reading Spurgeon's *Morning and Evening* devotional, kiss his sleeping wife on the forehead, and head off to work. He was looking forward to the same old same-old, except for his regular physical with Dr. Blair.

At 3:30 Sam found himself holding a magazine he wasn't really interested in and wasn't really reading, while complaining to himself about how doctors always overbook and make their patients wait. Soon he heard his name, got up and followed the nurse to the examining room. To his surprise, the doctor didn't tell him that everything looked great and that he would see him in a year. He was concerned about a few things that showed up during Sam's physical and scheduled a stress test and other follow-up examinations.

It was during the follow-up that Sam's world radically changed, more so than he even realized at the moment of first shock. Sam had very serious blockage in four arteries and needed immediate bypass surgery. The doctor wouldn't even let Sam go home. He was able to call his wife, but then was ushered up to a room and placed in bed. Surgery was scheduled for two days later. It didn't make any sense. He was tall and quite slim, he had always been very physically active, he didn't have bad eating habits, and he hadn't felt bad a day in his life. Yet here he was in bed facing bypass surgery.

Sam got little sleep that night. He kept comforting himself with the fact that he hadn't had a heart attack and so he wasn't dealing with major heart damage, but he was still confused and afraid. The next day was spent comforting his wife, Fran, in between being prepped for surgery. When the surgery was over, Sam came out of it a physically different person. For the first time in his life he felt like an old man.

He expected that the feelings of being elderly at forty-nine would pass after he recovered from surgery, but as the weeks went on, Sam began to wonder if he would ever be the same. The extended disability leave from work soon morphed into talks about whether he would ever be able to do his old job again. Eventually the discussions turned to whether the company had another position for him and then to final negotiations about his severance package. The shock of that first year was so powerful that Sam had little time to take it all in. Only after he came home, spending days thinking about what he would do with the rest of his life, did the weight of what had happened really hit him.

Sam was barely fifty, and he felt like he had no future. All of the people who had stood with him had gone back to their own lives. Even Fran had taken a full-time job and had begun to study for her master's degree three evenings a week. Sam hated his house because it had turned into his own personal prison. He hated going out because he envied everyone he saw. He hated to think about how his life didn't add up to too much. He reasoned that he had failed at much of what he should have done, and most of his dreams had evaporated unfulfilled. There were many things Sam could do. He was by no means an invalid. In fact, there were many job possibilities open to him, but he was not interested in any of them. Sam spent more and more time alone, and when he was with people, he was often silent and withdrawn. He had painted in his mind an idyllic picture of his pre-op life that made it much more attractive than it actually had been and a much darker picture of his present life than it really was.

Sam simply hated being Sam, and it wasn't getting better. He told me his story with tones of bitterness and discouragement. It was all he could do to live within the plot of his own story, let alone believe that there could be any kind of future for him.

Now, there are ways in which Sam's story is unique and extreme, yet imbedded in it are many of the elements of the typical midlife struggle (sudden awareness, interaction of thought and desire with that awareness, the disorientation that results, etc.). But one thing impressed me about Sam that I have observed in many people as they tell their stories. It is a very important dynamic for us as we think about the Bible and the struggles of midlife. Let me explain.

The Sidelining of Scripture

My youngest son is a good basketball player. He is a real student of the game and has wonderful hand-eye coordination. He protects the ball well and has a great outside shot. He is not a high jumper or a lightning-speed type of player. During the past year, when he longed to be on the floor, he spent much of his time on the sideline. His coach favored a fast, "run-and-gun" kind of game that simply doesn't play to my son's strengths. He was sidelined because his game simply didn't seem to fit the system.

In a similar way, I have been very impressed throughout the years by how the Bible gets functionally sidelined in the lives of struggling people. They are all committed believers in the Word of God, and they have not denied their faith in the truthfulness of Scripture. But in times of personal suffering, difficulty, and crisis, the Bible suddenly becomes functionally irrelevant. The way they think about what is going on in their lives is not dynamically shaped and directed by the overarching story of Scripture. And when Scripture is functionally sidelined, they begin to lose their identity, ethics, mission, and values. It simply doesn't seem to speak to their present game. Yes, they all believe that it speaks to life in a general way and that what it says is true, but there is a huge gap between the words on the pages of Scripture and the painful details of their lives.

Most often this gap is not revealed by the person saying, "Frankly, Paul, I don't think the Bible has a thing to say about what I am going through." It is more frequently revealed by an utter lack of mention of the Bible and its perspectives as the person is struggling to make sense out of his life. Let me give you another metaphor.

When you buy a car, there is an owner's manual in the glove compartment. It is there because it tells you everything you need to know, as the owner of the vehicle, in order to properly use and maintain your car. It is the most reliable automobile reference guide that you can put your hands on for the precise reason that it was written by the company that made the vehicle. Wouldn't it strike you as weird if the first time a light went out, a dashboard warning came on, or the radio didn't properly function, I would be confused and upset but not consult the owner's manual? Yet that is exactly what happens to many believers who get lost in the middle of their own story. They recognize that God's Word is true because it was written by the Manufacturer, but in times of trouble, they never take it out of the glove compartment of their lives. God's Word is our most reliable manual on the proper use and maintenance of a human life. It speaks with power and practical wisdom to every human experience. It is impossible for it not to address the issues of your life, because *life* is precisely what it is all about. Written by the One who knows everything from before creation to beyond destiny, it contains everything we need to live life as it was meant to be lived in the here and now.

As I listened to Sam tell his story, it struck me that if I had not known who he was and what he believed, there would be no hint in his narrative that God's Word in any way informed his perspectives on life. His belief in Scripture and the way he had dealt with the painful particulars of physical disease somehow existed in two different chambers of his heart. What I want to do in this chapter, as well as the whole book, is to bring the Bible to life. I want to bridge the gap of functional separation that often exists between the Bible and everyday life. This gap is particularly evident in times of personal trouble.

I want to do this by directing you to two psalms. One of the benefits of the Psalms is that they keep us honest. In the Psalms, biblical faith isn't presented as being neat and easy. Rather, the closer you get to really understanding the shocking honesty of the Psalms, the more you see how messy, chaotic, and question riddled the life of faith actually is. In our world, things happen that we don't understand. God regularly confuses us, and sin blinds us. The Psalms speak into this world with a gorgeous balance of honesty and hope. Let's look at two psalms together.

Finding Hope Where There is None

I want to take you to one of the darkest of the psalms, perhaps the darkest passage in all of Scripture. Its words are bleak, grim, and without hope. There is no relief within its stanzas and no resolve at the end. There is no hint of joy or expectancy.

There seems to be no friend to hold onto and no anchor of truth. The cry of this psalm is the final whimper of one who is at the end, about to give up. This psalm has the power to startle, and even offend you. You wonder why God isn't doing something, and you wonder what useful purpose it serves in the canon. Why would this psalm be written as a song for the choirmaster? How could the Sons of Korah, known for their jubilant chants, sing something so utterly dark?

In the face of the apparent hopelessness of Psalm 88 you begin to get hold of the amazing hope that it expresses. Enter the darkness of Psalm 88 with me, but search for hope as you do.

O Lord, the God who saves me,
day and night I cry out before you.
May my prayer come before you;
turn your ear to my cry.

For my soul is full of trouble
and my life draws near the grave.
I am counted among those who go down to the pit;
I am like a man without strength.
I am set apart with the dead,
like the slain who lie in the grave,
whom you remember no more,
who are cut off from your care.

You have put me in the lowest pit,
in the darkest depths.
Your wrath lies heavily upon me;
you have overwhelmed me with all your waves.
You have taken from me my closest friends
and have made me repulsive to them.
I am confined and cannot escape;
my eyes are dim with grief.

I call to you, O Lord, every day;
I spread out my hands to you.
Do you show your wonders to the dead?
Do those who are dead rise up and praise you?

Is your love declared in the grave,
your faithfulness in Destruction?
Are your wonders known in the place of darkness,
or your righteous deeds in the land of oblivion?

But I cry to you for help, O Lord;
in the morning my prayer comes before you.
Why, O Lord, do you reject me
and hide your face from me?

From my youth I have been afflicted and close to death;
I have suffered your terrors and am in despair.
Your wrath has swept over me;
your terrors have destroyed me.
All day long they surround me like a flood;
they have completely engulfed me.
You have taken my companions and loved ones from me;
the darkness is my closest friend.

The words of Psalm 88 are so dark, so desperate, and so lacking in any perceivable hope that it almost takes your breath away. You cannot help but be touched by its sadness; the pain of the writer's heart as it struggles to adequately describe what it is going through. To him, God is not only distant, but he has turned away his face (a metaphor of rejection). In the middle of deep darkness this person feels utterly alone. Closest companions have been driven away. There is no one who really understands, there is no one who really cares, and there is no one who can help. In a desperate attempt to get God to respond, the psalmist appeals to God's commitment to his own glory. Essentially he says, "God, I'm dying here. Will I be able to praise you when I'm dead? Will I be able to testify to your faithfulness from my grave?" Finally, this psalm ends the way no other does. Its final word is "darkness." The psalmist basically says, "I have looked around and I have realized that I do have one friend. His name is Darkness. Yes, he has become my closest friend."

In the cosmology of "I'm so happy and here's the reason why" Christianity, it would make no sense that Psalm 88 is in the Bible, and even less sense that this could be the experience of a true believer. Can a true believer get to the place where he has no functional joy or practical hope? Can a true believer feel forsaken and friendless? Psalm 88 offends the warm and fuzzy Christianity of modern Western culture. It confronts us with things we don't want to look at, let alone take time to consider. We tend to want a Christianity that is full of personal hope and happiness. We tend to want a Christian life of comfort and peace, whose rare problems are easily solved by a theological dictionary and a little bit of prayer. We just want to be happy, and that doesn't seem too much to ask of a God who owns everything and is in control of everything.

Yet, Psalm 88 *is* in the Bible, and it is there for a purpose. It is a vital part of God's revelation to us, and when we hear and understand its message, it will be easy to understand why it is the perfect psalm for midlife.

Psalm 88: Confrontation

You don't find many contemporary hymn writers rushing to put Psalm 88 to music. Yet we need to look at what this psalm forces us to see: Life in this fallen world is hard. The world is a broken place. We all will face the unexpected. Being a believer does not exempt you from moments of significant darkness. There will be times when it seems impossible to figure out what God is doing. There will be times when it seems as if your cries are going unheard and your prayers unanswered. There will be moments when it seems like you are utterly alone and that no one could possibly understand what you are going through. This psalm confronts us with a powerful reality; being in covenantal relationship with the Lord does not mean that I will escape the difficulties of life in a fallen world.

Think about it for a moment. Christians get old. Christians face disloyalty, dishonor, and rejection. Christians face physical disease. Christians face governmental corruption and injustice. Christians face moments of disappointment and sadness.

Christians face mistreatment. Sometimes our families break up, our cars crash, and our houses burn down. This is important for us to understand. The heaven that we all long for is yet to come. We live in the uncomfortable moment between the glories of our justification and the glory of our final union with Christ for eternity. And where do we live in-between? We live in a world that has been, and continues to be, devastated by sin. The signs are everywhere around us. This world groans, waiting for redemption!

Is this some mistake? Wouldn't it have been better, easier, and more efficient for us to be ushered into eternity the moment we believe? You could commit your life to Christ and just disappear. No more need to face the hassles of life in the fallen world. No more fear of what will happen. No more need of security devices and pain medication. But our continued presence in this groaning place is not the failure of the plan; it *is* the plan. As difficult as it is to accept, you are here because this is where your all-wise and all-loving Heavenly Father wants you. These experiences do not get in the way of what he is doing in and through you but are the means by which it gets done.

Psalm 88 confronts us with the fact that God is not after what we are after, or this Psalm would not be in the Bible. If God were exercising his awesome power to deliver your personal satisfaction and pleasure, then Psalm 88 would be an embarrassing testament to his complete failure. Psalm 88 calls us to confess humbly that we tend to live self-absorbed lives. We think that a comfortable life is a happy life. We want situations, relationships, and the surrounding creation to provide the pleasure that we seek, and we are disappointed, discouraged, or angry when they don't deliver. God is, in fact, working on our happiness and satisfaction, but it is of a higher order, and one that is only attainable when we have forsaken our own glory and learned to live in constant pursuit of his.

Psalm 88 also calls us to be honest. We have cried out to God and wondered if he has heard. We have felt like we were singled out particularly for suffering. We have gone through times when we have felt friendless. The struggle has not only been physical, relational, and circumstantial, but also intensely spiritual. *We too* have questioned God's presence, faithfulness, and love. We have second-guessed his plan. At times we have been tempted to wonder who really is in control. Beneath the "I'm fine, how are you?" veneer of Sunday greetings, we have all faced the hardship of the already-not-yet place where God has called us to live until all is prepared for our final destination.

We need a Christianity that gets beneath sugary greetings and theological platitudes and boldly takes the richness of redemption to the realities of what we daily face. We need a faith that stands in the middle of Psalm 88, unshocked and unafraid, and we need to confess how far we are from a Christianity that is just that sturdy.

Now what does this have to do with midlife? Everything! Let's be honest here; we find midlife hard because *it is hard*! We struggle with *the* plan because it is not *our* plan. We are disappointed because we age. We are dissatisfied because our dreams slipped out of our hands. We are discouraged that, in our sin, we failed many, many times. We are disappointed that good things come to an end and that people move on. Midlife exposes how much we struggle with the fact that God completes his work of redemption in us by keeping us in the middle of all of the harsh realities of the fall. Coming to Christ isn't an easy exit from the travails of the broken world. Rather, those travails are the workroom in which the redemption artistry of Christ is completed. But there is more.

Psalm 88: Hope

When you see the title of this section you may be thinking, "Wait a minute. I thought you said that this is the one psalm that is almost devoid of any hope. What in the world could be hopeful about a psalm that ends with 'darkness is my closest friend'?" If your hope lies in your circumstances, then there is no hope to be found in Psalm 88. If your hope rests in your ability to figure life out enough to solve your problems, then there is no hope to be found in Psalm 88. Yet I am convinced that this dark psalm brims with hope.

The hope of Psalm 88 is found precisely in the fact that it has no hope in it. It isn't wrapped with some pretty theological bow at the end. Psalm 88 is hopeful because of its stark honesty and profound darkness. Did you ever share a painful story with someone and realize that they just don't understand why it was so difficult for you? That kind of experience begins to get at the wonderful hope of Psalm 88.

First, Psalm 88 reminds me that the God in whom I hope really does understand the deepest issues of the human heart. He is never caught off guard. He is never confused or overwhelmed. With precision and sensitivity to detail, he can play back my experience to me in a way that has a powerful ring of truth. The struggles of Psalm 88 have an air of familiarity to me that should be tremendously comforting. God looks with loving understanding into the deepest caverns of the human experience. He hears with patience and mercy the most desperate cries of the human heart. He never minimizes, mischaracterizes, misunderstands, or mocks my struggle. With the skilled brush of one who really sees, he paints my experiences with the accuracy of one who really knows.

This God gets it! Because he does, you can come to him when you are utterly lost and confused and cry your hopeless cries with confidence. There really is one who knows and understands. There is really one who patiently stands with me in trouble. The darkness does not blind his eyes or prevent his care. The light of his understanding and love illuminates the hopeless hallways of this desperate psalm.

Yet, there is still more. Why is this psalm in the Bible? Maybe a better way to ask the question is, "How does Psalm 88 fit with the rest of the Psalms and the rest of the Bible?" Psalm 88 tells us how deep, how wide, and how far the arms of our Redeemer extend. God's grace is not wimpy. It extends, with life-altering power, to the deepest level of suffering that is the result of the damaging effects of sin on our world. It reaches into the most specific and troubling details of your life and mine. It receives the most desperate cries of our hearts, never turning a deaf ear. It addresses our most fearful and doubt-ridden thoughts. Our Lord redeems the lost and the lonely, the rebel and the fearful, the confused and the doubtful, the sinner and the sufferer, the poor and the forsaken, the rejecter and the one rejected. There is no thought so distorted, no emotion so powerful, no circumstance so horrible, no action so twisted, and no desire so desperate as to be outside of the reach of the Redeemer and his grace. Psalm 88 is in the Bible to remind us that the circle of God's grace is big enough to contain every experience that this broken world could throw at us. Now that is a reason for hope!

How does this psalm relate to the lostness, the aloneness, the disappointment, and the disorientation that many people experience during midlife? Because Psalm 88 is in the Bible, you can say to yourself, "What I am going through right now is not beyond the scope of redemption. The loving hands of a powerful Redeemer are long enough to reach into the details of this experience as well. This, too, is the kind of thing for which God has given me his grace!" You see, it is utterly impossible to get so lost in midlife that grace can't find you. It is inconceivable that you could experience a confusion so great that grace would not be able to understand it. **Here is the hope: you can never live beyond the reach of grace.**

Perhaps you are thinking, "How can you be lost and hopeful at the same time?" This question leads us to a second psalm. This psalm is a case study, a story of hope in the middle of a seemingly hopeless situation. It is a picture of remarkable rest in the center of deeply personal unrest. It is a story about being rejected without feeling alone. It is not a myth, but a real-life, heart wrenching story of one man and his son. And it happens right where you and I live, in this fallen world. Let's consider Psalm 4.

Up Against It, but Living with Hope

This psalm takes a bit of a setup to understand. It is a companion to Psalm 3. The title of Psalm 3 tells you when both psalms were written and what they are about. Psalm 3 and 4 are morning and evening psalms, written when King David was fleeing from his son Absalom. This real-life story (recorded in 2 Samuel 14–18) is full of mystery, drama, danger, and intrigue. It is a scandalous political drama, but more so, it is a sad family drama.

David was in the palace as the anointed king of Israel. Word came to him that his son had been seditious, doing everything he could to turn his father's subjects against him and to take the throne. The report comes that the hearts of the people are increasingly with Absalom. Imagine how hurt and devastated you would feel to realize that your own son had done such things against you! But there is more. Because Israel was a monarchy, the only way the throne could pass to Absalom was for David to die. David is hit with the crushing realization that his boy is not only intending to take his throne but his life as well! Unwilling to marshal an army against his son, David goes into hiding with a few of his most faithful and trusted followers. In Psalm 4 we find David and his loyal band, driven into exile by his disloyal and murderous son.

Answer me when I call to you,
O my righteous God.
Give me relief from my distress;
be merciful to me and hear my prayer.

How long, O men, will you turn my glory into shame?
How long will you love delusions and seek false gods?
Know that the Lord *has set apart the godly for himself;*
the Lord *will hear when I call to him.*

In your anger do not sin;
when you are on your beds,
search your hearts and be silent.

Offer right sacrifices
and trust in the LORD.

Many are asking, 'Who can show us any good?'
Let the light of your face shine upon us, O LORD.
You have filled my heart with greater joy
than when their grain and new wine abound.
I will lie down and sleep in peace,
for you alone, O LORD,
make me dwell in safety.

Take a moment to put yourself in this father's position. Try to feel the extent of his grief and pain. It shouldn't surprise you if David were bitter and angry against Absalom and maybe even in a crisis of faith. Why would God let this happen? What possible good could ever result? In moments of deep personal disappointment like these, we often let our hurt set the agenda for us. And when we do, we inevitably live to regret those decisions and the legacy they leave behind. This, too, is a danger of the midlife struggle. In moments of disappointment and disorientation, in the grief of regret and the sadness at the death of our dreams, we are very vulnerable to making decisions that will add further trouble to the trouble we are already experiencing.

Yet the remarkable thing about Psalm 4 is that it not only gives us a window into David's decisions, but we are allowed to peer into his heart. Let's take a look at how David is responding to this moment of personal suffering.

1. ***David doesn't run away from God; he runs to him*** (vv.1–2). You do not see David questioning God's faithfulness. He is not questioning the principles of the Word or the wisdom of God's will. He is not wondering if it was worth it to obey God for all these years. What David does is place himself once again in the hands of his Heavenly Father. He turns toward God, asking him to hear and do what he alone can do.

2. ***David reminds himself of his identity as God's child (v.3).*** We are always responding to life out of some sense of identity. Our sense of who we are powerfully shapes the way we respond

to the blessing or difficulty that we face. David reminds himself that he is one of God's *set apart* ones. Since he has been set apart for God's own possession, he can rest assured that God will always hear him when he cries. Shocked and confused as he may be about the trouble he is facing, he can be sure that God will hear and answer.

3. ***David examines himself (v. 4).*** This is very different from our normal instinct in times of trouble. It is so easy for us to lose sight of ourselves when we are dealing with hard circumstances or mistreatment by others. It is so easy to play the DVD in our heads over and over, wondering why we had to go through this. When we do this, we tend to grow more discouraged, bitter, doubtful, cynical, and hopeless with each repetition. But David doesn't do this. In the middle of this horrible situation, he examines his own heart. In times of trial, it is our hearts that are under attack, and it is our hearts that get revealed. It is important to know our hearts, to assess where they are weak and vulnerable to temptation, and to do what we can to guard them. Remember, the decisions we make in moments of difficulty are not forced on us by the situations we are in but by what our hearts think and desire in the middle of them.

4. ***David worships! (v. 5).*** Worship tends to be the last thing we think about in situations like these. We tend to skip our personal devotions. We permit ourselves to miss small group gatherings, or we decide against a ministry opportunity. When we do this, we withhold from God the one thing that he is always worthy of, the sacrifices of our praise and worship. There is nothing more appropriate, nothing more God honoring, and nothing more personally and spiritually beneficial in times of difficulty than to be devoted to worship. God is there, he is good, and he is worthy!

5. ***David prays for the people around him (v. 6).*** David was not alone. He had been followed by a band of committed men. David isn't so absorbed in his own moment of pain that he is oblivious to those around him. He doesn't ignore them, hoping they will go away. He doesn't give them an impatient and

angry lecture. Instead, he ministers to them. He asks God to make himself known so that they would experience his presence and enjoy his rest.

6. ***David rests (vv.7–8).*** We would expect David to suffer through grief filled, restless nights, unable to escape the pain that has filled his day. But again, David surprises us. He isn't an angry insomniac because he hasn't lost the source of his personal safety, stability, and joy. David's security was not about position, possessions, locations, or situations but about his relationship with God. Because God was the source of his rest, he could sleep as securely in the wilderness as he ever had in the palace! Even in this moment of great personal grief, he is able to lie down and rest.

Now, you may be tempted to respond, "This psalm doesn't help me at all! This guy is simply not for real!" Let me remind you of how real this man really is. He was a person just like us. He was quite capable of making disastrously bad choices. David's worst choices did not come amid difficulty but right in the middle of amazing blessing. We all can be as tempted by blessing as we are by suffering. Blessed by God to be the anointed king of Israel, he was not satisfied. He took another man's wife and arranged the man's murder. No, David isn't a plastic saint. He was a weak and vulnerable sinner, just like us. This is why this Psalm is so hopeful. The hero of this Psalm is not David. The great hero of this Psalm is the Lord! He is the one who gives remarkable faith to his people. He is the one who gives them the power to resist temptation. He is the one who is ever with them, even in the darkest of difficulties. It is his grace that gives wisdom to the mind and courage to the heart. The same God who was in the wilderness with David is with you in your difficulty as well. He is able to help when there seems to be no help. Don't say to yourself, "This is impossible, I will never respond that way!" Say, "David's God is my God, so what David did is possible for me as well."

It is true that in his wisdom God has chosen not to exempt us from the hardships of life in this fallen world. No, he does something more beneficial and wonderful than that. He delivers us from ourselves so that we can stand up under disappointment, weakness, disorientation, and temptation. And as he enables us to stand; we do more than survive; we grow and change. In the situation where we are most tempted to give up, we learn to persevere. In the times of personal unrest, we can know a remarkable peace and rest. We are not defeated, but rather, we emerge from difficulty with new maturity and a sturdier faith. Isn't this just the kind of hope a person in the throes of midlife difficulty really needs?

It is Real and It is Possible

I want to share a piece of my own story with you. I went to seminary hungry to learn and to prepare for a life of ministering God's Word to his people. I am very thankful to this day for what I learned there. I have said many times that not only did I learn a biblical worldview in seminary, but it is also where I learned to think. The one major deficiency in my seminary training is that it was almost entirely focused on the public ministry of the Word. I only remember one lecture in one practical theology course that approached the topic of what distinctly biblical counseling looked like. As for the private ministry of the Word, I entered the pastorate pretty green and unprepared.

At twenty-six years of age my wife and I, with our infant son, moved to Northeastern Pennsylvania. We were called by God to minister in a community where the American dream had died in 1950! It was old coal and railroad country. There was a dark negativity that sat like fog over this area of the country. The dream had evaporated and people seemed defeated. The downtown was in increasing decay, and there didn't seem to be any hint of a turnaround any time soon. In any place where life has been hard and dreams have died, you will find broken and hurting people. Yes, the public ministry of the Word was important, but there was a crying need for someone who could hear the individual stories of people and, with the light of Scripture, lead them out of their particular mazes of difficulty. Frankly, I was unprepared, and I was scared to death!

I will never forget my first call for help. It was like jumping into the deep end of the pool before you have taken your first swimming lesson. It was a broken and hurting family. The husband, Greg, was cross-addicted to drugs and alcohol, his wife Loretta was severely depressed, and their four children suffered from the results of all the above. I will never forget my walk up to that couple's house that first night. It was only a few blocks away from where Luella and I were living, but it seemed like I had walked for miles. I thought, *You have no idea what you are doing! What do you really think you have to offer them? You should have just said, 'I'm sorry, I can't help you!' Why did you agree to this? What are you going to say?* (Obviously, very positive, faith-based self-talk!)

By the time I arrived at their house, my hands were clammy, my heart was racing, and my head was in a fog. Loretta greeted me at the door. She seemed very thankful that I was there but very discouraged at the same time. Greg was upstairs vomiting, the results of the addiction that so enslaved him. I sat down on the couch with feelings of great dread. I think the biggest motivation I had was to survive the evening and get out of there as soon as I could. Because of my sheer terror, I suggested that we pray and I pleaded for God's help. I pleaded with him to do what only he could do. But there was a problem with my prayer.

As I prayed, I felt as if it were my job to call God onto the scene. This was the logic of the prayer; it was clear from looking around that God wasn't there, so it was my job to plead with him to come on the scene and do what he alone was able to do. However logical this is, the fact is that it is unbiblical. After the first hour, the unbiblical logic of my prayer had been thoroughly confronted. What I saw that night is something I never thought I would see, yet I have seen it again and again.

I saw the hand of God! In a place that seemed God-forsaken, in a place where it seemed as if the devil was having a heyday, and in a place where everyone seemed ready to give up—everywhere I looked, I saw the presence, the power, and the love of God. I was amazed, and it gave me new boldness.

There were so many things I saw that night that could only be explained by the presence of an Almighty Savior in the lives of this couple. When I looked at Loretta, I saw much more than the depressed wife of an addicted man. I saw a woman who, with feeble hands and a broken heart, still held on to her Redeemer. Yes, she was deeply discouraged, but she was not cynical, and she had not turned her back on the Lord. As I looked at her, I saw Christ and the persevering power of his grace. In all of the sin and failure, he had kept her.

But there was more. As I walked to their house that night, I anticipated an antipathy between them that is often the case when a husband and wife have stepped on one another's dreams. But it wasn't there between Loretta and Greg. There was warmth and affection that, for me, was completely unexpected. They had not stooped, in their mutual disappointment, to doing the kinds of things troubled couples do that make a struggling marriage even worse. It hit me that their marriage wasn't preserved because they had read the best marriage books and had applied the truths with faithfulness and discipline. No, they were together because of divine intervention. The Lord had stood between them, protecting them from themselves.

But there were even more indications of God's hand. There was a tenderness and approachability to Greg. His life *was* a mess, and he *was* trapped in the downward spiral of addiction, but he was a seeker. There seemed to be a genuine hunger for the Lord. Although he didn't know me very well, he was very open, self-disclosing, and almost without defensiveness. I knew what I was seeing. This was more than the strength of this man's character. This was more than sturdy resolve. I was seeing the presence and power of the indwelling Holy Spirit in operation. Right there before my eyes, the Holy Spirit was actively battling with Greg's sinful nature and giving him power to do what, left to himself, he would never have been able to do.

The children surprised me as well. Sure, they looked and acted like they had grown up in a very troubled home, but they were not out of control. There was a strength of relationship between Loretta and Greg and their kids that caught me off guard. The more I observed them that night and the more I got to know these little ones in days and weeks to come, the more I was persuaded that God, in the grandeur of his mercy, had built a wall of protection around them.

Then there was a real readiness for help. In my years of working with people, I have learned that not everyone who cries out for help really wants it. Old patterns of self-righteousness, self-excusing, and blame-shifting are often hard to break. Old discouragement often hardens into bitter cynicism that is difficult to break through. People tend to argue and reject the very help they once seemed so desperate to get. They defend the logic of the very decisions that led them into such a desperate condition. But, Loretta and Greg were in a very different place. Yes, they threw some blame around, and there were places where they were too ready to defend themselves, but there was a readiness for help in it all. They really were seekers, and the thing that surprised me the most was that they were not entirely without hope. It was dim and flickering, but it was there. I thought of the prophecy in Isaiah 42:3 of a pastoral Messiah that was to come. It says of him, "A bruised reed he will not break, and a smoldering wick he will not snuff out." These were bruised people. Their faith smoldered, but it was there! Their Messiah was there as well. He had not broken them, and he had not quenched their faith. He had been faithful to the prophecies of what he and his ministry would be like.

For the first time that night I did something that was to become a theme in my ministry: I pointed to the concrete signs of the presence of a living and active Redeemer. He is there, and if he is, then there are visible signs of his work. Underneath the trouble of troubled people is a great, more fundamental form of trouble. The big trouble is that they *do not see God*. Again and again I have heard believers tell their stories in godless ways. They see much sin, suffering, damage and destruction, but they do not see *him*.

So, time and time again, I have functioned like Elisha. Surrounded by the Syrian army, Elisha's servant says in great fear, "Oh, my lord, what shall we do?" And over and over, I have echoed Elisha's response: "Don't be afraid. Those who are with us are more than those who are with them." When the servant looks again, he sees that the hills are covered with chariots of fire of the Lord! Yes, they were surrounded but not just by the enemy. They were surrounded by the Lord and his mighty army (See 2 Kings 6:15ff.).

In the middle of the disappointing realities of life in a broken world this is what we need. We need eyes to see him. Day after day I am like a tour guide, walking people through their own lives saying, "Look here. Oh, look over there! Stop and notice this. Have you ever seen this before?" Each time I point to the evidence of a Redeemer who is still on site and still doing what he has promised to do. I have learned that a significant part of my job is to stand in the middle of people's lives with them and to be used of God to give them eyes to see. My job is to help them come out of hiding and to look through the fog of fear and destruction. My job is to help them see the powerful hand of a loving Redeemer who is not confused, uncaring, or inactive. I want them to see that, in the middle of all of the trouble, there are blessings that need to be recognized. I want them to see that this is the only real reason for hope. Sam couldn't look at himself or his circumstances and find any reason for hope; Greg and Loretta couldn't look at one another and find reason for hope, but as they saw the Lord, there was hope to hold on to.

I have seen the pages of Scripture come to life in the real lives of people. I have entered many Psalm 88 lives, and I have seen many Psalm 4 responses. Why? Because the God who understands the depths of our trouble (Psalm 88) is with us in them, helping us to do what we would never be able to do alone (Psalm 4). The hope of these two psalms is *real and possible* for me and for you and for all of God's children.

Perhaps you are in the middle of your life and you have lost your way. You wonder what your life has been worth. You wonder if it has really made a difference whether you lived or died. You wonder why God wasn't with you more and didn't give you more. In your disorientation and distress, *remember* and *see*. Remember that your Lord really does understand, with amazing detail, everything you face. Remember that he really is with you in every place of life in which you find yourself. And remember, because these things are true, there are evidences of his presence and power in your life right now. Look for him in the hallways of your life. Grab hold of the hope that his presence can give. Remember, *it is real, and it is possible*! Look again and keep looking until you see the one thing that can give you reason to continue: Him.

Chapter 3

The Death of Invincibility

After thirty, a body has a mind of its own.

—BETTE MIDLER

You know you're getting older when all the names in your black book have M.D. after them.

—HARRISON FORD

There's no fooling myself anymore. I can do all the mental gymnastics I want, but the fact is that physically I am not the same person. I am not in possession of the same level of energy I once had. Although I am not grossly overweight, my body has morphed into the thick profile of a middle-aged man. My omnipresent bifocals sit on my face as a dead giveaway that my youth has passed me by. The tightness and tone of my muscles has given way to a flaccidity that is a testament to the athleticism of another era. When I get up in the morning, my body talks to me in ways that are new and often not enjoyable. My stomach, once impervious to the most violent of cuisines, has developed a sad new sensitivity. It is all very hard to face.

In my youth, I never realized how much comfort I received from the strong and robust condition of my body. I never realized how much my physical condition contributed to my feeling alive and secure. These new feelings of physical weakness and vulnerability are one of midlife's unsettling realities. And no matter how hard you work, there simply is no denying them. Yet it isn't just a body thing. These changes reveal struggles that are intensely spiritual; and therefore, worthy of our attention.

Have you walked down the street recently, seen your reflection in a showroom window and wondered what in the world happened? Have you mourned the fact that you're simply not able to live and work at the frenetic pace that was once your norm? Have you been all too aware lately of the lines on your face or the newly minted blotches on your skin? Have you tried to demonstrate your once-dominant athletic prowess to your grown children, only to pay the painful price for days? Have you felt the encroaching dread of old age? Then this chapter is for you. There is help here for the physical issues that often become so powerful in midlife struggles. The goal of this chapter is to examine these struggles in a way that is culturally relevant and gospel rich.

The End of an Era

One event from my teens captures the death of physical invincibility very well. It was summertime, and my Dad and I went out to play tennis. He was a sporting goods salesman and had always been quite athletic. We arrived at the court that evening ready for some intense father-and-son competition. We warmed up with a few volleys, and I served the ball to my Dad. He netted it. Then he walked up to the net, bent over, let out a groan of pain, and told me he could not straighten up. I was tempted to ask if we could keep playing, because it was the only way I could ever beat him!

In a moment, my robust and athletic father had turned into an old man. It actually scared me as I helped him walk off the court and gingerly eased him into the car. Fortunately I was able to drive, so before long we were getting Dad the medical help he needed. As he limped around in obvious pain for the next several days, it was disorienting for all of us, but even more so for him. His back had issued a stern warning on the court that evening: You are no longer a young man! In one moment he had been forced to reevaluate his physical health and capabilities. As we rode home from the court that night, he quietly stated the obvious: "I guess I'm just not as young as I used to be."

Weakness and aging are significant parts of the midlife struggle. It is unavoidable; all of our bodies age and change. There are things we once did that we cannot do any longer. And when we forget who we are, giving way to delusions of youth, we pay the price physically. The early evening one-on-one basketball tournament with our teenage son leaves us with pulled muscles. The whole-house spring cleaning leaves us stiff as a board. The hike up the mountain leaves us gasping as if God had suddenly deoxygenated the world. We may have many good physical years ahead of us, but we do not have the physical vitality of our youth. It is a hard fact to face.

But the nasty little signs are there. Aging is a process and not an event, so the signs sneak up on you: wrinkles, rashes, spider veins, graying hair, loss of hair, hair where it shouldn't be (in your ears), muscle loss and softening, weight gain, loss of flexibility, loss of energy, chronic aches and pains, vision loss, sagging skin, skin discoloration, tiredness, hearing loss, stiffness of joints, and the list goes on. These are not things you want to think about. You don't want to admit that you don't comb your hair anymore; you rearrange it on your head. You don't want to admit that you have to use more makeup to cover the splotches that somehow just appear on your face. You try to convince yourself that you are forgetful because of your busy and active life. You have a terrible battle maintaining the weight that once was your norm without any attention or change of habits. You try to ignore the stiffness that greets you as get out of bed. You avoid reading glasses until your arms just can't extend enough to make the newspaper legible. It isn't a catastrophe. There surely are things of greater importance in your life. Deep inside, you hate what's happening to your body and the incontrovertible physical evidence that you are not what you once were. You are middle-aged and getting older every day.

A Dangerous Intersection

Why does the natural process of aging discourage us so? Why are so many plans and products designed and sold to us to help us deal with it? Why do we tend to do so many things to recapture or retain our youth? More important, why do these natural physical processes so often lead to deeper, more spiritual struggles?

Four factors come together at midlife that have the power to make aging a huge struggle. Many people get disoriented and derailed when these four factors intersect at midlife. They are: *a universal awareness*, the *assumptions of youth*, the *focus of our culture*, and a *condition of the heart*. Let's first consider them separately and then examine their collective impact at midlife.

A Universal Awareness

There is a *universal awareness* deep inside of every human being, even though we may not be able to wrap words around it. It is the grand contradiction, the piece jammed into the jigsaw puzzle that shouldn't really be there. The very subject makes us uneasy. It's unnatural and we all know it: *People are not supposed to die.* Like a knife rammed into the heart of creation, sin brought death into the world and all the aging, sickness, and decay that goes with it. We can philosophize about it all we want, and we can give it our best existential twist, but there is no getting around it: death is fundamentally unnatural. It wasn't supposed to be part of the story. This awful, unavoidable abruptness wasn't supposed to be the final chapter.

Ever since the fall, all people everywhere have mourned the reality of death. This universal distaste for death is part of a universal yearning for the glories of what was meant to be. In the tranquility of God's creation-majesty, death was not part of the picture. Life would give way to life, again to life, and the pattern would go on into eternity. But in a horrible moment of cosmic destruction, death stuck its ugly face in the middle of the story. We all know that it should not be there. Things shouldn't end this way. You can't look at a lifeless body without being overwhelmed with how weird and unnatural it all is.

So when we see wrinkles, when the body begins to ache, and when weakness resides where strength once reigned, a visceral dread grips us all. It's not so much that we don't like being forty or fifty. It's not so much that we want to continue to play touch football or work at a frenetic pace. No, it is the awareness that we are closer to the one thing in life that simply shouldn't be—death. Though few of us recognize it, embedded in this dread is a longing to return to what was supposed to be. It is a longing for a place where life and death no longer battle, where death has once and for all been completely defeated.

Each time we dread aging or mourn a death, we are crying out for a Redeemer to defeat death forever. Aging, sickness, deterioration, and death preach the Gospel because they point to the utter futility of living a life that ends this way. Redemption makes the story rational again, because in defeating death, it gives each redeemed one a story that ends the way it was meant to end—with life.

Midlife struggles are dyed with all the life-and-death drama of the Gospel. These struggles are not weird or unnatural. They make sense. When you listen below the surface you will hear the horrible cries of the fall mixing with the awesome celebrations of eternity. In the dread of aging and death, the drama of redemption bubbles to the surface.

The Assumptions of Youth

Allow me to share one vivid memory from my teenage years. My friend Brad and I had planned on the night for weeks. For us, Big Bob's was the gourmet center of the universe, unparalleled in its culinary delights. We had heard that it offered edible wonders so amazing that we could not resist their siren call. I cashed my meager paycheck from stocking shelves at JCPenney, all one dollar and sixty cents an hour of it, not caring if I spent the entire check that evening. We were attracted to Big Bob's not only because of the glorious cuisine but because of the bragging rights that we would garner as a result of eating there.

Like all customers of upscale restaurants, we had to wait in line, right under the bug zapper, for about twenty minutes until we were given a paper menu (with a maze and a word puzzle on the back) and shown to our pink Formica-topped table. We didn't need the menu because we knew what we were there for. As we waited excitedly for the waitress to arrive, we had more the mentality of conquerors than diners. What had brought us to Big Bob's were three amazing delights whose renown had been published person-to-person throughout our community. First was the Monster Burger, a stunning thing, seven inches in diameter after cooking, and offered with anything a human being could possibly conceive atop such a piece of meat. The bun looked like two edible Frisbees, a bakery achievement on its own. Then there were the Monster Fries. They came spilling over the edges of what looked like a picnic basket for a small family. The fries were offered plain, slathered with gravy, drowned with cheese, or liberally sprinkled with any spice the diner could imagine.

Brad and I never considered sharing. We each ordered a Monster Burger and an order of Monster Fries. They were the kind of single-portion servings we had always dreamed of but had never been fortunate enough to experience. Our eyes were on the prize, the third and final culinary magnet that had drawn us to this place. It was called "The Kitchen Sink," twenty-four scoops of ice cream and seven different toppings, luxuriously presented in a glass punch bowl. That night we ate everything, including the Kitchen Sink! We even used straws at the end to drink up every last drop of the seven-topping slurry that was at the bottom of that punch bowl.

I don't even remember feeling stuffed. We left, looking for places to share our tale and ended up that evening in bumper cars, careening into one another, without even a twitch of intestinal uneasiness. We never thought of the stress we were inflicting on our bodies with this type of meal.

There is a vast difference in the way I now think about food, diet, restaurants, and menus. I carefully examine the ingredients on food containers. I count calories. I even understand the danger of trans fat. When I examine a menu, I find myself considering both health and taste. I think about what the meal will do to me after it is over. I think about my heart, my veins, and my intestines. I am conscious about my weight and am regularly scanning the relative condition of my health. I don't eat many of the things I would readily enjoy and have learned to eat many things that I wouldn't have considered in my Big Bob days. I am actually now more attracted to food for its quality than its quantity and really do believe that often less *is* more. I am simply not the same guy who found such delight at Big Bob's. Midlife has changed my perspective.

Delusions of Invincibility

We live much of our lives joyfully oblivious about our physical bodies. Physical health is like oxygen; you don't think about it and you aren't grateful for it until you begin to lose it. In our youth, we tend to forget how dependent, weak, and physically vulnerable we actually are. We don't think about the magnificently interdependent and perfectly balanced systems of the body that must work in unceasing union with each other in order for us to retain our health. Sure, in some distant sense, we all know that we are getting older, but we live like we're basically invincible.

As we move into our twenties, we continue to live with a happy invincibility. Our attention is on new relationships, a new place of work, or perhaps the new task of parenting children. Our schedules are incredibly full, and the days fly by. Most of the time our bodies simply aren't the focus of our attention. Eventually, in subtle and not-so-subtle ways, we begin to experience the death of our own invincibility. Yet, we are so skilled at not facing the facts. We tell ourselves that a certain pain has come because we did too much gardening, or that the shirt doesn't fit because the cleaners shrank it, or that the gray hair that we are seeing is premature.

No matter how hard we work to maintain the delusion, we cannot fight the stark reality of every creature in this fallen world: everything that lives is in the process of dying. This world and everything in it will pass away. Physical invincibility is a delusion. As compelling, powerful, and delightful as it may be, it is a lie.

The Focus of Our Culture

The third factor converges powerfully with the assumptions of youth to shape our experience of midlife. We not only live with feelings of invincibility; we also live in a culture that is obsessed with the human body. In the comprehensive secularization of our culture, all that's left standing is physical man. Life is reduced to physical people living in a material world. The most important things in life are the things that you can see, touch, taste, or hold in your hands.

A culture that assumes the centrality of the physical world will end up with body obsession. As a popular television ad once asserted, "Appearance is everything!" We spend billions of dollars every year on products, processes, technology, and institutions that all promise to make us more muscular, more beautiful, and more youthful. Endless websites tout the latest fat-burning chemical, muscle-defining equipment, or wrinkle-reducing cream. Billions of dollars are spent in research in a rush to discover and market the next miracle product. Book after book is written to give you the secret to being the fittest and most beautiful you.

Experts have even begun to posit that "aging is an option." Websites take names like, "Youthful Forever," "Youthful Essence," "Fountain of Youth," "Always Youthful," and, the name I like best, "Renewman." Each site promises you permanent youth if you purchase the right set of products.

Then there is the whole body re-sculpting industry. It is no longer targeted at the idle rich. It is no longer just the fascination of the Hollywood elite. Millions of average Americans are reshaping, altering, and re-sculpting their bodies. Your eyes, chin, lips, forehead, ears, breasts, abdomen, thighs, calves, etc. can all be reshaped. And if anything sags again, it can be reshaped once more. The American Society of Aesthetic Plastic Surgeons says that there were 8,470,363 cosmetic surgery procedures done in America in 2001. Over seven million of these procedures were done on women and one million on men. These statistics do not include millions of nonsurgical procedures such as Botox and collagen injections, chemical peels, and laser hair removal. There are few things we spend more time and money on than our personal appearance. It is a cultural addiction, and all of us live under its influence.

Let me detail some of the elements of the physical obsession that dominates Western culture.

1. ***The youthification of Western culture.*** It is an amazing thing. If you are over forty-five, you won't see yourself very much on prime-time television. Yes, there is the occasional midlife or senior character who exists in the background, but the culture depicted in prime-time is shockingly young. Whether it is in sitcoms, dramas, or reality shows, it appears that in Western culture few people live much longer than thirty-five!

We all know that what dominates the popular media is somehow reflective of the ideals, values, and perspectives of the surrounding culture, or it would not be so consistently presented. The problem is that a youth-obsessed culture will tend to despise aging. In his book, *Growing Old in America*, Andrew

W. Achenbaum says that a positive view of aging existed in America for almost two hundred years. The elderly were typically esteemed in their communities and were consistently presented to young people as examples. Old age and what it represented were so esteemed that people actually found artificial ways of appearing older (powdered wigs being the best known example). Achenbaum's comments point us to the difference between our cultural perspectives and Scripture's.

The Bible looks at youth and aging in the exact opposite way from our culture. While the Bible esteems the vigor of the young, it views old age as a sign of blessing and repeatedly calls on us to honor the aged (Isa. 46:4, Lev. 19:32, Prov. 23:22, 1 Tim. 5:1). The tendency of modern Western culture to despise aging and to worship youthfulness is one subtle indicator of how far it has moved away from a biblical perspective on life. In Scripture old age is a sign of God's covenantal faithfulness. It is also connected with functional wisdom. We, on the other hand, crave youth, dread getting old, and quickly put out to pasture all those who have lived long enough to have acquired some functional life-wisdom. This ageism is part of the oxygen of our culture. We all breathe it in daily, and it has affected the way each of us views who we are and where we are going.

2. ***The affluence of Western culture.*** Recently I was visited by a friend from India. I asked him to give his impression of Americans. He hesitated for a bit, and I assured him that it was okay to be honest. What he said next I will never forget. "Because you have so much, you complain so much." I was taken aback by the power of his analysis. It seems like it would be the other way, but it is not. Sinners not only struggle with want; they have a terrible time handling blessing. Sin makes all of us scarily self-absorbed and endlessly ravenous. When we have everything we need, we complain that we do not have more of everything, that others have a better everything than we have, or we manufacture new things to crave. We worry more and are depressed more easily. We have the time and

money to pay attention to things that we were once too busy to notice.

My Indian friend gave me another simple, but revealing, example. His host had taken him to a grocery store to pick up bread. He was astounded that there was an entire aisle dedicated to a seemingly endless selection of breads. He watched as people walked up and down the aisle, looking for the specific type of breads that they had in mind. He saw disappointed customers walk away empty-handed because the one type of bread that they had their hearts set on wasn't available. This scene was a hermeneutical vignette, making sense of the mentality of our culture.

Our affluence appears to have solved most of the physical problems that dominate the world. We don't forage for food. We don't wonder if we'll have shelter. We don't have to deal with many of the diseases that are the result of poor sanitation and a contaminated food and water supply. Our affluence has also put a lot of free time on our hands. Yet the luxury of time has not led us to happiness and contentment, looking for ways to serve others. Instead, we are dissatisfied and discontented. We obsess over our self-esteem or the percentage of body fat we are carrying around. Like emotional archeologists, we intensively examine our past for any pottery shard of our family history that may explain why we are the way we are and do the things we do. We carefully parse our words, lest anything we say could in some way be construed as being intolerant of anyone who in any way is different from us. We invest an amazing amount of time and energy examining how we feel and how we feel about how we feel in comparison to how we are told we should normally feel. We have plenty of time to recognize each new wrinkle and each new instance of midlife pain. And we have the time and money to preen. Our affluence allows more and more of us to spend more time and money than ever before, doing anything and everything we can to look, smell, and feel the best we can. Every day we spend a shocking amount of money on cosmetic luxuries. We exert amazing efforts to be the best physical specimens we can be. It is not just a focus. It is an obsession.

It is not wrong to think about our identity and past history. Our emotional state is important. It's not wrong to want to look nice. Yet, there is something spiritually unhealthy about the way, in our affluence, we have been so captured by these things. The third world person does not wake up to deep concerns about identity, past history, or present beauty. He prays for food and shelter and is quite content with things that we would reject out of hand. Our affluence does not make us selfish; it simply enables us to afford more sophisticated expressions of selfishness.

3. ***A culture of leisure.*** One of the most subtle but significant shifts in Western culture has been the seismic shift from a labor-based to a leisure-based culture. Leisure can be defined as the freedom provided by the cessation of work or duty. In other words, work time belongs to someone else, while leisure time belongs to me to spend as I please (although biblically not even my free time is *my* time). My identity is no longer shaped by my calling to work but by my right to play. Work is viewed as the price we have to pay to get the leisure we really are living for. Work doesn't really excite or engage us; it isn't viewed as what we were put on earth to do. We are far, far away from the days when work was viewed as a fundamental way that we image and worship God. Now we tend to identify ourselves by the toys that entertain us in the moments of leisure that we live for. Whether a boat, a BMW, a widescreen plasma TV, a vacation home, or a $1000 fly-fishing rod, our leisure toys have become our identity markers.

Many things could be said about this subject, so let's attempt to simplify it and focus on how it affects the subject at hand. First, it looks as though we actually have a work-based culture. In fact, many would say that our problem is that many of us work too much. However, what has radically changed is not the number of hours we work per week, but our basic *atti-*

tude toward work. We tend to see work as more of a curse than a calling. We put in our time because we have to, or because our work enables us to pursue the things for which we are really living. What causes us to work more than we should is not our love for work, but our craving for the things that added work will allow us to experience or purchase.

Second, and not unrelated, is a shift in the way we view leisure. We all need retreat from labor; that is the principle of Sabbath. We are not limitless in ability or energy. Work must always be approached with a view toward the need to rest both our bodies and our souls. So, the pursuit of leisure is right and proper when it is a *means* to an end. Distracting entertainment, quiet relaxation, and rejuvenating activity all serve us well in their proper place, but they were never meant to be the thing that we live for. This is where the significant change has taken place. Leisure has become the end rather than a means to the end. It has become the thing we live for.

When a culture craves and focuses on leisure, it will naturally focus more on entertainment. This is why the entertainment industry is so dominant in our culture. And entertainment tends to focus on pleasure. I want to be entertained in a way that brings me pleasure. The more focus on pleasure, the more life gets defined as being all about the personal pursuit of what makes me happy. Thus a culture of leisure is scarily individualistic and self-absorbed. Life morphs into an unceasing pursuit of comfort, ease, and individual satisfaction. This kind of culture will tend to curse all the life experiences that are toilsome, painful, and difficult. "The good life" becomes the easy, pleasure filled life.

A self-absorbed, pleasure-obsessed culture will be intolerant of all the painful, discomforting, and embarrassing physical changes of midlife. If food is what brings me pleasure, then I will curse the fact that I now have to watch what I eat. If exercise is what makes me feel good about myself, I will hate the fact that I am not able to do physically what I once did. If the beauty of youth has been my source of identity, I will curse the evidences of old age that are harder and harder to hide. A pleasure-obsessed, leisure-driven culture will tend to curse aging and all the physical changes that go with it.

4. ***The death of eternity.*** Perhaps the most powerful leaven of the Christian worldview is its focus on eternity. We are the people who "fix our eyes on what is unseen," because "what is unseen is eternal" (2 Cor. 4:18). We know that this world is wasting away. We know that we now live somewhere in the middle of the "already" and the "not yet." We know that the best of life is yet to come. Eternity reminds us that no one has the power to take away the things that are really worth living for; the things you cannot touch, taste, weigh, quantify, or hold in your hand. When you have one eye on eternity, this present physical world looks entirely different. Yet in a culture that has presided over the death of eternity, it is very hard to hold physical things in their proper place. Consider what Paul says: "outwardly we are wasting away, yet inwardly we are being renewed day by day" (2 Cor. 4:16).

If you do not have a robust belief in a real afterlife, you are left with the first part of Paul's statement. You look at yourself in the mirror and cannot believe what is happening to you. You don't want to even think about what you will look like in ten years if these physical trends continue! Only in light of eternity does the second part of Paul's confession bring any comfort. This earth-suit of my body is wearing out, but that is not the end of me. Paul doesn't deny that this physical process of decay is happening, but he recognizes another glorious and unstoppable process. It cannot be seen with physical eyes or evaluated with medical instruments, but it is as real as anything I experience in the physical realm. My inner man is being daily and progressively renewed. It is strategically and progressively being prepared for life in eternity.

Viewing myself from the vantage point of eternity helps me to see both processes at once. Yes, the physical me is in the process of aging and decay, but that is okay because after the body has served its earth-bound purpose, I will be given another body for eternity. And even though my body is wasting away, my heart is progressively being changed and renewed. I am growing in strength of character, and therefore I am being prepared to live forever in paradise with my Lord. This is why Paul says that he does not lose heart. He can face his physical condition with hope and encouragement because he sees the unseen. He sees redemption, renewal, growth, change, and restoration. Only when viewed from eternity can physical aging be put in its proper place.

5. ***The rise of cosmetic technology.*** A recent *New York Times* article tells of how upper-middle-class teenage girls prepare for the first day of the new school year by having all kinds of cosmetic procedures. A quick nose job, chemical peel, a bit of liposuction, collagen lip implants, a visit to the tanning salon, along with the normal work on the nails and hair, make that first day a whole lot easier.

Notice the emphasis here. For these girls, preparing for school has little to do with examining your attitude and gearing up your mind. But it has everything to do with employing the finest in cosmetic technology to be the best physical person that is technologically possible. Consider for a moment how this affects all of us. When you live in a culture where beauty once beyond your dreams is now both surgically possible and even affordable by the middle class, everyone living in that culture will be affected by the new standards of physical beauty that the technology produces.

It is hard enough for the average middle-aged person to live in Western culture without constantly mourning the loss of his or her youth, but it is even harder when the surrounding culture has increasingly elevated standards of physical appearance. When your culture obsesses over the size and shape of one's nose, the fullness of one's lips, or the relative tightness of one's abs, all who live in that culture will tend to curse aging and all the physical changes it brings with it.

6. ***The media ideal.*** I have often thought that televisions should be sold with a required warning label: "Danger: Unre-

alistically beautiful people inside." The media image of human beings doesn't look much like what I see when I walk the streets of center city Philadelphia. The daily norm in my community includes masses of average-looking people, occasionally punctuated by specimens of rare beauty. It looks little like what television, movies, advertising, and magazines push on us: masses of beautiful people punctuated on rare occasions by the average-looking Joe—who sticks out like a sore thumb!

When popular media dominates the thoughts, desires, and expectations of the culture, its projected ideals become the "norms," even when these "norms" are far from what is actually normal on the streets. These ideals have a powerful ability to shape the way we see ourselves and others. They stimulate desire and dissatisfaction, excitement and disappointment. The stars in the popular sitcoms or movies stay young because they *are* young, or because they will soon be replaced by younger stars. But we don't stay young! We gain weight, lose our hair, wrinkle and weaken, get diseases, break our arms, and bloody our noses. We age, we suffer, and we die; yet we live with a world of utter unreality projected all around us. It makes us uncomfortable with being normal and disappointed with the fact that the ideal has never been nor ever will be within our reach.

7. ***The death of the Inner Man.*** If I were a doctoral student at Temple University here in Philadelphia, and I proposed to the faculty that I would like to do my dissertation on the relationship between the heart and human behavior, I would probably get confused looks or be laughed out of the room. We don't talk much about the heart in modern Western culture. Heart language pops up on Valentine's Day and in halftime speeches about determination, but the inner man, the heart as the Bible describes it, is not given serious attention. Instead it has been replaced by a widely received determinism. There are typically two kinds of determinism that most people accept. First is the environmental/experiential determinism that says that you are the product of your environment or that you are

what your experience has made you. Second is the biological/physiological determinism that posits that your behavior is caused and controlled by biochemical processes within your body. The Bible teaches that our hearts are constantly interacting with everything around us, while our culture assumes a relatively passive inner person. It is true that your environment influences you, as does the operations of your body, but neither has the power to bypass the heart.

What does this have to do with midlife and physical aging? Everything. When you are in a culture that underestimates the rich inner world of the heart, that culture will tend to think of the physical you as the real you. Would this not add power to the experience of physical aging? If the real me is the physical me and my body is progressively growing older and weaker, would it not reinforce my feelings of discouragement and dread as I face the realities of aging?

A Bad Place to Grow Old

When you add all of these cultural influences together, it is not hard to understand the culture's inordinate focus on the physical body. Just don't be too quick to think that it hasn't affected you. Consider whether any of the following scenarios resemble your life:

- You're on your third go-around on the Atkins low-carb diet.
- As a wife and mother, you spend much too much time and money on your personal cosmetology.
- Your basement is a graveyard of exercise implements, each an artifact to fitness dreams gone by.
- You maintain a disproportionately high clothing budget in order to keep up with the latest styles or your latest sizes.
- You purchased that motorcycle, not because you have always wanted to ride around on two wheels, but as an attempt to hold onto your youth.

- You've stood in front of the mirror and stretched back the skin on your face and neck, wondering what you would look like if you could afford to get it all surgically lifted.
- You dress younger than is appropriate or seek the company of those who are half your age.
- You say your relationship with God is the most important thing in all of life, but you have, in fact, invested a lot more time, energy, and money on your physical self than on your soul.
- You subtly struggle with envy toward those who are young and attractive.
- Stop and take a look. The evidence is probably there that you too have breathed in the oxygen of the surrounding culture, and it has affected the way that you view yourself.

Now think for a moment how the things we have discussed come together to produce great struggle in midlife. At the very moment that the signs are everywhere in my physical body that I am not what I once was, I am also being bombarded with the message that aging is a curse to be avoided at any cost. It is no surprise that our culture no longer esteems old age and that there is a major industry focused on selling anything that has the perceived power to turn back the clock.

A Condition of the Heart

So far we have considered three factors that make midlife such a struggle: the *universal awareness* of the unnaturalness of death, the happy *delusions of youth* and the obsessive physical *focus of our culture*. Yet together they are not enough to explain why physical aging so often becomes a spiritual crisis in midlife. None of these three factors would have the power they have to disorient and discourage us if they were not empowered by a fundamental condition of heart. This condition of heart is *cause central* when it comes to midlife struggles.

There is a little phrase in 2 Peter 1:4 that is tremendously helpful here. Peter says that God has given us everything we need so that we can "escape the corruption in the world *caused by evil desires*" (italics mine). Let this phrase sink in. Consider how radically different its viewpoint is from the way we normally think. We all tend to blame our surroundings for what we think or do ("It's peer pressure!" "If you had these kids, you'd be angry, too." "It's that music he listens to!"). And although it is quite appropriate to understand and evaluate the influence of the surrounding culture, it is vitally important that we get the order right.

What Peter proposes here is stunning. He does not say that we are corrupt because the culture around us is. In fact, the opposite is true. The culture is corrupt because we are! The culture hasn't produced the condition of heart, but the condition of heart has produced the culture. When you think about it, it could not happen the other way around. Culture is simply what results when human beings made in the image of God interact with God's world. Culture is not like some fog that you drive into, over which you had no influence or control. When a culture is a certain kind, it is always because of the people that are in that culture. This means that cultural change always means change in people, because culture is the people and people shape the culture.

Think of it this way. You look at a married couple and say to yourself, "They really have a bad marriage." You are not saying, "Isn't it a shame that a bad marriage has fallen upon them." No, what you are recognizing is that the things that this couple has thought, desired, said, and done to one another have produced a troubled marriage. The rocky and conflicted culture of this marriage has been formed by the people in it.

It is humbling, but it is true: if we are going to understand the huge struggle of physical aging, we can't just look at the culture in which we live but must also examine our hearts. This struggle, like every other human struggle, has its source in the heart, and the only real solution is in heart change. You and I must humbly confess that the problem starts with us. This confession is vital, but it must be followed by a clear understanding of what our heart problem actually is. Only by doing both of these things will our all-too-typical struggles with aging be replaced with a new freedom and joy.

The Great Replacement

It wasn't long into my adult life that I realized I wouldn't make a very good Stoic. I tend to find much too much pleasure in the physical things around me. Whether it is a fine painting, a delicious meal, or a well performed piece of music, it is very easy for me to define the good life as one that contains liberal amounts of each of these. That is why I have found the insights of Scripture on the human heart to be at once convicting and encouraging.

How does Scripture help us to understand both the nature and the power of the midlife struggle? The answer can be found in a very simple, yet profound sentence in Romans 1. This sentence provides not only an interesting insight into human motivation, but provides us with a paradigm for understanding human life on this side of eternity. Romans 1:25 says, "They exchanged the truth of God for a lie, and worshiped and served created things rather than the Creator—who is forever praised. Amen." Because of the worship language in this passage, it is possible to miss how comprehensive this insight is. There is more being said here than the fact that we tend to serve a whole catalog of God replacements. Yes, we all tend to have that inertia away from the Creator and toward the creation, but there is something else being said here.

Romans 1:25 alerts us to the fact that there is an innate tendency in every human being to replace the *spiritual* with the *physical*. We all do it in various ways. The truth of the matter is that life can be found only in the Creator. Yet we seek to find life in the material things, the love of another person, the security in a physical situation or location, or in physically experienced pleasure or comfort. Idolatry, in its simplest form, is when I replace the worship of God with some physical image or object that I can see and touch. The reason this is so tempting is obvious. The idol can be seen, touched, or somehow physically experienced. I can sit in a lavish house, look around and say, "What a good life I have!" I can feel the lips of someone who loves me caress my cheek. I can hear human applause or glory in the beauty of a certain place. I can relive the physical comfort of a wonderful meal or the physical pleasure of an enjoyable sexual relationship. A certain physical person with a real voice can compliment me on my appearance or my work. It is not hard to understand how tempting it is to replace the spiritual with the physical.

If sin sets us on a trajectory away from the Creator and toward the creation, then it also sends us away from the spiritual and toward the physical. So appearance will trump character. Personal pleasure will trump purity of heart. The love of a person will trump the love of God. Material things will trump spiritual realities. Security of situation and location will trump security in the Lord. Physical pleasure and comfort will trump the satisfaction of the soul. The present will trump eternity. This inversion of what was meant to be is all around us. It is one of the principal dangers of life in a fallen world.

We were never wired to live for the glories of what is seen. At best, these shadow glories were meant to point us to the one and only glory really worth living for, the glory of the Lord. There is always a terrible price to pay for this great replacement. It destroys relationships, it distorts culture, it scars people, and finally it leads to death. The oxygen of the glory of God that we were meant to breathe cannot be found elsewhere. When we take in the deoxygenated gases of the creation, our lungs collapse and our hearts atrophy. The problem is not that the physical things are evil in themselves. The problem is that they can take God's place in our hearts. Desire for a good thing becomes a bad thing when it becomes a ruling thing.

Creation cannot and will not sustain us. In our distorted vision, we look at the shadow (the creation) and we see life. But the shadow has no life of its own and can give no life. The shadow is a shadow because it reflects what is alive. In the same way the creation is not self-starting or self-sustaining. It always reflects the glory of the Creator because it is completely dependent on him for its very existence. Physical things by their very nature have no power to offer what the Creator alone can give.

No passage better captures the danger of looking to a physical idol for life than Jeremiah 10:1–16:

Hear what the Lord says to you, O house of Israel. This is what the Lord says:

"Do not learn the ways of the nations
or be terrified by signs in the sky,
though the nations are terrified by them.
For the customs of the peoples are worthless;
they cut a tree out of the forest,
and a craftsman shapes it with his chisel.
They adorn it with silver and gold;
they fasten it with hammer and nails
so it will not totter.
Like a scarecrow in a melon patch,
their idols cannot speak;
they must be carried
because they cannot walk.
Do not fear them;
they can do no harm
nor can they do any good."

No one is like you, O Lord;
you are great,
and your name is mighty in power.
Who should not revere you,
O King of the nations?
This is your due.

Among all the wise men of the nations
and in all their kingdoms,
there is no one like you.
They are all senseless and foolish;
they are taught by worthless wooden idols.

Hammered silver is brought from Tarshish
and gold from Uphaz.
What the craftsman and goldsmith have made
is then dressed in blue and purple—
all made by skilled workers.
But the LORD *is the true God;*
he is the living God, the eternal King.
When he is angry, the earth trembles;
the nations cannot endure his wrath.

"Tell them this: 'These gods who did not make the heavens and the earth, will perish from the earth and from under the heavens.'"

But God made the earth by his power;
he founded the world by his wisdom
and stretched out the heavens by his understanding.
When he thunders, the waters in the heavens roar;
he makes clouds rise from the ends of the earth.
He sends lightning with the rain
and brings out the wind from his storehouses.

Everyone is senseless and without knowledge;
every goldsmith is shamed by his idols.
His images are a fraud;
they have no breath in them.
They are worthless, the objects of mockery;
when their judgment comes, they will perish.
He who is the Portion of Jacob is not like these,
for he is the Maker of all things,
including Israel, the tribe of his inheritance—
the LORD *Almighty is his name."*

The Creator/creature line is the great divide. Nothing on this side of the line is comparable to the Creator. Further, every thing on this side of the great divide depends upon the awesome God, who is on the other side of the line, for its existence and moment-by-moment continuance. Think about it. Behind every powerful physical thing stands the God of glorious power. Behind every moment of physical beauty is the God of awesome beauty. Beneath every physical wonder is the God of awesome wonder. Above every moment of love there is a God who is the source and definition of all true love. Still, our temptation to replace the spiritual glories of the Creator with the physical glories of the creation greets and grips us every day. It is a constant and inescapable struggle. We deify our physical bodies, physical pleasure, material possessions, the security of a place, the love of a physical person, etc.—while at the same time forgetting the spiritual glories of intimate communion with the Lord of Lords, the King of Kings, the great Creator.

Be Afraid, Be Very Afraid

It is important for us to realize that the struggles of midlife are a window to deeper, more fundamental struggles. If all of us tend to replace the spiritual with the physical, then it is quite easy to understand how physical aging could become such a huge emotional and spiritual struggle. We were never meant to get identity from our physical bodies, but we do. We were never meant to get our sense of security and safety from our physical bodies, but we do. Physical strength and health were never supposed to be the source of our hope, but they often are. The thing we have to get a hold of is the realization that our struggle with midlife physical changes actually reveal idols that have been with us for a long time. Aging pumps them up to the surface. Many of us need to confess that we have not been functionally trusting God at all. And when the thing that we have been trusting (our physical body) fails us, we become sad, angry, envious, discouraged, obsessed, and depressed.

Yet physical things still have a great power to seduce us. Because our hearts are deceitful, they can migrate from worship of and service for the Creator, to worship of and service for the creation without us even knowing it. Because of this, it is worth noting the dangers that are resident in this replacement.

1. ***Physical things are impermanent.*** Everything that is physical decays, grows old, grows stale, wears out, or falls apart. Physical things are in a constant state of change. Nothing that you are looking at today will be exactly the same tomorrow. Despite their appearance of permanence, physical things are really transient and unpredictable. Because this is true, they are not a reliable place to place your hope. They will always fail you because they will all pass away.

2. ***Physical things are deceptive.*** They appear to deliver what they cannot in fact deliver. That is why Scripture reminds us in many passages that idols have eyes that cannot see, ears that cannot hear, and mouths that cannot speak. Jeremiah even says that you have to nail them to a platform or they fall over, and you have to carry them around because they cannot walk (See Jer. 10:1–16; Psa. 115:5, 135:16; Hab. 2:18, 19; Isa. 41:23, 46:7). Every promise of every idol is a lie. For all of their attractiveness, they cannot give me what I am looking for. It will never happen. To seek life in idols is an act of personal and spiritual insanity. It will never be found.

3. ***Physical things are impersonal.*** Worship in its purest form is a relationship. I was created for a relationship with God. This personal relationship of communion, love, allegiance, worship, dependency, and obedience is to be the axis on which my personal world revolves. My worship of God is intensely personal. My spirit connects with the Spirit in a communion so profound that it is impossible to wrap words around it. Human beings were made for this foundational connection of spirit to Spirit. Trying to replace that with something that I can see, touch, taste and use—but that I can never have a relationship with—robs me of my humanity.

Notice something else: You and I have some control over the physical things in our lives, even our own bodies. You can alter the shape and physical condition of your body. You can diet. You can do physical exercise. You can change the way you eat. You can put on makeup or invest in new clothes. You can even go so far as receiving plastic surgery. You can control *things*, but you cannot control God or your relationship to him. Proper worship is not only putting God where he belongs in your life but also surrendering control of your life to him. Impersonal things so easily seduce us because they put us in control, the place where every sinner tends to want to be. Here is one of idolatry's great allures, yet it is at once also one of its greatest dangers. You and I were never meant to be in control, and when we are, we always make a mess out of things.

4. ***Physical things are enslaving.*** Here is one of the cruelest tricks of idolatry. What we think we have under control is, at that moment, in the process of enslaving us. Our desires for physical things morph into "needs," and when they do, we become completely convinced that we cannot live without them. You see this dynamic as people relate to their own physical bodies. What was once a desire to be fit morphs into a time-and money-draining life focus. A desire to be slim morphs into deadly anorexia, or into an unceasing pursuit of the next diet miracle. A decision to have some cosmetic surgery done morphs into a sad obsession with altering the look and shape of one's body. A desire to look nice, morphs into constant anxiety about appearance and an unrelenting envy of those who look as you would want to look. The enslaving, addicting quality of idolatry must not be understated or ignored. Like every other kind of idolatry, the worship of physical things enslaves us, even if that physical thing is our own body.

5. ***Replacing spiritual things with physical things is deadly.*** What is the danger of worshiping physical things? In a word, death. Let me offer another metaphor. When the coal miners of Northeastern Pennsylvania went down into the deep mines, they would take a caged canary with them. They kept careful watch over the canary, knowing full well that if the canary was gasping for breath or dead, they had little time left. These min-

ers of old knew that breathing any gas other than oxygen wasn't an option; to try to do so would lead to death. In the same way, it is important that we remember that life can only be found in the Creator. Any physical thing that appears to be life-giving is a delusion.

Trying to find life outside of the Creator exposes me to that which can only bring destruction and death. Putting physical things in the place of the Creator is always destructive to life as God ordained it to be. When I feed on that which cannot give life, I am therefore *not* feeding on the life-giving, grace-bestowing nutrients that can only be found at the feet of the Creator. Jonah said it this way, "Those who cling to worthless idols forfeit the grace that could be theirs." You see, we should be much more afraid of the subtle ways we replace the spiritual with the physical than we are of the normal experiences of aging.

Putting It All Together

The struggles of physical aging that so often characterize midlife are the fruit of a deeper struggle. The struggle of struggles is the struggle for the heart. There will be a day when this struggle is finally over, and God will own our hearts unchallenged for eternity. But today the struggle still goes on. So, God, in the grandeur of his redemptive love, will do what is necessary to reclaim our wandering hearts. These painful moments are not the result of his unfaithfulness and inattention; they are rather the product of his lovely grace. He loves us with an eternal and jealous love. He did not shed the blood of his Son for us only to lose us to some physical thing in the creation.

God fights for us with the full might of his redemptive hand. He is willing to make us uncomfortable and sad. He is willing to bring us through suffering and grief. He is willing to shake and unsettle us. He is willing to squash our dreams and let the air out of our hopes. He is willing to let what we have craved slip like sand through our fingers. And he does all of these things because we are precious to him. We are the apple of his eye. He will not share us with another. He will not allow us to live in the delusion that we have found elsewhere what can only be found in him.

So, our struggles with physical aging are the struggles between idolatry and grace. The Lover of our souls is using the occasion of midlife and the reality of aging to expose and deliver us from idols that resided in secret and ruled us. Reject the self-pity, envy, and discouragement that are so tempting at this time. Look to heaven and be thankful. You are being rescued. Celebrate the One who again and again delivers you from what, by yourself, you would be powerless to escape. Don't mourn the death of your hope in the physical. Celebrate this death, for it is a welcome to a new life of renewed and vigorous love, service, and communion with your Redeemer. Say to yourself with Paul, "Yes, outwardly I am wasting away, but I have real hope and real joy, because inwardly I am being renewed every day. What my life is really about can never be weakened by age or destroyed by years!"

Chapter 4

The Leaves are Off the Trees

Regrets are the natural property of gray hairs.

—Charles Dickens

For all the sad words of tongue or pen,
The saddest are these: "It might have been."

—John Greenleaf Whittier

I love the fall, but I hate autumn. I love the delightfully moderate weather of fall, when the sweltering heat of summer is gone. The sun is still bright, the days fairly long, and the temperature is as about as close to perfect as it will ever be this side of eternity. It is wonderful to be outside and not be sweating or shivering. But autumn is a very different thing. Autumn is a time of harvest, a time when you realize that you cannot go back and do it again. This year I wasn't ready for autumn. I wanted to glue the leaves back on the trees. I wanted to turn back the garden clock and help my flowers have a better start.

Midlife is a time of harvest. The leaves are off the trees and there is no putting them back. The world won't reverse on its axis. Clocks won't turn back. If childhood is the spring of one's life and youth is the summer, then middle age is the autumn. It is the time when each of us in very important ways reaps what he sows.

For much of your youth and adult life, you live wondering how it will all turn out. You are planting, watering, and weeding. You are looking forward. You envision the harvest, but it is cloudy and unclear. So you keep working and refuse to give up hope. Then all of a sudden, you find yourself spending most of your time looking back. It is disorienting and uncomfortable at first. When you've spent your life planting, it seems weird and unnatural to harvest, but you have no choice. You are in your own personal autumn.

Looking back is wonderful and dangerous, delightful and sad. It can be filled with joy or stained with tears. It can soar with thankfulness and plummet with regret. The mix of these extremes makes it hard. And it is particularly hard for the fruit of thankfulness not to be totally covered by the leaves of regret.

I wish I could look back and only be thankful, but I cannot. Let me give you one example. This September our last child left home. It was a wonderful time and a sad time. Luella and I have recounted the myriad of ways that we have experienced the gracious and glorious care of the Redeemer. We have talked about our love and thankfulness for each one of our children. Again and again we have shared how much we have been protected and guided by the wonderful wisdom of the Word of God. We have talked about our thankfulness for the body of Christ, for good preaching, for Christian schools, and for the many books and tapes that helped and supported us along the way. God placed us in the path of wise brothers and sisters who walked the road before us and cautioned us about what lay ahead.

It *has* been a time of thankful reminiscence, but the fact is that none of our children, no matter how spiritually inclined, turns out like we would have imagined or dreamed. They make choices that you and I wouldn't make. They go through the bumps and bruises of young adulthood, sometimes bloodying their noses in unnecessary ways. They may share your faith, but they don't share every one of your values. And along the way they can be quite candid about your weaknesses and failures and how they have determined to avoid them. So, it's hard to look back at your life as a parent and only be thankful, because honest looking back will include recounting many moments of weakness and sin.

We *weren't* the parents that we wanted to be. Yes, we were very dedicated to do it God's way, and we were always looking to learn. We sought to make God's presence obvious to our children, and we talked much about the Gospel. We endeavored to be faithful in correction, instruction, and discipline. But in all of this there was one huge and glaring problem: we did it all as sinners. There were so many times when our sin got in the way. In midlife, these are the moments you tend to remember. Let me recount one for you.

My kids were all young, and I was a young pastor. I wasn't being paid very much, but I wanted to do something nice for my family, so I began squirreling away money until I had saved enough to take us all to Hershey Park, the big amusement park in our area. I was dreaming of a day of familial amusement-park bliss. I thought of our children riding a ride and saying to the person next to them, "This ride is fun, but I find a much greater enjoyment being the child of that man down there who worked so hard so we could enjoy this day."

We had packed a cooler full of food and a cooler loaded with five cans of soda. I have four children, so I had purchased four different kinds of soda (in order to avoid global, nuclear war). Two of these were the same special kind of soda that I could not resist. There were only two cans left on the shelf at the store, and in a moment of parental brain cramp, I grabbed both cans. We arrived at the park, all of us excited about the day before us, when one of the kids asked if he could have something to drink before we all went into the park. It didn't seem like a dangerous request. Instantly my children realized that there was only one can of the magic soda left, for one child had sneaked a can on the way there, and chaos erupted. They were kicking and pushing. They were throwing ice at one another. They pulled at one another's clothes, all the time reinforcing their physical fighting with name-calling and verbal threats. I couldn't believe it! We weren't even in the park and my day was already spoiled. So much for a peaceful day of familial amusement-park bliss.

I wish I could say that I stood back and gave God thanks for revealing the hearts of my children and giving me such a golden ministry moment. No, I was immediately angry too and I jumped into the fray. "So you want to fight," I said. "We don't have to pay all this money so you can fight with one another. You can fight for free! I'll drive us home, put a cooler in the back yard with one can of soda in it, and you can fight forever, since that's what you really love to do!" As I was yelling and waving my hands, my kids quit fighting, because they were watching the people staring as their father was losing it in the middle of the parking lot.

How many more moments of selfishness and sin were there in our family history? How many more times when my plan got smack dab in the way of God's plan? Probably too many to number. What happens in midlife is that as you begin to look in the faces of your older teen or young adult children and watch them respond to life in a fallen world, many of your memories are filled with regret. You simply weren't always able to be the parent you wanted to be or to do the things you had committed to do. Much of the time you were in the way of what God was doing, rather than being part of it. But now there is nothing that you can do about it. The leaves are off the trees.

Midlife is a reflective time. In your youth, even though you have not reached your goals, you are still able to tell yourself that you have time. But the more life you have behind you, the more dreams give way to reflection, and before long you are spending much more time looking back than looking forward. You become a regular spectator on the person that once was.

And you don't always like what you see. The person on the screen of your memory struggles much more than you ever wanted to struggle, and it is hard to admit that it is actually you that you are watching. You wish you could do it the right way this time. You wish you could have wiser eyes, sharper ears, a clearer mind, and a more tender heart. But there is no going back.

In a World Where Regret Lives

There was a time when there was no reason in the world to regret. Everything people thought, desired, said, and did was completely in accord with the will of the Creator. Imagine being a husband at your twenty-fifth anniversary celebration, looking back on your marriage and not having a single thing to regret. Imagine being a mom sitting with your adult children and reminiscing about your years of parenting and literally having nothing to regret. Imagine pondering your relationship with God over decades and finding nothing to regret. Imagine reflecting on your every thought, word, and action without a twinge of remorse or guilt. This was the way it was meant to be.

God made a world of remarkable unity, harmony, peace, and love, where no regrettable thing would interrupt the tranquility he had created. There was work, but it was never done begrudgingly or irresponsibly. There were relationships, yet they were never marked by selfishness, disloyalty, or anger. There was heartfelt worship, service, and obedience to God, but never a moment of rebellion or idolatry. Imagine with me for just a moment what it would be like to live in such a place. What would it be like never to feel regret, never to experience remorse, and never to lug around the heavy weight of guilt? Don't let yourself think that what I am describing is totally unrealistic. In fact the world was once this way.

But on that horrible day with the snake in the Garden, the beauty of the regretless world was shattered. It still lies in pieces all around us. There may be no more common human experience than regret. It is with you all the time. It is like black dye on the white sheets of our existence. You can close your eyes and wish for pure white, but when you open your eyes, you see the black stains of regret everywhere. There is never a day when it is not right to regret a thought, a desire, a word, or a response. It marks the best of family moments. It stains the sweetest of romantic encounters. It leaves spots on the best of friendships. It colors the best of your intentions. The idle word, the impulsive choice, or the wayward desire all cause you regret. You wish you could take back choices. You wish you could grab your words out of the air. You wish you could relive situations and rewrite the script of relationships, but you cannot. The leaves are off the trees, and regret is your harvest.

This is our world, a place where regret lives. It is the class that I blew off and learned nothing. It is the job that I never took seriously. It is the giving in to cravings that have led to too much weight and failing health. It is the career that I allowed to command too much of my time and energy. It is the ministry opportunity that I let slip through my fingers. It is the times I let the opinions of others have too strong a hold on me. It is the conflict that I let grow and fester. It is the debt that I let consume me. It is the material things that I let command my eyes and control my heart. It is money that was squandered while being tightfisted in the face of need. It is the big house that I had to have but didn't really need. It is not enough time with my kids and too much time for me. It is being too tired and too busy ever to be consistent in personal worship of the Lord and study of his Word. It is being driven too much by envy and motivated too much by greed. It is not taking greater advantage of the resources of the body of Christ. It is not saying "thank you" enough or being more willing to help. It is not being patient and understanding enough with others. It is being to willing to respond to evil with evil. It is universally human while being intensely personal. We all live in a place where regret lives.

Where Regret Points Us

In the face of this crushing regret, we are not without hope. Regret is a longing that points us to our need. Beneath each moment of regret is a cry for a better place. The sad songs of regret call us to listen for the joyful hymns from the other side. For there will be a day when the last regret is felt and the final remorse will die. On the other side there will be no more bad choices, unwise reactions, inappropriate thoughts, or evil desires. One of the brightest, most wonderful realities of eternity is that we will be delivered from our weakness and sin and therefore freed from regret. Embedded in each mundane flash of regret and every huge load of remorse is a deep and abiding longing for a better place, a place where failure gives way to victory and sin gives way to righteousness. Until that day, we look back and we feel the searing pain of regret. It is the culture of the Fall, and therefore, the universal experience of all of us.

From Astronaut to Archeologist

It is not something that you just decided to do. Without realizing it, you progressively slipped from living like an astronaut into living like an archeologist. The lifestyle of the young is all about launching with courage and expectancy into worlds unknown. It's all about new trajectories, new locations, and new discoveries. You aren't really discouraged by the distance between you and where you want to be. You rocket from destination to destination, living for the thrill of discovery. You like the pseudo-danger of placing your feet on turf that they have never touched before. You want the next day to be different, and you are not at all afraid of change.

But as you get older you change occupations. You begin to face the fact that you are living with a fundamentally different mentality. You no longer launch toward what could be; now you spend your time uncovering and critiquing what once was. You have taken on an archeologist's approach to life.

Midlife is like a long-term dig into the mound of your existence, and it is often hard to face what you've uncovered. This change takes place because at some point you were no longer able to convince yourself that things would be different or that you would have time to do it a different way. Your past took on more power than your future. It can be discouraging work, but in our midlife years we all seem to be drawn to digging.

It is dangerous work, because this dig does not have scientific objectivity. You are uncovering deeply personal moments fraught with drama and consequence. You uncover yourself as you never have before. It can be a bit breathtaking, even paralyzing. Many of us get stuck and never come out of our archeological hole. It's as if the dirt has fallen in on us and covered up the light. We want so much to be able to go back and walk the streets of our past. There are people we would love to see. There are conversations we would love to redo. It puts a knot in your stomach and a tear in your eye. You try, but you simply can't shuck your guilt or bury your remorse.

Why is Regret so Painful and so Costly?

You know how you remember some moments in fine-grained detail? Well, this was one of those moments for me: Luella and I went out to eat (I can remember exactly where we were sitting), and I could sense that she was unusually serious. I asked her if something was wrong. She said we really needed to talk about our relationship. Then Luella, very kindly and carefully, began playing the "video" of my responses to her and to our relationship. At first I was very defensive. I really wanted to believe that I was not like that man in the video, but the more I "watched," the more troubled I became. I was stung by my selfishness and insensitivity. I was surprised at how often I was irritable and impatient. I was shocked at how committed I was to my agenda and how quickly I became angry when anything or anyone got in the way of it.

I was stunned to recognize how fully I had bought the myth of my own righteousness. Sure, in some theological sense I knew that I was a sinner, and yes, I would acknowledge my need for grace, but day-to-day, I thought of myself as a righteous man. I lived with feelings of arrival that kept me from habits of humble self-examination. In fact, I was so convinced of my righteousness that when Luella would come to me with appropriate and loving complaints, I would instinctively think that she was the one with the problem. I was quite skilled at turning the tables on her. Her attempts to lovingly confront me often ended up with an examination of her sin!

I am deeply persuaded that this is precisely where the Bible dissects and exposes midlife regret. The reason regret has the power to depress, derail, and paralyze us is that regret calls me not only to confess that I have failed, but also to let go of the myth of my own righteousness. The archeological work of midlife exposes who I have been all along. The problem is that what has been exposed doesn't jive with who I thought I was for all these years. Scripture says that if we "claim to be without sin, we deceive ourselves and the truth is not in us." (1 John 1:8). It says this because we are so easily blinded to the depth and consistency of our sin. We tend to underestimate how susceptible our hearts are to living under rulership other than the Lord's.

In our self-righteousness, we tend to recast our own history. When we play back the video of our actions, reactions, and responses, we don't come across as angry and selfish as we really were. Then, when others confront us we feel misunderstood and falsely accused. It is hard to see how self-assured and self-reliant we actually were. It is hard to hear yourself defend yourself, arguing for your own righteousness to another. Yet God knows how crucial it is for us to see these things. So, as we brush the dirt of time off the artifacts of the past, God puts us in a position to see that any good thing we uncover is the result of his grace. In this way midlife can be the occasion of profound and lasting spiritual change. It can be a time where in a deeper and more personal way I understand the Gospel and the true extent of my daily need for the grace of Christ.

Romans 7 and Midlife Regret

Midlife provides a window into our hearts. This is such a good thing. It is good for the delusions to die. To the degree that we have bought into our own righteousness, to that degree we will fail to pursue Christ and his grace. Many of us tend to lack an appreciation for the grace of Christ because, at the level of our daily functioning, we simply don't think we need it. Midlife can help you see yourself with clarity and humility, and in so doing, bring you to your knees. This in itself is a sweet grace. God can use the archeology of midlife to bring you to stand with Paul in Romans 7:14ff, and make his confession your own:

> *We know that the law is spiritual; but I am unspiritual, sold as a slave to sin. I do not understand what I do. For what I want to do I do not do, but what I hate I do. And if I do what I do not want to do, I agree that the law is good. As it is, it is no longer I myself who do it, but it is sin living in me. I know that nothing good lives in me, that is, in my sinful nature. For I have the desire to do what is good, but I cannot carry it out. For what I do is not the good I want to do; no, the evil I do not want to do—this I keep on doing. Now if I do what I do not want to do, it is no longer I who do it, but it is sin living in me that does it.*
>
> *So I find this law at work: When I want to do good, evil is right there with me. For in my inner being I delight in God's law; but I see another law at work in the members of my body, waging war against the law of my mind and making me a prisoner of the law of sin at work within my members. What a wretched man I am! Who will rescue me from this*

> *body of death? Thanks be to God—through Jesus Christ our Lord!*
>
> *So then, I myself in my mind am a slave to God's law, but in the sinful nature a slave to the law of sin.*

We all need to make this confession because each one of us tends to underestimate seriously the presence and power of indwelling sin. No matter how soundly biblical your theology is, that indwelling is the one doctrine that all of us have trouble believing. Yes, we can believe it for others, but it is hard for us to imagine that it really applies to us.

The reason regret tends to hit us so hard in midlife is that for years we have been convincing ourselves that the problem isn't really us. Perhaps the biggest and most tempting lie that all of us tend to embrace is that our greatest problems exist somewhere *outside* of us. This is an attractive distortion because we are surrounded, in this fallen world, by people and things that aren't operating as they were designed to—so there are plenty of available things to blame. I can always find someone in my life who hasn't responded to me properly. I can always identify a difficult situation that I have had to go through. We all tend to take the unrealistically demanding boss, the consistently rebellious child, the all too impatient spouse, the rude neighbor, or the gossiping extended family member as proof that the seeds of what we are harvesting, in fact, belong to someone else.

There is an important spiritual dynamic in operation here. Because we are believers, the heart of stone has been taken out of us and has been replaced with a heart of flesh. This means that when we think, desire, say, and do what is wrong, we experience a God-given unease of heart—conscience. When this happens we all seek heart relief. There are only two ways to find this relief. We can place ourselves once again under the justifying mercies of Christ and receive his forgiveness, or we can erect some system of self-justification that makes what is wrong acceptable to our conscience. An angry father who has just ripped into his rebellious son will tell himself that it is vitally important for his son to respect authority. This justification recolors his sin of anger against his son. Or a wife, who has developed regular patterns of gossiping about her husband's sin to her friends, will tell herself that she is seeking prayer and accountability. She now feels comfortable doing something that the Bible calls sin. Or a teenager who lies to his father about what he is doing tells himself all the time that he has to because his father just "lives for control."

It's an old argument that goes something like this, "His sin makes my sin not sin." We have all used it, and it does us harm. Our growth in grace, our relationships with others, and our harvest as God's children have all been crippled by our strategies of pseudo-atonement. We have been given a Savior who is magnificent in love and grace, yet, in the face of his mercy, we function as our own replacement saviors again and again.

Notice how radically different this is from Paul's perspective in Romans 7. The whole logic of the passage is based on the fact that Paul is locating his struggle *inside* of himself. For Paul, the foundational war is not a war with difficult situations (in many places Paul recognizes they exist) or sinful people (Paul tells stories elsewhere of having to deal with them), but a war with the gravitational pull of sin within. Romans 7 can be uncomfortable for us because it takes us to the very place of self-indictment that we have tended to work so hard to avoid. In our skill at avoiding this place, we have set ourselves up for the shock of regret that tends to hit so hard at midlife.

The Great Surprise

Let me posit some reasons why the regrets of midlife hit us so hard, and how they can become occasions for significant spiritual renewal.

1. ***We have tended to be our own personal con man.*** Kris Lundgaard points this out so powerfully in his wonderful book, *The Enemy Within*. A con man appeals to something for which you have a very strong desire. Perhaps he offers you something you normally would not be able to afford at a seemingly reasonable price (the tract of vacationland in Florida). Or maybe he offers release from an area of personal obligation (quick and easy freedom from debt). The "hook" of a con man always offers you something that you crave. In our sin, we offer ourselves spiritual vacationland that is in reality a stinking swamp of sin. It gives us what anyone who is aware of his sin craves: freedom from guilt. Yet it is the deepening awareness of sin that God uses to draw us into greater dependence on him and into a greater celebration of his grace. When we play the con man and offer ourselves false atonement, we take ourselves off the moral hook. In doing so we not only get in the way of his sanctifying mercies, but we also set ourselves up for moments of shock and dismay when it becomes quite clear that we were not, in fact, as righteous as we thought.

It pains me to confess that along the way I thought I was a much better parent than I now know that I was. I was much more convinced of my nobility as a husband than I now am. In fact I have come to recognize my own con games. For example, I am pretty domestic, and for years I have done most of the cooking in our house. I have always endeavored to be available to my children. When Luella would attempt to confront me lovingly with my sin, I would turn the tables and remind her of my dedication, labor, and availability around our house. My argument was that her problem was not *my* sin, but *her* discontent! I now realize that I was making that argument as much for me as I was for her. What I got from it was not only freedom from guilt, but a personal appraisal of righteousness.

2. ***We have signed a premature armistice agreement with our sin nature.*** In the war with Iraq, the United States learned that one of the most important decisions in a time of war is when to declare victory and sign a peace agreement. If this is done too soon, the enemy is given an opportunity to do more damage with covert war than he did in traditional front line combat. This leads to confusion and a loss of troops who have

been led to believe that major combat is over and have therefore let down their guard. The cessation of the major battles does not mean the war is over. A good general knows the difference between a series of single battle victories and total victory in the larger war.

This is exactly what we often fail to remember in our war with sin. Because God has brought us to himself and delivered us from many sins, we begin to live with a peacetime mentality. Yes, we *are* new creatures, and yes, the controlling power of sin over us *has* been broken, but the presence of sin still remains. This means that the great moral and spiritual war still rages on within us. This is not a time to invest in the luxuries and leisure of peace, because shooting, bombing, and pillaging is still going on. The sin inside of us is the fundamental enemy of every good and beautiful thing to which God calls us. It cannot be reconciled with the holiness which God has ordained for us. Sin and holiness are eternal enemies. Holiness will only reign in our hearts when sin has been totally eradicated.

Because of the wonderful atoning work of the Prince of Peace, the war between us and God has ended. But the war of hostility inside of us still rages on. The problem is that we tend to think that the enemy within has been conquered long before that is actually true. We live as if there were peace when there is no peace. And because we think we are at peace, we turn our attention to other things, becoming even blinder to the war that is being fought in our hearts in every situation and relationship this side of eternity.

Let me give you a personal example. I am an agenda-oriented, planner sort of person. I always know what I want to accomplish each day, and I instinctively estimate the time each task will take. I like to think ahead and preplan, trying to solve any potential problems that could arise. I have tended to think that my way of living is *the* responsible way of living. I am married to someone who tends to live much more in the moment. Luella is amazingly sensitive to what is going on around her and quite willing to be flexible. She is not at all bothered by changes in her plan or schedule. Luella actually thinks that life is more important than the plans that we make in the midst of it.

Early in our marriage I expressed lots of anger toward Luella for her seeming inability to get with the plan (mine, of course!). I said and did unkind things. Luella became quite forthright in confronting my behavior. I began to confess to my anger, and it began to abate. This was a good thing, but the problem was that I saw that victory as the end of the war, when really it was just the beginning. I had confessed my angry behavior, but not my heart that was behind it. Because of this I continued to lose the battle. I was not lashing out in anger any more, but I was constantly irritated and quite skilled at finding ways to manipulate Luella into serving my agenda and schedule. In declaring peace much too soon, I was blinding myself to the continuing battle and temptation that I was succumbing to almost daily.

We cannot allow ourselves to confuse the single-battle victories of sanctification with the ultimate cessation of conflict when Christ returns. Sin and righteousness, the flesh and the Spirit, are at war. There is no peace, only battles won and battles lost. Peace has been purchased. It is guaranteed. It will come. But until then, the war of wars never ceases. The delusions of victory, and the feeling of peace that follows, set us up for the shock and disappointment of midlife regret. We sadly have to admit that we are still being bombed by an enemy—sin—that we believed we had long since defeated.

This is why Paul ends his letter to the Ephesians (6:10–24) the way that he does. His summary of all that he has said about the body of Christ: communication, forgiveness, marriage, parenting, and the Christian in the workplace and the world, is to call us to arm ourselves for war. Paul reminds us that what makes each of these dimensions of life difficult is that each one is a spiritual battleground. Each one is a location where the great war between the Spirit and sinful nature takes place. Our struggle is not with flesh and blood. People and situations are not our problem. Our problem is that all our relationships and situations are taking place in the middle of war. The Christian life is one of serving in an armored division in the middle of an ongoing war. When we forget this, we declare victory and peace too soon and set ourselves up for the rude awakening of regret in midlife.

3. ***We have fed the beast while being surprised that we have been bitten.*** I once saw a report on television that most zookeepers get bitten when they are feeding the wild animals under their care. It makes perfect sense. Feeding is a moment when the beast is most ravenous and the zookeeper is nearest. Recently in Las Vegas, a famous animal act performer was viciously mauled. It happened because he was alone on stage with a six-hundred-pound tiger that was refusing to obey. In a spontaneous act of authority, the trainer bonked the cat on the forehead with his microphone. In anger, the tiger lunged at the trainer, clamped his jaws around his neck and dragged him off stage while the audience sat paralyzed with horror. The trainer was all too relaxed and in dangerously close proximity to the beast. If he had not been, he would not have wound up in the hospital fighting for his life.

The Bible presents the devil as a roaring lion, seeking to devour (1 Peter 5:8). Perhaps like the zookeepers, we most often get bitten when we have been feeding the beast. We get ourselves in trouble when we feed the beast little morsels of our heart and life. No, we don't want to be swallowed up, but we tend to be naive about the danger we put ourselves in.

Let me give you an example. Brent was committed to being a pure and faithful husband, but he didn't realize that at work he was feeding the beast. The first morsels he offered didn't seem that dangerous. It was merely lunch in the company cafeteria, and he told himself that she was the only person who was sitting alone. It would have been rude not to sit there. The conversation was easy, so three days later Brent sat with her again. He was not consciously attracted to her, and the thought of unfaithfulness was still abhorrent to him, but he was moving closer to the lion with tasty morsels in his hand.

Brent and his female coworker were sent across town on assignment not too many weeks later. They decided to have supper together because they had been too busy to stop for lunch that day. On the way home he was thinking about how much he had enjoyed their dinnertime conversation. It was then that Brent realized what was going on. No, he hadn't technically committed adultery, but he was daily moving closer to the beast, and if he continued he was surely going to be bitten.

All of us tend to be much too naive when it comes to the presence, power, attractiveness, and danger of sin. All of us, in our own individual ways, feed the beast every day. We harbor bitterness or envy. We permit a brief lustful look or thought. We permit moments of anger against our children or our spouse. We allow ourselves to be comfortable with our materialism or our greed. No, we aren't committing the "big" sins, but we are sowing subtle and acceptable seeds of sin that will someday reap a harvest of regret. The regrets we face in midlife result from being much too casual in our battle with sin. If the devil is a roaring lion on the prowl for food, then we should do everything we can in our daily living to stay at a safe distance.

4. ***We have bandaged our wounds without healing the disease.*** If you had sores on your body that continued to reappear, you wouldn't be satisfied with putting ointment and bandages on them. You would know that there must be some infection or disease in your system that is causing the sores. The sores aren't your real problem; if you treated the disease, the sores would go away.

So it is with our struggle with sin. It is very tempting to think that bandaging the sores will alleviate the disease. Perhaps you are a father who has struggled with disciplining your children in anger. You know this is wrong, and you always feel remorse afterward. You have not only consistently confessed your anger to your children but have even delegated discipline situations to your wife so your anger would not have an opportunity for expression. Now all of these things are well and good, but they must not be confused with getting at the cause of your anger, and therefore, producing lasting change. You have unwittingly bandaged the sore without treating the disease.

Listen to the words of Christ to the Pharisees in Matthew 23:25–26:

> *Woe to you, teachers of the law and Pharisees, you hypocrites! You clean the outside of the cup and dish, but inside they are full of greed and self-indulgence. Blind Pharisee! First clean the inside of the cup and dish, and then the outside also will be clean.*

Christ is basically saying, "You guys have it all wrong! What you are attempting to do will never work. You try to exchange bad behavior for good behavior (the outside of the cup and dish), but that will never work, because the heart (the inside of the cup and dish) has not been addressed. Only when the heart changes will lasting change take place in your behavior as well." The angry father has to get at the attitudes, desires, and thoughts of his heart that are the causal system behind his regular struggle with anger. Perhaps he is bitter against his children for the way that they have complicated his life and commandeered his time. Maybe he is angry for the way they consistently interrupt the relaxation that he looks forward to nightly. Perhaps his anger is rooted in problems with his wife, and he is irritated that she tends to put the burden of discipline on him. The possibilities are myriad. The point is that if his anger is ever going to be defeated and replaced by gentle and patient discipline, he must see and repent of the issues of heart that are the true cause of his struggle.

We all tend to be satisfied with the Pharisees' approach. We'll hold our tongue. We'll walk away. We'll avoid a tough situation. We'll make changes in relationships, situations, schedules, and locations. All of this fools us into thinking that we have dealt with the "disease," when really all we have done is alleviate symptoms. We think lasting change is taking place, but the causal system in the heart has not been addressed. If our battle with sin could have been solved by behavioral techniques or strategic changes in situation, location, relationships, or schedule, Jesus would not have had to come to earth and suffer and die. The golden promise of the new covenant work of Jesus Christ is a new heart! There is no other way. There is no other hope for fallen, sin-riddled humanity. Christ came not to bandage symptoms, but to cure our diseases.

Again, what does this have to do with midlife regret? Our externalism (dealing with the symptoms of sin) tricks us into thinking that we have dealt with much more than we actually have. Because of this, when we enter the looking-back period of midlife, we are caught up short. We begin to see that patterns that we thought we had dealt with in fact continued. We realize that what we thought we had conquered continued to plague and defeat us throughout the years. It really does become a time when we cry out with Paul, "What a wretched man I am!"

Consider the four things we have looked at here and their impact on the regret of midlife. If it is true that we have tended to play the con man with ourselves, explaining away our sin; if we have declared victory too soon in our war with sin; if we have fed the very beast that we have tried to escape; and if we have dealt with sin's symptoms while leaving its causes unaddressed, it is no wonder that we are surprised, shocked, and saddened by our legacy. When our harvest comes in, it hurts to admit that it is really ours. This is a very significant moment. For now you see, probably with greater clarity than you were ever able to along the way. Because of this, this is a moment fraught with both danger and potential. This moment of personal honesty and truth can be crushing and paralyzing, or it can be the beginning of a remarkably new phase of redemptive insight, change, and personal celebration.

Biblical Strategies for Dealing with Regret

Jason slumped on the chair in my office with his head in his hands. He looked like a completely defeated man. Without lifting his head, Jason began to talk, quietly at first. "This is not how I thought it would turn out. I thought it was my job to do the best I could to provide for my family. I know I was always busy, and I know that I was gone a lot, but I thought they all understood that I was doing it for them. I thought Jeanie knew I loved her and that I would do anything I could to make her life comfortable. Now my kids are grown and gone, and it's just Jeanie and me. I don't have much of a relationship with my kids. They don't hate me, but there is a distance between us that is pretty painful. You see, there weren't many nights that I was there to read to them and put them to bed. I was only occasionally there for family worship. I attended some of their recitals and games, but there were so many that I missed. Much of the time I was around I was exhausted, irritated, or preoccupied.

"Sure, we had a great house and we took the most awesome vacations, but there were so many things I failed to do. I let my business get in the way. I let it set the agenda. Jeanie and I really do love one another, and we have been looking forward to these years of being alone together. But there is a distance between us that we simply can't seem to bridge. It feels as if we don't even know one another. When we go out, we talk about what we did that day and then sit in silence. I could hide from it all by working more, but that doesn't excite me anymore either.

"Then there's my relationship with the Lord. I have always been faithful in church attendance and giving, but for years my personal relationship with God has really been on the back burner. I've had a lousy devotional life and have done almost nothing that you could call ministry. I sit in church and go through the motions. I sing words that I know are true, but they don't grip me. I listen to what I know are good sermons, but they don't seem to engage or motivate me. I pray, but they're cold, perfunctory prayers; more the prayers of a man who knows he is supposed to pray than a man who loves to pray.

"So, here I am. This is my thirty-year legacy. I have little to show for all my hard work but a big house and nice cars. There is so much I would like to redo, but I can't. I don't know what to do, and I don't have much hope. Paul, I'm not sure why I'm here saying these things to you. Jeanie has been concerned about me and suggested that I talk with you. I guess I just want to get this off my chest."

Your story may be different from Jason's, but if you are alive and well and in your midlife years, you are experiencing some degree of regret. You may mourn your business choices. You may be carrying around a heavy weight of parental guilt. You may linger over things you did, or failed to do, in your marriage. Perhaps you regret not being more serious about your relationship with God. Maybe you've visited and revisited missed opportunities for ministry. If you're a sinner living in a fallen world, it is impossible for you to look back at a legacy of perfect choices.

You and I will have reason to regret until we are finally home with our Lord. Think about it: no reason anymore to want to unthink a thought, unsay a word, or undo a choice. We will not only be in remarkable peace with our Lord, but we will also be at complete peace with all of our choices and behavior. We will have passed over into a regretless eternity. There will be no more weakness, immaturity, and failure. Therefore, in the middle of your regret, live with one eye on a regretless eternity to come.

It is vital that we arm ourselves with biblical strategies for dealing with regret. Remember, you are not about to die. You are in the middle of your life. There is much that is before you. You can participate in a real turn in your story. As God's child, you have reason to step forward in faith, hope, and courage, embracing the new life that is always available to you because of the person and work of the Lord Jesus Christ.

The following strategies provide a way of turning regret into a whole new harvest of good in your life and in the lives of others.

1. ***Enjoy the freedom of confession.*** What is confession? It is the freedom to say about yourself what both you and God know is true, without fear of rejection, condemnation, or punishment. Confession is more than an obligation; it is one of the wonderful freedoms of our new life in Christ. Think about this as you are doing the archeological work of midlife and uncovering the pottery shards of past failures. Because Christ lived perfectly, died sufficiently, and rose victoriously, you and I can come out of hiding. We are free to own up to, without fear, the darkest of our thoughts and motives, the ugliest of our words, our most selfish choices, and our most rebellious and unloving actions. We are freed from our bondage to guilt and shame. We are freed from hiding behind accusation, blame, recrimination, and rationalization.

Confession is powerful and effective. It turns guilt into forgiveness. It turns regret into hope. It turns slavery into freedom. It turns you from mourning over your harvest to planting new seeds of faith, repentance, and hope. You see, you are not trapped! Things are not hopeless! Your Lord, the great Creator and Savior, is the God who never changes, but at the very same time he is the God who promises and produces deeply personal change. The changes he makes in us are so foundational that the Bible's best words describing them are "new creation." God's plan is to change us so fundamentally that it is as if we are no longer us; something brand new has been created!

Confession is not only owning responsibility before God and the appropriate people (those whom my sin and failure has affected), but it is refusing to be stuck in our regrets, and refusing to give up hope. It is believing that not only does God forgive me, but he has promised to change me. And as he changes me, I will plant different seeds in my circumstances and relationships, which will grow a whole new harvest of good fruit.

A few years ago we had an ugly, unusable, inner-city back yard. It had a fifteen foot high brick wall at the back so it was very private—but it was all weeds and mud. Every time I looked at the yard, I would be discouraged and overwhelmed. We never took visitors out back; in fact, we were embarrassed when anyone got a glimpse of it. One day I was looking at a magazine and saw a little yard like ours that had been reclaimed. It had been turned into a wonderful little garden retreat. The next time I stood on our back porch, I looked at our little yard with hope. I saw with new eyes. Confessing my hopelessness and laziness to my wife, I began to go to work. The changes took many seasons, but when we moved from that house, we left a very different yard. The weeds had given way to a beautiful lawn. That ugly wall was now the backdrop for ornamental shrubs. The mud had given way to an English cobblestone patio. This place of embarrassment had become our favorite retreat.

As you look at the mud and weeds of your past, think about the sweet promise of hope that is found in 1 John 1:8–9.

> *If we claim to be without sin, we deceive ourselves and the truth is not in us. If we confess our sins, he is faithful and just and will forgive us our sins and purify us from all unrighteousness.*

Notice that when you come to God with humble and honest confession, he not only promises to *forgive* you, but also to *change* you as well. That is what it means when it says, "purify [you] from all unrighteousness." When you confess, you change, and the people and situations around you are affected because you are saying and doing different things.

Now, with this promise in your heart, stand on the porch of your present life and look with hope at the yard of your past. Force yourself to see a beautiful new lawn, gorgeous shrubs and flowers, and a quaint stone patio. The changes you want for your yard are possible, so start with embracing the freedom of confession. Not only are you free to own your failures honestly, without fear, but you are free to embrace the hope of change. All of this is yours because God knew you would be a sinner, so he sent his Son to live like you wouldn't, to pay the debt you couldn't, and to give you hope you wouldn't have any other way.

2. ***Embrace God's forgiveness.*** In a fallen world, we don't really expect much forgiveness. A politician's youthful rebellion is detailed in every major newspaper decades after it happened. The married woman still talks about her father's coldness and insensitivity years and years after she left the home. The stupid choice made early in one's career is resurrected with every new job application. The poor financial choices wreak havoc on your credit for years. Your mother-in-law continues to treat you as the arrogant and impulsive person you were in your youth. In a fallen world your record tends to go with you, and it gets stuck in your face over and over again. In a fallen world it seems very hard to outlive your past.

This is why God's promise of full and complete forgiveness is so unusual and so wonderful. God, who sees and knows everything about me, even my most secret thoughts and desires, has promised and purchased for me a blanket of forgiveness that is so complete that it is impossible to comprehend. The Bible says that God's commitment to forgive and accept us is so profound that he purposefully forgets what we have done. This doesn't mean that he is weak and forgetful, but that he chooses not to think of us in light of all the wrongs of heart and behavior that we have committed. Forgiveness means that God chooses not to remember the darkest, most shameful, and most regrettable parts of you and me! And if God turns from these things, I am free to turn from them and move on as well.

Listen to David, who experienced this forgiveness in the face of huge regret:

For as high as the heavens are above the earth,
so great is his love for those who fear him;
as far as the east is from the west,
so far has he removed our transgressions from us.
(Psa. 103:11–12)

Or hear the Lord speak of his new covenant through the mouth of Jeremiah:

> *"This is the covenant I will make with the house of Israel*
> *after that time," declares the* LORD.
> *"I will put my law in their minds*
> *and write it on their hearts.*
> *I will be their God.*
> *and they will be my people.*
> *No longer will a man teach his neighbor,*
> *or a man his brother, saying, 'Know the* LORD,'
> *because they will all know me,*
> *from the least of them to the greatest," declares the* LORD.
> ***"For I will forgive their wickedness***
> ***and will remember their sins no more."***
> *(Jer. 31:33–34, emphasis mine)*

Think about it. God, whose memory is exhaustive and complete, chooses to remove our sins from his memory. Even though our sins are a direct affront to his authority, a devaluing of his wisdom, and a rejection of his love, he is so great in mercy and grace that he is willing to erase them from his memory! And because God does this, he releases us from our bondage to regret. We do not have to live in the paralysis of remorse. We do not have to live looking backward. We are free to move on.

You see, God's promise of forgiveness is a welcome to new life. It is an invitation to leave regrets behind and to get up and live again. It is a God-given opportunity to do new and better things. God's grace gives us new moments to plant new seeds that will lead to a new harvest of good things. Because of God's promise of forgiveness, you can look your failure in the face and not be overwhelmed or paralyzed. He lifts your burden of guilt and regret and welcomes you to plant and harvest once again.

3. ***Embrace God's sovereignty.*** One of the sweet things that the Bible reminds us of again and again is that, contrary to appearances, our lives are never out of control. No, they are under the careful, wise, loving, and powerful care of the Lord. He truly is sovereign. It is nearly impossible for us to look around and see it in operation, but there is no situation, relationship, or circumstance that is not controlled by our Heavenly Father. The story of our lives has been carefully administrated by him. He always is in charge. He always knows what he is doing and why he is doing it.

Now, his absolute control is exercised in such a way that it never turns you into a robot. He accomplishes his sovereignty through the choices that you and I make and the actions that we take. His sovereignty does not invalidate our choices, and our choices do not remove his sovereignty. In the operation of the universe, the issue of the sovereignty of God and our responsibility is never an either-or; it is always a both-and. So, I am called to believe, choose, follow, worship, love, and obey, while at the same time entrusting myself and my life to God's sovereign care. I live knowing that I am responsible for the choices I make, while at the same time knowing that God controls the details of my life for my good and for his glory.

This balance is very important during the struggles of midlife. It is right for you to look back and examine your choices. It is right to confess the things that were your responsibility that you did wrong. It is right to recognize the harvest that has come from the decisions you made and the actions you took. But you must never do that in a way that forgets the always-wise and always-good rule of the Lord. Let me give you some examples.

It drives Jim crazy that, as a father of four children, he didn't receive good parenting instruction until his kids were in their teens. Mary came to Christ at age thirty-five and struggles with the legacy of her early adult life. Jamal got married very young and now looks back and says he wasn't really ready. George says he came into "major money" before he was mature enough to handle it. Maria wishes God had taught her more before she had made a series of early adult choices. Frank and Doris wish they had known, in the first twenty years of their marriage, what they know now.

Each of these people struggles with a particularly important aspect of God's sovereignty: *his timing*. Because God is the definition of true wisdom and the author of order, his timing is always right. He never gets things out of order. He never does something too early or too late. He is always able to decide between "what is best" and "when is best." He always knows when to act, when to speak, when to wait, and when to withdraw. He always responds to our cries for help at the right moment.

Yet in the midyears of life, it is almost impossible to look back and not revisit the question of God's timing. You will come across a good parenting book and think, "I wish I had read this fifteen years ago." Or you will hear a good series of messages on marriage and think, "Where was my pastor in the early days of my marriage?" As you are looking back, it is important to embrace the freedom and comfort that God's sovereignty gives you. You can take responsibility for what you did, while at the same time, you can rest in God's timing. He gave you eyes to see at just the right moment. He taught you important truths at just the right moment. He gave you that mature Christian friend at just the right moment. He brought you to that new church at just the right moment. He placed the book in your hands at just the right moment. He gave you wisdom through your personal times of worship at precisely the right moment. He knows who you are. He knows what you can bear and what is going on around you, and his rule in your life is always exercised at just the right time. So look back, with honesty and humility, but do not forget that it has all happened under his control. He is always wise, loving, good, righteous, and on time!

4. *Clarify your identity.* Human beings are always measuring their potential. The toddler stands wobbling in the middle of the room and wonders if he can manage the few steps needed to get to his mother's knee. The kindergartner scans the other children in the room and nervously wonders if she will be able to keep up. The teenager, heading to his first job, measures his potential for success in his mind. The college freshman careens from excitement to dread, wondering if he'll succeed or fail. As you scan the sins, victories, and failures of the past, you wonder whether you will be able to do it all in a different way. Are you trapped by your past? Are things now the way they will always be?

I am persuaded that your assessment of potential is always rooted in your sense of identity. "What can you do" questions are always attached to "who you think you are" answers. The longer we live, the more we will tend to take on a sin and problem-based identity. The blinders are off, and we are no longer deluded. We have seen our harvest. It is tempting to let these things define us. Perhaps bad choices have led you to a divorce. Divorce is very difficult human experience, but it is not an identity. Or maybe you are left being a single parent. Again, this is a very significant human experience, but it is not an identity. If I take these experiences on as if they were identities, they will define how I assess my potential.

The Apostle Paul, who was very aware of his own struggle with sin (remember Romans 7), offers us very helpful words here:

> *I have been crucified with Christ and I no longer live, but Christ lives in me. The life I live in the body, I live by faith in the Son of God, who loved me and gave himself for me (Gal. 2:20).*

Paul's identity is not sin or problem-based, but grace-based. He is essentially saying, "This is who I am—a child of God. That means that when Christ died, I died; and when Christ rose, I rose to a new life. Not only that, but the living Christ dwells inside of me. Because this is true, I keep telling myself that it is no longer I living by myself and in my own power, but Christ living in me. So, my potential is as great as his grace and his power."

As you do the archeological work of midlife, remember who you really are in Christ. Don't let an unbiblical sense of identity rob you of your hope and your potential. Remember that not only have you been forgiven, but also the resurrected Christ now really does live inside of you! He is your potential! He is your hope! You can change! Things can be different! As you look forward to the years to come, remember that Christ *is* your identity and step out with faith and courage.

5. ***Plant a new harvest.*** The one comfort for farmers and gardeners everywhere is that today's harvest will be followed by another season of planting and harvest. Until we die, no harvest is the final harvest. Our God is the author of new seasons. He is the giver of new seeds, new roots, and new fruit. He causes fruits and flowers to grow where weeds and thorns once were. He is the God of the new harvest.

In midlife God calls you to turn from mourning over your previous harvest to planting new and better seeds. Maybe you mourn about the harvest of your parenting. Plant new seeds. Maybe that means working to restore distant or broken relationships with your adult children. Or it could mean being a wise and godly grandparent, sowing spiritual seeds in the souls of the next generation. Perhaps you mourn that your life was controlled by your career. Take advantage of the time and economic freedom that midlife affords and plant new seeds. Work less and invest in family and ministry more. Perhaps you mourn the fact that you did not study Scripture more diligently in your youth. There are many opportunities to increase your knowledge of God's word and your potential for ministry (internet study, evening Bible schools, etc.). Perhaps you mourn over a selfish life, where all you earned was spent on a more comfortable life for you. Commit to finding specific ways that you can give and serve. Ask yourself: which of my gifts, experiences, resources, and wisdom can I use to serve others?

As you assess your harvest, live with a "new seasons" mentality. The final chapter has not been written. You have many productive years behind you, but you now have the wisdom of age and experience. You may now be less encumbered with economic and family responsibilities. Take advantage of the new season that God has given you and step out and plant new seeds.

6. ***Celebrate eternity.*** Paul makes a critical observation in 1 Corinthians 15:19. He says, "If only for this life we have hope in Christ, we are to be pitied more than all men." You see, this life that God has called us to doesn't make any sense without eternity attached to it. It is only the hope and promise of a resurrection out of this life and of an eternity to follow that enables us to continue to live in this fallen world. This world *is* a terribly broken place. Nothing in us or around us operates consistently the way it was meant to. Things regularly take place that were never meant to happen in God's original creation plan. Sin still twists our desires and distorts our thoughts. It still drips, like a horrible black dye, and stains every situation and relationship in our daily lives. You are surely wiser than you once were, but you have not escaped your sin. Just because you are a better-trained and better-equipped soldier doesn't mean that the great war with sin is over.

So here's what to do. Accept the fact that you are a sinner living in a fallen world, keep reminding yourself that Christ really does live inside of you, and keep your eyes on eternity. Start celebrating early. Let the anticipation grip you, like a child three minutes from Disney World. Keep rewinding and playing the video of eternity in your head. The day really is coming when we will not only be rescued from this terribly broken world, but we will finally and forever be rescued from ourselves. We will actually escape the sin inside of us. We will be perfect, holy, and without any sin whatsoever.

In that final place, there will be no midlife regret. There will be no things that were poorly done or left undone to fret about. There will be no words to take back. There will be no difficult moments of confession, repentance, and reconciliation. There will be no unwise investments and impulsive decisions to regret. The world will finally operate as it was meant to, and we will think, desire, act, and speak in the right way all the time.

Whether you're aware of it or not, every moment of regret is a longing for eternity. Every instance of remorse is a cry for a better place. Every time you feel guilt and shame, your heart reaches out for a day when they will be wiped away. Let your longing grow. Let your celebration begin. Live with your eyes on eternity. It is the only way to make sense out of what is going on now. Your lodging is being prepared right now. Have hope!

Standing in a Pile of Your Own Leaves

You're now in the autumn of your life, and you're quite aware that the leaves are off the trees. You're standing in a pile of the leaves of your marriage, your parenting, your extended family, your friendships, your work, and your ministry. These leaves of the past have grown wrinkled and dry, and you know you cannot put them back on the tree. It's tempting to sit down in the pile and examine leaf after leaf and wish you were holding a new bud from a new sapling, but you aren't. The harvest has come in, and it is what it is. Yet in all of this there is hope because your Lord is the Lord of new seasons. With the new season comes the freedom to plant new and better seeds. With the new season comes the expectation of a new harvest of new fruit.

Stand up and walk away from your pile of yesterday's leaves. Take the seeds of a new way into your hands, press them into the soil of your life, and thank God that you will live to see a better harvest.

Chapter 5

Towers to the Sky

People don't fall in love with what is right in front of them. People want the dream—what they can't have. The more unattainable, the more attractive.

—Xander

Yes, everybody's dying to be someone else, but I'll live my life if it kills me. —E.E. Cummings

We're all dreamers. It didn't stop in Genesis 11 with the Tower of Babel. We all conjure up visions of our own personal earth-bound heaven, and we all are committed to realizing what we have dreamed. So, we get up each day, look at the pile of bricks we have been given, and with the mortar and trowel of our time and energy, we try to construct our tower of dreams. Some of our dreams are unrealistic and irrational. Some of us dream about what is in our reach. Some of us are afraid to dream, but we do it anyway. It is inescapable; there is always some grand vision that has your heart. There is always something that motivates you, that magnetizes your energy, and that gives you reason to press on. Let's admit it: we're all just a bunch of stone masons, working hard to construct our own personal towers to heaven.

The dream captured Greg earlier in life than for most people. He knew from a young age what he wanted to do with his life. Greg was in love with buildings. Even as a preschool child he was always drawing houses or constructing some kind of toy edifice out of available materials around his house. He was interested in doors, windows, porches, and roofs. Even while young he noticed the minor differences between his house and the other houses on his cul-de-sac. He loved looking at picture books about buildings and the real estate section of the paper.

By the time he was in high school, Greg had become quite the armchair architect. He was the only kid in his high school who subscribed to *Architectural Digest.* He took the only drafting classes offered in the high school curriculum. Greg couldn't wait until he graduated so that he could go to college and pursue the one thing that interested him. Trips to the big city were always followed by months of dreaming. Greg would dream of winning the contract to design a major urban skyscraper, winning a major architectural award, or being interviewed in a national magazine as one of the influential architects of his generation. Architecture was Greg's sport, his hobby, and his music. If they made posters of architects, Greg would have had Frank Lloyd Wright's at the head of his bed.

Greg's parents were quite supportive of his interests, helping him find summer classes to take at the community college and part-time office boy work at a local design firm. Even though his math grades weren't great, Greg was accepted to a university with a strong architectural school. He couldn't believe that he was actually allowed to concentrate on the one thing he had always wanted to do! He groaned through the general education courses but thrived on every course in his major. He loved every aspect of what he was studying: the art, the engineering, the physics, and the design. He was sure that he was on the road to realizing his dream.

Greg didn't graduate with honors, but he did reasonably well. No offers came from the big national and international firms. However, Greg wasn't disappointed. He told himself that he had to "pay his dues," that "his time would come," and that sooner or later he would be "discovered." After about eights months of sending out resumes all over the country, Greg accepted a job at a local architectural firm. He was disappointed that he had landed at a small firm that did such uninteresting work, but he was convinced it was just a matter of time before he got his break.

Greg settled into his work and became a very respected and trusted employee. He worked his way up the ladder and after several years was running a design team. Yet Greg still looked for the break that would get him national attention and cause the "big boys" to come calling. Contract followed contract, and year followed year, and Greg had a very successful career. He and Megan had three wonderful boys, a church they loved, and a beautiful house. Yet all was not well with Greg. He was now forty-two and a partner at the firm he had associated with right out of college. Everyone else thought Greg had a dream life, but it was harder and harder for him to hold onto his dream. It no longer seemed likely that he would get that dream project. He was stuck, dead-ended, designing strip malls and industrial parks.

It became increasingly apparent to Megan that Greg was *not* okay. He was often sullen at home, spending hours alone in his office staring at his computer, missing precious moments with his family. He was easily irritated and often impatient. She wondered what had happened to the optimistic man she had married. When Greg wasn't working or sulking around the house it seemed he was spending money. Megan tried not to overreact to the Porsche, but it *was* hard for her to justify, given that they were soon to enter the college years with their children. The car was followed by a $3,000 stereo and a 50-inch plasma television.

It wasn't that Greg was losing it, but there were increasing signs of an internal struggle within him. He seemed much too fixated on his age. He talked as if he were an old man, and he seemed to be obsessed with all things youthful. He became more committed to exercise than ever before, and although Megan at first saw this as a good thing, it soon became clear that Greg was trying to recapture something. Megan's concerns became more focused one evening when Greg came home with about five hundred dollars worth of new clothes. It was so unusual for him. He had always been so thrifty. That evening as Megan was getting ready for bed, he called to her from the bathroom and asked if she thought it would be weird if he colored his hair. She wanted to ask him what was going on, but she decided to wait for a better time.

About a week later, Greg and Megan went out for dinner. Greg had been quiet for most of the night, so Megan mentioned how distant he had been and asked him what was wrong. "It's my job, Megan. It just doesn't excite or motivate me any more. I know I should be thankful that I have a job and that God has used it to give us a comfortable life, but I've gotten so I almost hate it. I sit in boring meeting after boring meeting talking about designing the next strip mall. Megan, it's making me crazy. I can't remember the last time I enjoyed my work as an architect; I'm not going to go any further than this. I'm trapped in the middle of my own career."

That night Greg introduced the possibility that he might just quit. He had read an account of a high-powered lawyer who had liquidated all his assets and bought a vineyard. Greg said that this former lawyer was happier than he had been in years. He told Megan that he had found a little vegetable farm outside of town and said, "Maybe if I bought that farm, I could get my life back." Megan was lovingly able to get Greg to consider that perhaps what he was dealing with was about something bigger than his job.

In Good Company

There are thousands of Gregs and Megans who are going through the same thing. The situation is hard to face, and it is easy to get into greater trouble. We don't realize how common it is for us to measure what we presently have with what we'd dreamed of. We don't realize how influential our dreams are until we hit midlife. All of a sudden we feel cheated, conned, and stuck. What satisfied us before doesn't do it anymore. It is like living in temporary housing. You're okay with the inadequacies because you know it's temporary, but you would respond quite differently if it was going to be your long-term dwelling.

We're okay with the in-between as long as it's in-between, but when we begin to assess our age and the distance between us and our dream, there is little around us that isn't dissatisfying. We begin to feel as if life has passed us by, as if we're older than we actually are. We begin to feel that our world is confining and claustrophobic. At the same time we feel helpless to change it all, and we mourn every decision we made that seemed to trap us where we are. Standing in the mortuary of your dreams is not a happy place to be.

In midlife it is easy to think that the things around you are driving you crazy. You are convinced that your wife or husband has changed, so you feel differently about them. Or you tell yourself that anyone living with your kids would be as irritated as you are. Or you're convinced that your pastor simply isn't the communicator that he once was. Your friends seem stuck, and you don't like your neighborhood, your car, your clothes, or your yard. It feels like the walls are closing in on you, and sometimes it seems as if you can't breathe.

The truth is that nothing around you has changed that dramatically. You have changed, whether you realize it or not. The tower to heaven that you have been building for years has tumbled down at your feet. It's hard to see clearly through the thick dust of your crumbled dreams. You are further from your self-constructed heaven than you have ever been, and there's not much on earth that attracts or motivates you. Maybe it was the tower of the perfect family, the tower of a dream career, the tower of a certain lifestyle, or the tower of successful ministry. The point is that you had a dream that you thought you could realize, and it has slipped through your fingers.

One of the reasons midlife is rocky is that we're all dreamers and tower-builders. Midlife is a war between our dreams and reality, and too often, people, families, and churches are its casualties. In fighting to keep our dreams alive, we tend to do all the wrong things.

The Beauty of Imagination

One of the things that separates us from the rest of creation is our ability to imagine. Human beings don't operate by instinct or biological causality. We have the astounding ability to "see" worlds in our minds that may not yet exist. It is a powerful ability that gets right to the heart of who we are and how we operate, and there is a fundamental reason that we were wired this way.

We were made for relationship with God. But there is a huge gap between us and the Divine. Our world is the world of sight, sound, and touch, but God lives in a world of unseen realities. So God gave us spirits in order to commune with Him and to do what we were created to do. One of the primary functions of the spirit, the inner man, is the ability to imagine, to "see" God. Imagination in this sense is not conjuring up what is unreal, but what is real, only unseen. God hardwired us with the ability to "see" what cannot be seen, to commune with one with whom we cannot physically converse, and to love the one whom we cannot touch. We are creatures of imagination.

So human beings are wired to dream. It is what gives us station and dignity among the rest of creation. We don't just give God glory by means of our existence, like the rock, the flower, or the fish. We can "see" and commune with Glory himself.

We were made with the ability to cross the great divide between the physical and the spiritual.

It starts when we are very young. That game we call "make believe" in children is the imagination beginning to flex, grow and develop its muscles. As a young parent, I looked out of our kitchen window one afternoon and saw our son, Ethan, sitting on the sidewalk by himself. I walked out to him and said, "Ethan, why are you out here all by yourself?" He said, "I'm not, Dad. Joe is with me." I couldn't see anyone else, so I asked, "Joe, who?" Ethan said, "My best friend, Joe Fakeny." (Interesting name, don't you think?) As I interviewed Ethan further, I realized that in his imagination he had dreamed up a whole family and a community where they lived. As he sat in that yard, he "saw" Joe and he "heard" what Joe said to him. This was just the beginning for this little boy; throughout his life he has "seen" what is not visible.

We all do it; our dreams simply change as we age. The child in Sunday school sees the Red Sea open up, the walls of Jericho falling down, the hot furnace fires of Babylon, and the rough-hewn cross of Golgotha. The teenage boy dreams about college and what his dorm life will be like. The twenty-something imagines his ascent to a successful career. The new Christian sees his heart being cleansed by the blood of the Lamb. The couple with four children sees themselves alone together again, enjoying their post-parenting years. The person under conviction sees the darkness of his heart and the gravity of his sin. The dear old saint, sitting alone in her nursing home, sees the other side and imagines what it will be like to have her travail finally end.

This ability to imagine is wonderful, mysterious, practical, holy, mundane, and amazing. Whether listening to someone describe a place you have not been to, or reading a novel and imagining what each character looks like, or listening to a sermon and seeing God, it is a remarkable ability. It is particularly significant for believers because we accept the fact that there is a God who really does exist, who cannot be seen, touched, or heard. As Eugene Peterson says in his book, *Subversive Spirituality*, for a Christian, whose largest investment is in the invisible, imagination is a very important thing.

The Danger of Imagination

Yet, as with most wonderful things God has made, the Fall has made imagination dangerous as well. It is wonderful that the imagination has a profound capacity to direct the course of our lives. It is dangerous that there are so many unworthy things that can capture our imagination and thus misdirect our lives. This fact should not be overlooked. Each of us is in pursuit of a dream. You may not realize it, but you spend much of your waking time in a world of unseen realities. You dream at your desk, in a meeting, at the kitchen table, driving the car, walking the dog, in the middle of a long shower, and a hundred other times during the day. Part of your humanity and your sanity is an imagination that is healthy and limber.

Now what exactly is a dream? *A dream is imagination coupled with desire and projected into the future.* For example, I want to be comfortable, so I dream that someday I will be very successful in business and will purchase a luxurious house in an elite community. I play and replay the video of a succession of promotions and of exactly what that house and that community will look like. The more I replay my dream, the more detailed it gets and the more it has control of me. Each day that I work, I am a person in pursuit of a dream.

Before long the dream is not just a faint and distant hope for the future. It becomes a prized possession. I become convinced that life without the dream would be unthinkable and unlivable. My sense of identity, purpose, well-being, contentment, and satisfaction becomes directly connected to the realization of the dream. Something has happened here that is very dangerous. My imagination has been captured and is now controlled by some aspect of the creation.

It was never meant to be this way. All other dreams were meant to be subservient to God's dream. Yet in the pursuit of my "essential" dream, I have been slowly building my own personal tower to my own personal heaven. It *has* me. It defines me. It motivates me. It guides and directs me. It gives me a reason to get up in the morning and a reason to press on. Every day I get out my mortar and trowel and put another few courses of bricks on my personal tower to the sky. I'm still going to church, and I haven't forsaken the faith, but in a profound and practical way, God is out of the picture. I am not in a place of overt rebellion to him, yet I am not serving him. I don't have time for the Lord because all of my daily time and energy is invested in my dream. I was given the capacity to imagine so that everyday my "eyes" would be filled with him, yet now another dream obstructs my vision of his glory.

The crushing disappointments of midlife are directly tied to imagination and the dreams that have captured our hearts. Over the years, a crucial shift took place. Our vision of the only Glory worth living for was progressively replaced by a competing glory-vision. It became more than a hope for the future. It somehow became the thing that we were living for. It consumed our imagination, shaped our behavior, conditioned our emotions, and structured our plans. We just didn't realize it. We put our life's hope in the wrong thing, and it disappointed us in the long run.

It's not that what we dreamed for was necessarily ugly and sinful. We may have dreamed wonderful, wholesome dreams. The problem is that our dreams tend to become a replacement glory for the one Glory that was meant to shape every aspect of our existence. Having your imagination filled with the glory of God in a way that gets you up in the morning and gives you a reason to press on is the only safe place for your heart. All other dreams will fail us, no matter how clearly we are able to imagine them or how successful we are at achieving them.

That security-giving dream of the perfect white picket fence marriage turns out to be a life in a row home in the city with a man who is all too busy. That dream of the ultimate career success ends in a dead-end job that bored you after the first several months. That hope of the quintessential family gives way to the sad realization that you're all a bunch of sinners. That one special thing that you always wanted to accomplish never gets done because you lived each day under the tyranny of the urgent. You made the money that you dreamed you would make, but when you did, the reality of the money didn't live up to your dream. We all face those emotion-laden moments when our dreams die, or when we finally got what we wanted, but it simply wasn't what we thought it would be.

We set ourselves up for disaster when we allow our dreams to capture our hearts. Think about it. None of us is in control of enough things to guarantee that our dreams will come true. As we exercise our imaginations, we all tend to pretend that we are sovereign and that the world will operate according to the rules of our imagination, but it never does. Even if we could guarantee the realization of our dreams, we would still be disappointed because the things that we give our hearts to will never give us what we hope they will. They won't give us true identity. They can't give us real meaning and purpose. They aren't able to give us the stability, security, and purpose for which we seek. These are all things that will only be found in God. To look for them elsewhere is setting ourselves up for huge and lasting disappointment, but we all do it all the time. And when our dreams fail us, rather than being disappointed with ourselves, we tend to be disappointed with God and wonder why he doesn't love us more.

Dreams Die and Disappoint

There are several principles of the imagination that can help and protect us as we consider or even struggle with this aspect of midlife crisis.

1. ***You will dream.*** As was stated earlier, it is impossible to be a rational, breathing human being and not dream. Imagination and the ability to dream future dreams are vital gifts from God so that, though we cannot see, hear, or touch him, we can still have a relationship with him. The ability to project forward and think about where you would like to be is a good thing as well. Responsible living requires us to plan, so we must be able to "see" our goals in order to determine how to reach them. Dreams are born at the intersection of imagination, desire, and the future. To be alive is to live in the service of some kind of dream.

2. ***Your dreams will compete with the Lord for your imagination.*** Dreams are compelling because when you are dreaming, the world and all that is in it is utterly compliant. (When you dream about a world that is imperfect, you usually call that a nightmare.) In the world of personal imagination, you reach all of your goals, get everything that you want, and do not have to deal with any detractors. You are sovereign over it all. Dreaming makes it hard to deal with the resistance that we face in the real world. Because the dream world is much easier to live in than the real world, dreaming is magnetic.

The great irony is that the closer you get to capturing your dream, the more likely it is that the dream has captured you. At this point you are a person in danger. You may not see it coming, but increasingly you become convinced that life, to be real, must include the dream. What was once a distant hope becomes something that you cannot live without. Your pursuit of the dream gives you meaning and purpose. The accomplishment of the dream gives you identity. You will even judge God's love and faithfulness by whether or not he gives you the dream. Your dream has begun to compete with God for the rulership of your heart, and if things continue in this way, it will functionally replace God as your source of security and hope.

A subtle transition takes place, and you don't even recognize it when it happens. You have exited God's "big sky" country, where life is moved and motivated by the grand and expansive purposes of the kingdom of God and have entered the narrow confines of your own claustrophobic little dreams. The problem is not that you are demanding too much from God; the problem is that tragically, you are willing to settle for far too little. Our dreams are puny in comparison with the amazing things God wants for us. God's "dream" stretches from before the foundations of the earth through human history and on into eternity. It includes the ultimate war and the greatest victory. It solves your greatest problem and gives you reason to get up in the morning with hope. It guarantees your place in the most magnificent celebration in the universe. It imparts stunning wisdom and gorgeous love. God's dream fixes what has been broken and reconciles what has been divided. It unites you with the Lord Creator, the Sovereign Savior, the great I Am. It is more than you or I could ever ask for, bigger than our biggest dreams, and beyond the furthest reaches of our imaginations. It assures us that we will be liberated from personal slavery and unalterable personal destruction. Yet, in our blindness we are more attracted to our little self-designed dreams, and we experience great personal anguish when they slip through our hands.

3. ***Your dreams will either die or disappoint you.*** The fact is that the vast majority of our dreams simply die. They crumble before we ever get a chance to experience or enjoy them. They do this because the real world doesn't behave the way the world of our imagination does. In that fantasy world there aren't any obstacles or competitors in the way of my dream, but in the real world there are many deep valleys and high peaks between dream and realization. I'm not in control, and people don't always do my bidding. The real world is a place of unrealized dreams and unfulfilled plans.

Why do dreams die? First of all, because the world we live in is a broken place and therefore does not operate the way it was intended. People do bad things to one another. They get cheated, overlooked, and passed by. Institutions are marred by bad motives or unhealthy competition. People step on one another to get what they want. People refuse to work with one another while jealously holding on to what they want. The human conversation is infected with a virus of deceit. People plagiarize and slander. People get addicted to what is harmful, while rejecting what is good. People suffer and get sick. People get hurt and die. Dreams die because the world in which you dream is a terribly broken place.

Dreams also die because there is a God. Nothing exists outside the scope of his plan. Everything lives under his careful orchestration. It is impossible to arrive in any situation before he does, because he is everywhere, controlling all things according to his own wise counsel and for the purpose of his own glory. As much as he has blessed us with the ability to dream, decide, and plan, our will is not ultimate. It is hard to accept that we are not ultimate, that we are creatures of a sovereign God. It is hard to give up our delusions of control, sufficiency, and autonomy, but to be authentic human beings with real integrity, we must. It is not wrong to dream if embedded in your dream is a remembrance of who you are and who God is. You are creature, and he is creator. Many of your dreams will die, but all of his purposes will stand.

Even if your dream comes to fruition, it will not fulfill you. It won't provide your fundamental identity. It won't give you emotional security. It won't give you that profound sense of meaning and purpose that you are actually seeking to get. How many people have fulfilled their dreams, only to feel empty, hungry, and lost once more?

I had the occasion of working for two years for a very wealthy man. It was clear that his wealth-driven dreams could not deliver what he was really looking for. He owned so many cars that he had no more room on his property to park them. He had more than he had imagined, yet he was empty. Still searching, he reached for the next dream, hoping it would satisfy. In the final analysis, dreams almost always disappoint us because they cannot give us life. When we place our identity, purpose, sense of well-being, security, and hope in our dreams, they will always come up short.

So Your Dream Has Died

Fred had always wanted to be in full-time ministry, but his current situation was not what he had envisioned. He had done very well in college, become a student leader in the premier campus ministry, and after graduation was hired as full-time staff. He loved teaching, discipling, and mentoring students, but he knew he needed more training. After some months of research, Fred enrolled in seminary. He loved every minute of it. He did well and became president of the student body. Summers were spent in various parts of the world on short-term missions trips. Before he had graduated he had been hired by a megachurch to develop their student ministries. Fred couldn't believe it; his life was like a dream!

After five years at the big church, Fred longed to be a senior pastor. It didn't take long for him to receive a call to a small church in the Midwest. With great expectation, Fred and his wife, Darla, moved with their two young children. The church struggled for the first few years, but Fred's giftedness and hard work began to pay off, and the church began to grow. Fred's dream was still in place, but then it all started to evaporate. He began to have greater and greater trouble getting his elders to follow him. They seemed critical of everything he did, even his preaching. Eventually it got so that he had to drag himself to his office, and within a year he resigned. Fred was devastated, but he told Darla that they would move on and get a fresh start. In a new church, hundreds of miles away, the new beginnings never happened. Without knowing it, Fred had carried his hurt, anger and bitterness with him. He was more self-protective, distant, and defensive than he had ever intended to be and never got off to a good start with his leaders. Before long, he and Darla were discussing their exit.

One night sitting alone in his living room, Fred faced the fact that he could not handle another pastorate. At the same time, he didn't have many other marketable skills. Over lunch with a friend, Fred learned that a local ministry was looking for a Director of Development. It interested Fred. He had found that he had raised his support quite easily when he was in the campus ministry, so he pursued this new possibility.

Seven years later, with a donor list in his hands, Fred sat as his desk examining the death of his dream. This was not where he was supposed to land. This was not the "ministry" that he had always dreamed of. He knew many guys from his class in seminary that didn't have half the gifts that he did, but were enjoying success in pastoral ministry. He hated the thought of the next fund-raising call. He loathed the thought of another uncomfortable lunch, trying to get a person he did not know to give to the ministry. He envied his seminary friends and dreaded their calls to see how he was doing. He felt like a complete failure and forsaken by God. He lived in a cloud of despondency, forcing the friendliness that his job demanded. Fred told himself (and God), "I didn't want much. I never asked for a mansion and a Mercedes. I didn't want to be Billy Graham. All I wanted was to be a pastor. Was that really too much to ask? I did all that study, all that training for this? I just don't get it!"

As Fred sat at his used oak desk in his small windowless office, he couldn't imagine sitting there day after day until he retired. The thought almost made it impossible for him to breathe. He knew he should be thankful for his place in God's kingdom work, but he couldn't muster up a little contentment, let alone heartfelt thanks.

Sadly, Fred had been ensnared by several traps that easily ensnare us at the funeral of our dreams.

1. ***The envy trap.*** Why is it that when we're suffering, we focus on those who aren't? Why is it that when we are disappointed we seem to notice those who are delighted? Why is it that when our dreams slip through our fingers, we are all too aware of the person who has achieved his dream? It is so easy to be captured by envy. It is so easy to think that somehow God has gotten a wrong address, that the success our neighbor has enjoyed was meant to fall on us. It is so easy when your dream

has died to think that all the wrong guys are winning, while the good guys have gotten hammered (see Psalm 73).

Envy is more than sadness in the face of unfulfilled dreams. It is not only being angry that I don't have something, but being angry that someone else does. It is a wish that God would take away what he has given you and return it to me where it rightfully belongs. When envy rules your heart it will control your eyes. Envy will cause you to notice the success, fortune, prosperity, possessions, relationships, and joy of others. Envy will cause you to be much too vigilant and to pay far too much attention on how God has blessed others. Envy will cause you to be sad when you should be happy, to be angry when you should be grateful, and to be disappointed when you should be experiencing the rest of contentment.

Envy makes it impossible to keep the two great commands. First, it destroys loving worship of God. Envy debates his wisdom, doubts his sovereignty, and questions his love. It accuses God of failing to be the good and wise father that he has promised to be. Envy brings God into the court of our judgment and sucks the life out of our intimacy with him. We simply don't tend to pursue joyful fellowship with someone we think has failed us. Envy also robs me of my ability to love my neighbor, making him a competitor at best, and at worst a thief, because he possesses things that I am convinced rightfully belong to me. I cannot celebrate with him. I do not share his joy. My envy does not wish good for my neighbor, but rather wishes him ill. Envy is a moral cancer that eats away at your heart.

2. *The bitterness trap.* Bitterness is not only about not liking what you have been left with, but feeling in your heart of hearts that you deserve more. Again, Psalm 73 is helpful here. Asaph complains, "Surely in vain have I kept my heart pure; in vain have I washed my hands in innocence" (v. 13). He compares what he has with what others have and basically says, "I've obeyed for this? I do all the right things and obey God, and what do I get? Nothing! These guys couldn't care less, yet they get all the good stuff. It isn't fair. It just doesn't make any sense!"

Many of us are tempted to look back during midlife and do an accounting. We add up all of our hard choices, good decisions, and disciplined labors and compare them to "good" things in life that we think we have earned a right to. If the good results do not match the labor that we have invested, then we tend to feel that we have been the victims of a cosmic con. It feels like a whole-life bait and switch.

There are probably more silently angry people than you and I are aware of. They live with the feeling that somehow they have been ripped off. They think back at all they have done and simply can't understand why they don't have more to show for it. They worked hard. They tried to be honest. They didn't take advantage of others. They tried to be contributing members of their community and their church. They endeavored to be good parents, loyal friends, and faithful spouses. Yet, when they take that whole-life personal accounting they don't have much to show for it. The more they think about the injustice of it all, the more bitter they get. And to make matters worse, there are many people they see every day who seem to have it all but neither appreciate nor deserve it.

Bitterness focuses on a boss that never recognized what you were capable of, a spouse who never got their act together, a rebellious child who destroyed the family dream, or a church that failed to recognize your ministry potential. In reality, however, your bitterness is more vertical than it is horizontal. As believers we deny that life is orchestrated by fate, luck, chance, cause and effect, or some system of natural laws. We affirm that the world and everything in it is controlled by a Person who orders and rules everything by his wisdom, power, and goodness. It's hard to admit, but when we are angry, we are in reality angry at God. In our bitterness we summon him to the court of our judgment and charge him with being unloving, unkind, unfair, or unfaithful. We hold before him the evidence of others who were blessed when we were not. We resurrect incident after incident that "proves" we were not given what we rightly deserve. We point a finger at the Almighty and say, "If you had kept your part of the bargain, I would have gotten my dream!"

This deep and personal bitterness against God produces a cruel harvest. It will suck the life out of your passion for the Gospel, your delight in worship, your zeal for ministry, and your trust in the only place where true wisdom, life, hope, and peace can ever be found. Bitterness sucks the oxygen out of your spiritual universe and replaces it with a toxic gas that you cannot see or smell. With every breath you are killing the very cells of your heart, and yet you may not be aware of it at all.

3. ***The doubt trap.*** The two traps we have already discussed lead you into a third trap. I have already stated it, but it is worth repeating and reemphasizing: the emotional and spiritual roller coaster of midlife disappointment is really fueled by doubt about God. All of our difficulty with people and circumstances is the fruit of a functional theology of cynicism. We aren't denying God's existence or ostensibly forsaking the faith, but we are less and less willing to put our lives in God's hands and rest. When I talk with people who profess to be believers but are dealing with a major life disappointment, I will encourage them to place their life in God's powerful and loving hands and rest. Again and again they will look at me with a surprised expression as if I am too naive or ill-informed to understand that this doesn't really work. Some may even harbor secret disappointment that Scripture calls us to run with our fear, pain, and grief to the very One whom we think is a major part of the problem. One man captured it very well: "How often can I be knocked down before it is alright to say, 'I'm not going to get up anymore'?"

4. ***The bargain trap.*** It is often tempting to try to strike bargains with God, but life is not a series of strategic negotiations with God; it is a moral drama of wisdom and foolishness, right and wrong, true and false, and good and evil. It plays itself out in even the most mundane situations of our daily lives. At the center of this moral drama is what defines our happiness. Perhaps there is no more important human thought than, "If I had ________, then I would be happy," because what holds your happiness controls your heart, and what controls your heart conditions your emotions, commands your choices, and shapes your behavior. Because of this, God will not bargain with us. He knows that unless we find our ultimate happiness in him, we will become hopelessly enslaved to things that can never deliver the life that we are seeking. These false messiahs always disappoint us, leaving us more despondent, bitter, and ultimately morally bankrupt. In the purest of jealousies, God fights for our souls, refusing to participate in any bargain that would tempt us to search for life outside of him.

Yet, many people have argued with me that there *are* bargains in Scripture, in which God seems to have willingly participated. One of the prime examples is Hannah, whose story is found in 1 Samuel 1 and 2. Hannah was married to a man who had two wives. Peninnah, his other wife, had given birth to many children, but Hannah was barren. In Old Testament culture, where the family depended on many children for its wealth and continuance, barrenness was a curse. In her grief, Hannah went to the temple to pray saying, "O LORD Almighty, if you will only look upon your servant's misery and remember me, and not forget your servant but give her a son, then I will give him to the LORD for all the days of his life, and no razor will ever be used on his head" (1 Samuel 1:11). At first glance this does look like a bargain with God, and in fact, God did give Hannah a son. However, the passage needs closer examination.

If you are striking a bargain with God, it is only *after* you have received what you wanted that you rejoice and experience peace. But this is not how Hannah responded. Once she prayed, she did two things that demonstrate this was not a bargain with God. First, she went and got something to eat. What a fundamentally human observation Scripture makes here. You know that deep emotional upset robs you of your appetite. Many people who are going through extended times of disappointment and grief lose a significant amount of weight. Hannah's eating pictures a woman at peace. She is not waiting for the birth of her baby for her peace to return; she has it now. Second, "her face was no longer downcast" (v. 18). The slumped shoulders, hanging head, and sad face of a woman in pain were gone. Hannah walked away from her time of prayer with her head high and a smile on her face. Note again that she was not waiting for something for her joy to return. She had it already!

Hannah's prayer was not a negotiation with God in order to get her dream, but an abandonment of her dream for a better one. Rather than being consumed by her own purpose, she is choosing to be consumed by God's. Rather than attaching a happy life to the success of her own kingdom, she finds life in the success of God's kingdom. Hannah is essentially praying, "Lord, I don't want this child for me; I want this child for you. I want this child so that he and I may in some way be part of the good things that you are doing on earth for your people." Hannah is not negotiating with God for her dream. She is letting go of her dream for a son, to lay hold of something infinitely better—God! This is why she is able to go away in happiness and peace.

4. *The denial trap.* Some of us will not face the fact that we will never realize our dream. We invest an amazing amount of time and energy doing everything we can to keep the dream alive. In a tragic allegiance to our dream, we may even begin to contradict our own values and break our own rules. Joe always told himself that he would not be like his father who sacrificed his family on the altar of career success. Yet somewhere in the middle of his life, Joe, too, became obsessed with a career dream that wasn't happening. He reasoned that if he were more dedicated, more knowledgeable, more skilled, and more available at work, the dream would be just around the corner. So he accepted assignments that meant disruptive moves for his family, enrolled in courses that ate up his time, and worked far more hours than any husband and father should ever work. There were even many Sundays where he could not get up for church because he had worked on Saturday until almost dawn. He continued to deny the death of his dream even though his family and his relationship with God were paying a terrible price.

Tess's dream seemed so biblical. All she ever wanted was a wonderful marriage to a godly man and a life of serving the Lord together. But as the years went on the dream that had once been held with an open hand had become an obsession. Benny was not the "dream" husband. He found personal conversations to be difficult and uncomfortable, and he struggled with personal issues that sapped him of his vitality and joy. Yet Tess reasoned that if she were a better homemaker, then Benny would respond differently. So Tess spent far too much time and money decorating their house. It became more of a museum than a home and an uncomfortable place to relax and rear children. She thought that if she were more alluring and attractive, then Benny would respond more affectionately. But with all her diets, exercise, and an inordinate amount of money spent on makeup, clothing, and lingerie, Benny was still not a participant in the dream. She concluded that she and Benny needed time away with one another, so she planned exotic and expensive vacations for just the two of them. The only lasting result was debt. But Tess would not give up. She forced Benny to read one marriage book after another and dragged him to one seminar and one counselor after another. She was sure that marital bliss was just around the corner; she simply needed to figure out what to do to get there. Meanwhile she had done more to drive Benny away than to woo him.

Some of us are all too skilled at denying the death of our dreams, and in our dutiful allegiance to them, we sacrifice many of the things that we once said were so important to us.

So What Do We Do with Our Dreams?

1. ***Dream vertically.*** Remember why you have been given this ability: so that the eyes of your heart could be enthralled

with a vision of him and his kingdom. Following the Lord doesn't curse you to a dreamless existence but welcomes you to the grandest and most glorious of dreams. This dream is too big to wrap your grandest thoughts around, spanning beyond the furthest reach of your imagination. It is the only dream worth living for, the only dream that can deliver, and the only dream that, when held tightly, won't wreak damage on you and those around you.

So dream wide, dream high, and dream well. But focus your dreams vertically and not horizontally. The horizontal dreams may or may not come, but they will never deliver what our hearts hunger for. Dreams will either die or disappoint, but they can never give us life. Before the foundations of the world were formed, our lives were inextricably tied to God. This is what it means to be human. There is no other way. Our hearts were always meant to belong to him, and whenever they are taken away by anything else, bad things result in and around us.

2. ***Recognize the power of your dreams.*** It *is not* wrong to dream of a great marriage, a wonderful family, a successful career, or years of meaningful work in ministry. These are good dreams, but we must recognize their power. Our dreams, however, also have the power to tempt and seduce us. They compete for the allegiance of our hearts. Our dreams are like armies of desire, involved in an all-out war that continues in every moment of our life. It is not just a war for our heart; it is a battle for our very humanity. For whenever your heart becomes functionally ruled by anything other than the Lord, you are then outside of the purpose for which you were created.

Here's what happens. Yesterday's dream becomes today's demand. Today's demand morphs into tomorrow's need. What once got my attention has now become the thing that I cannot live without. Remember this dream principle: the dream for a good thing becomes a bad thing when that dream becomes a ruling thing. This is the danger of our dreams.

3. ***Greet your disappointment and pain as a loving warning.*** God is not playing games with you. His actions toward you are always loving and always wise. Your ability to experience pain is God's system of warning. It is meant to tell you that something is wrong that needs to be corrected. Consider our ability to experience physical pain. God ordained this physiological warning system so that we would know that some organ of the body is broken or not operating as it should. Similarly, our moments of deepest heart disappointment are God's alarms sounding, alerting us to spiritual dangers that we would not be aware of any other way. In the painful realization of the death of your dream, hear the loving alarms of your Lord and Redeemer. These are not the sounds of unfaithfulness and inattention. They are the sounds of grace. He is alerting you to the life-altering danger of a wandering heart before it is too late. Your pain is an instrument of his love. Your disappointment is a tool of his grace. The noise of the crumbling bricks of the tower of your dreams is the sound of a gracious warning sent with love from your Father in heaven.

Also realize that this moment of pain is a moment of rescue. It may seem impossible to imagine life without your dream, but the dream that died would have never done for you what you wanted it to. The mournful dirges of your broken dreams are really the hymns that celebrate your rescue. In your pain sing with joy, for you are being rescued from your bondage to a cruel master, a false messiah. Your cell is being unlocked and you are being transported to a new and better kingdom. His kingdom has come with grace and glory right into the real world that you live in every day. Open your eyes and see what you could have never planned, achieved, or imagined. You are eternally loved by God; you are eternally his son or daughter; what he wants for you is always right and best; and what he has planned for you is immeasurably better than anything you could have dreamed for yourself. See and smile, even in your disappointment, for you are being rescued.

4. ***Fix your eyes on a better dream.*** Instead of bitterly and remorsefully looking back, look forward. You have years ahead of you to pursue a better dream. Ask yourself what better dream God has for you in your work, your family, and in the body of Christ. Look for the place he is calling you to, to restore the things that were broken in the years you were captured by your dream. God has a better dream, so be determined not to settle for anything less.

5. ***Celebrate the fact that God is the God of fresh starts.*** Remember Moses, David, Peter, and Paul, all people in Scripture who in the middle of their lives were rescued by God and set on a new and better pathway. You do not have to wallow in remorse. You have been graced by God with the opportunity to start fresh once more. Celebrate! Your life is not over; you are only in the middle, and because of his grace, your best and brightest years are still ahead of you. Throw yourself into life with enthusiasm, a life ruled by vertical rather than horizontal dreams. Know that only when your dreams belong to the Lord can you experience the best and brightest of lives.

Chapter 6

Lost in the Middle: Don's Story

Happiness is inward, and not outward, and so, it does not depend on what we have, but on who we are.

—Henry Van Dyke

Vitality shows not only in the ability to persist, but in the ability to start over.

—F. Scott Fitzgerald

In preparing to write this book, I had the privilege of interviewing a longtime friend who is now one of my heroes of faith. It is a remarkable and holy thing when a person is willing to open the front door and invite you into the interior of his life. I have never walked through a person's inner house without at one time or another wanting to weep, wonder, scream, or rejoice. As I listened to Don's story, I had all of these reactions. And I was amazed that Don was not only willing to disclose these things to me, his friend, but to you as well. Through his story you will see the powerful hand of your loving Redeemer, without which Don would not have survived, and you and I would have never heard it. Don's story dynamically illustrates the fact that God is on center stage during the most profound moments of midlife lostness.

I have chosen to place Don's story at this point in the book so it can function as both a summary of what we have examined so far and a bridge to that which follows. His life puts flesh and blood on midlife crisis, moving it from a set of abstract characteristics to concrete personal realities. His is a story of regret, of physical weakness, and of the crushing death of a dream. Embedded in it are all of the biblical themes we will consider in the remainder of this book. These themes make sense out of midlife struggles and push us toward the fresh starts of grace. Read Don's story as your own story. Sure, the details are very different, but Don is a human being living in the same fallen world that each of us lives in, a son of the same God that has fathered us. In his story he is fighting the same moral wars we each fight in little and big moments every day.

No One Runs to Hear Bad News

"It had been going on for a while, and I did my best every day to deny it. I guess we all have that ability, you know, to convince ourselves that what we are feeling and experiencing is not really happening, or at least, that it's not as bad as we think it is. You tell yourself over and over, sometimes many times a day, that you are not really feeling what you're feeling. You adopt the old 'ignore it and it will go away' strategy. If that doesn't work you try to fight whatever you are trying to deny. So I ate better, slept more, and tried to be more disciplined with my workouts, but something became harder and harder to deny because it just wouldn't go away. The numbness in my legs was undeniably there.

"I guess it had to be there long enough and constantly enough to break through my denial and drive me to a doctor, the first of what seemed like an endless succession of doctors that year. At times it seemed like a full-time job—I was on the year-long physicians' tour. That first Thursday afternoon I sat in the waiting room with about 12 other I'd-rather-be-anywhere-else souls, anxiously anticipating the moment when the nurse would appear, bellow my name and beckon me back to the hallways you never enter unless something is physically wrong with you. I sat, waiting for my turn, holding a magazine that I wasn't really reading, telling myself that what I had been experiencing physically was really nothing. The doctor would laugh, tell me I was in great shape, and give me a clean bill of health. I half-wondered if the lady next to me could hear my rapidly beating heart.

"My name was called, and I was ushered down the hallway and told to sit on the examining table. You feel so vulnerable and alone as you wait for the doctor to arrive. He had treated everyone in the family, but that familiarity wasn't too comforting. Not much came out of that first visit. No life-altering diagnosis. I received his professional concern and reassurance, but not much beyond that.

It Can't Really Be True

"I was in the middle of my life, and something was wrong with me that I did not understand and could not escape. I spent that year being interviewed, inspected, poked, and evaluated by doctor after doctor. Each told me that there was definitely something wrong but none really seemed to know what it was. Finally I found myself in the office of a neurologist. He told me what I was searching to know but didn't really want to hear. I had multiple sclerosis. MS! I had MS! Not joint problems, or aging difficulties, or arthritis, but a life-altering neurological disease for which there was no cure. This couldn't be happening! I was a dedicated father and husband. I was the chief breadwinner in my family in the middle of an exciting career! I had three young sons who needed me! I was an elder in my church! Not this, not now! This couldn't be happening to me!

"As I drove home that afternoon, it seemed like an impossible thing to tell my wife and my boys. How could I help them understand what I didn't understand? How could I help them not be afraid when I was so afraid? What about my career? All of this happened at an amazing time in my job. It was like I was on a career rocket ship. Thirteen months before being diagnosed, I was given my first management position with benefits, including long-term disability.

"There was so much going on. The owner of the business I worked for had passed away, and the man who put me into my new management position took over the business. He let me know that someday I would run the plant.

Excuse Me, the Timing is All Wrong Here

"It seemed weird that these two things would be happening at once. The best possible thing in my career was colliding with the worst possible thing in my body. Soon, however, with the wonders of modern medicine, things went back to normal. My twice-a-year steroid treatments seemed to keep the MS in check. I wasn't yet going through a real crisis of faith. Except for physical limitations like not being able to do sports with my boys, life was pretty much the same as before my diagnosis. All of my dreams were still attainable, including the dream of paying cash for my son's college education and the dream of owning a vacation home at the shore where all of us could gather for years to come.

"I was getting lots of support and encouragement at work, and it was all very exciting. I didn't have a college business degree, but I had risen to the top because I had tried to employ biblical principles in my leadership of the people at work. God seemed to be honoring the principles of his Word and blessing my efforts.

"Four years passed. There were regular steroid treatments and growing pressures at work, but life was good. I had a relapse-and-remission form of MS, so there were physical ups and downs, though they never seemed to keep me from doing my work. But over the four years since I had been diagnosed I had built up antibodies to the medications. This was my first real big setback, but even it turned out for good. I was given a new drug that helped me more than the previous ones had.

"At work the promises kept coming. I was told that one day I would own a piece of the company. I was asked to be the primary mentor of the boss's sons. Here I was, a sick man with no formal education but with more power and potential than I thought I would ever have! There were occasional bad physical episodes, but there was always hope of getting up out of them, and I always did.

"A year or so later, the heat really cranked up. A down-turning economy brought my company to its knees. There was more stress at work than I had ever experienced before. I was out to prove that I could handle it all and succeed, even with MS. I was not even going to consider having my wife work. Our goal had always been for her to be at home while our boys were in school. I worked high-stress, 14-hour days. I retained my position as elder in our church. Yet it was all taking a toll with regard to my MS. I was continually needing to up my steroid dosage, soon shifting from once every six months to once every six weeks.

"Then something amazing happened at work: my secretary came to Christ. Seeing me work through my MS was an important piece of what brought her to Christ. I thought to myself, 'Both the stress of my job and MS are worth going through for this.' Sure, I was sick, but life was good and all of my dreams were still fully in place.

"Things stayed pretty fulfilling and exciting for me. Even though I was dealing daily with a major disease, it didn't dominate my thinking. The company I worked for continued to grow, and I was now the corporate vice-president. I had a six-figure income, a company car, and was responsible for two hundred and fifty employees. I had more than I ever dreamed I would have. I was overseeing the plant managers, mentoring the boss's sons, negotiating with the union, dealing with customer relations and using biblical principles in each area. I thought I was in a very good place. The next three or four years seemed like the best of times. I had it all: a great family, a fantastic career, and a relationship with God. I loved God and he appeared to be blessing me richly. Things were good.

"Then the attacks began again, while at the same time work was getting increasingly more hectic. There were things going on in my body that I just didn't want to face. I loved my life. I loved my job. I loved the lifestyle that I was able to provide for my family. I did not want anything to get in the way of what God had helped me achieve and what we were experiencing as a family. My pastor mentioned the option of going on disability because he was genuinely concerned for me, but that was unthinkable. I could not quit. I could not give in. I would not let myself consider that I might not be able to continue doing what I was doing. All my eggs were in one basket, and it could not be taken away from me!

And Then the News Got Worse

"In January of the next year I went in for a routine MRI. The news was devastating: I had a hole in the base of my spine. It was very serious, and it was permanent. It seemed like I was looking at the end of my wonderful world. I immediately wondered if I was going to be able to keep up with the expectations of my boss and if this would mean the end of the rocket ship rise of my career. This news hit me much harder than my original diagnosis. This one seemed to be the deal breaker. Because of my career fears, I hid the truth from the people around me who could end my career, yet I was crying out inside.

"Questions assaulted me. What in the world was going on? Why now? For twelve to thirteen years I had fought to make it all work. I had been unwilling to cave in and give up, even when those around told me it was okay to do so. It seemed like God was giving me the ability to press on, to walk when I could not physically walk, and to deal with brutal medications. I don't think I was so much angry as I was discouraged and confused. Did I go through all of the suffering for this? Did God do those daily miracles for me, only to take it all away when I was right in the middle of harvesting everything I had planted for years? I cried for help to get through it all. I continued to seek counsel and all my counselors returned to the same themes: to pursue the Lord and slow down. I think I suffered during this time more from the stress of it all than directly from the disease. I needed to keep the dream going. After all, not all of my sons had finished college, we hadn't bought the vacation house at the shore, and I couldn't even think about my wife going back to work.

"Meanwhile things were the worst they had ever been at work. We simply weren't paying our vendors, so I was dealing with upset customers, while trying to keep my integrity. I found myself asking God for forgiveness for the ways I tried to keep the company afloat. On more than one occasion I seriously stretched the truth. I found myself struggling with practical issues of faith—trying to keep God and his way first. I finally knew I had to be honest with my boss. When I told him, he wondered out loud if the company was going to make it. He had promised me years ago that he would never let my disability insurance lapse, but now that seemed like a promise he might not be able to keep. He told me to go on disability now because he was not sure how long he would be able to continue to pay for it.

If I Say This, It's Over

"I knew that day when I walked in to talk to my boss that my career was over. I had been coming home totally wiped out. My wife told me again and again that if this is what it takes, she didn't want me there at work anymore. How could this be happening? Everything I had ever hoped for would never come to pass, just when things were right at my fingertips. At times I had wanted out, but I wanted to prove to the people at work that this God that I had talked about could get me through. What would they think about me and God now? It rocked my faith more than I thought was possible. My dream had become my idol, my job was my way of getting it, and the whole thing was based on my assumption that my physical health would remain okay. I was in the middle of my life and though I didn't know it, I had lost my way.

"It was a year of spiritual struggle and personal crisis. I had believed in my physical invincibility, and I was sure God would make my dream happen if I kept trying to serve him. But in ways I was unable to see at the time, my relationship with God had dwindled. It was my dream that had kept me going, and in subtle ways the dream had pushed him aside. My whole life had become my job and what it could do for me. When my idolatry was revealed, it seemed as if God wasn't there. I reached for him, but I could not find him. I couldn't experience the sweet fellowship with him that I had once known. I was increasingly depressed, and I found it almost impossible to sleep at night. It felt like I was turning my back on everything I had said and stood for. I had told people that no matter what, God would get them through, but he hadn't gotten me through. More than a blow to my faith, quitting my job was a blow to my pride, because it had all been about me. I was tempted to believe that God wasn't in this, but in my heart of hearts I knew he was.

"God *was* with me, and he was at work in me. Just because I had trouble seeing him didn't mean he wasn't there. God brought his people and his Word into my life. I read Hebrews 11 over and over again. I studied the lives of Abraham and Moses. It was hard to accept the utter death of my dream, and it was devastating to face the reality that I probably would never work again, but I began to take baby steps of faith once again.

The Enemy Within

"I don't know how else to say it, but I *was not* the same man that I had been fifteen years before. My heart *was not* in the same place it once was. My relationship with God *had not* stayed in the same place. But it had all been masked by my continuing participation in the things that sincere Christians do. I didn't quit going to church. I didn't resign as an elder. I continued to be involved in ministry, but my heart was more and more ruled by a burning desire to succeed at my job, because my job was the key to achieving all the dreams that I had set my heart on.

"Without any conscious decision to forsake him, I was actually far from God. He was no longer my life. When my career was taken away from me, it was as if God wasn't there. I thought that all that I was doing was for the Lord. I thought I was demonstrating every day that God could get me through, no matter what, but it was really all about me. I was confronted with my pride in my own life.

"It's tempting to think that when you turn back to God, he is right there waiting for you and everything in your relationship is immediately restored again, but that is not how it happened for me. Of course God is always there because he promised never to leave me. The problem was that I had drifted away from him! The habits of heart that were once a daily part of my life had been replaced by other habits. I was not the same person, so turning became more of a process than an event. I couldn't seem to let go of *my* work, *my* team, and the things that *I* had built. I kept coming into work, even though I was on disability. I wanted so much to be there because it had become the thing that defined me and gave my life meaning.

"Those first few months on disability were a huge struggle. I had been the main driving force at work. I had helped build this business. I had defined employee and customer relations. I had been let into the highest levels of planning and power. The owner had chosen *me* to mentor his sons. I had gone from almost nothing to a six figure income. I was not supposed to be sidelined. I was not supposed to be on disability. This was not supposed to be happening. What about all the things I had counted on and planned toward? I was beginning to see what had happened in my heart, but it was hard. It was like being in a war. I wanted to experience inner peace, but there was none. Questions and confusion flooded my heart. I wanted to be right with God, but I could not imagine what life would be like without my job.

"Taking disability made me feel like a loser, like half a man. I was supposed to be strong, disciplined, and persevering. I was supposed to be able to get up every day and contribute to my job and to my family. But I had been relegated to a taker. God began to use this fact to reveal the idolatry of my heart. I had tried to find "life" outside of him.

Seeing God

"At the same time God was doing more than revealing the depth of my idolatry; he was revealing himself to me. He used Exodus 33 (where he showed Moses his glory) to show me his purpose, his presence, and his glory. I began to see God and his loving and powerful hand. I had many reasons to be thankful. God had given me many good years physically, filled with more wonderful activity than I ever deserved. I had a wonderful wife who was my best and dearest friend. I had participated in important and fulfilling ministries in my church. I had dear and faithful Christian friends. I had been taught well from God's Word. My life was very rich, and the God who had given me all of those gifts was with me in this moment.

"In my pride I was headed for disaster. God had given me many more years of strength and success than you would ever think a person with MS could ever have. What was actually a gift had become a demand, so I was determined to push and push and push. If God hadn't intervened in my life I would have pushed until I was in a wheelchair. Still, with all the insight that God was giving me and with the ability to see his presence in my life, it was *not* easy. I was faced with some of the hardest decisions of my life which not only altered my life but also the lives of my wife and my three boys. I could see God's hand in it all, but I had no vision for what was on the other side.

"I was facing big losses and changes financially. My disability was taken care of, and amazingly my company was covering my medical insurance, but my financial life would never be the same again. There would never be that vacation home at the shore. I would not be paying cash for my sons' college educations. I would have to refinance my mortgage and be careful with what I spent. God was faithful in meeting our needs, but I could no longer finance my dreams, and I was no longer the productive and successful person that I loved being.

"Once you face your loss, the next question is, 'What now?' The things that used to occupy my thoughts had been taken away. There was a huge hole in my life, and I didn't know how it would ever get filled. What would I do with all of my time? What could ever be half as fulfilling as my work? How would I use my gifts and experiences? What would it be like to get up in the morning and not go to work? What would it be like not to be the person that people sought to solve their problems? My first few glances into the future looked pretty bleak and empty.

"But through the ministry of brothers in the body of Christ, God was beginning to build a new vision in my heart. I had always been good with people. I knew how to mentor and encourage them, and God wanted to use that for his kingdom. He was in the process of turning me from my kingdom to his kingdom, and he was about to make me more busy with his kingdom work than I ever thought I could be. There would be opportunities to continue to be salt and light at my former company as I did some consulting work on personnel issues. My days and weeks soon began to fill up with ministry opportunities. I had many opportunities to counsel and disciple struggling men. I was asked to be a founding member of the board of directors of a very exciting missionary foundation. Because I had time, I was able to help the foundation get properly incorporated. I found myself with several marriage counseling situations. I was not sitting at home feeling like a loser and wondering what to do with my time. The Lord had graciously filled my schedule with people and meaningful things to do. I began to see that there really was life after my career.

"I now know that my midlife crisis was not the end. I had gotten lost in the middle, but by God's great grace I was not lost for long. The crisis was actually a rescue from the bondage to something that I didn't even know had that kind of hold on me. And it wasn't just a rescue; it was a welcome to a brand new start. Even though my disease makes it impossible for me to work in a traditional way, I get up and work every day, and I am looking forward to many more years of useful labor in God's kingdom. I don't know what my physical future holds, but I do know that I am God's child, that he is with me every moment, and that his grace is greater than any weakness or disappointment I will ever face."

Making Sense of it All

Although it doesn't seem to make sense that God would allow such a thing to happen to such a good man right in the middle of his life, you can stand back from Don's story and see that what has resulted is very good. Yes, questions still plague us. Did these good things have to cost so much? Does everyone have to hit the old midlife wall before they really begin to experience the fullness of their identity in Christ and the grandeur of God's kingdom work? How *do* things become more important than they should? How is it possible for us to change so significantly and not know it? Do I have to look over my shoulder and wonder when God will lay me low, like he did Don? How *do* I recognize when my job (or physical condition, or appearance, or relationships) has become more than a job to me? Why is it that so many people lose their way right in the middle of their lives?

You can't throw abstract theology at Don's story and make sense out of it. The only way to make sense out of it is by viewing it through the lens of another story. Don's drama is actually a mini-chapter in a much greater drama. Though Don was dealing with significant and personal issues, he was not on center stage in his own story. In fact, his story is not really *his* story. Only when Don saw his story embedded in the larger story did he begin to know true life and hope once again.

In this way Don's story is our story. We too, live in the middle of our own mini-drama. Perhaps yours doesn't feel like a *mini*-drama, but a gargantuan and impossible one. You feel the heat of the spotlight, as if it's all about you. You are afraid that you are about to make a mess of things. But you, too, are just one chapter in the world's most significant story. You are most lost when you cannot see beyond your personal drama, because the details of your little story do not provide enough information, reason, and wisdom to help you make sense of what it really is.

In the rest of this book, we are going to examine the larger story and how it helps us to make sense out of, and know what to do with, the powerful struggles of the midlife years.

The World's Best Storybook

When our children were young, we spent a lot of time telling and reading stories to them. We read the great fables, taking them to imaginary worlds of mystery and wonder. I would make up series of stories to tell my children. One of the series they loved the most was about a boy (Flippy) and his frog (Hoppy). Night after night we followed Hoppy and Flippy on adventure after adventure. I also told them stories about Billy, an average neighborhood kid who had discovered a container of antigravity paint. Night after night they would follow Billy and his band of friends on yet another gravity-defying adventure. These stories were meant to teach, entertain, and amaze, but all the great stories that have ever been told are unable to contain the wisdom and wonder that is to be found in the world's best storybook, the Bible.

As I have written before, it is vital that we do not approach the Bible as an extended theological outline, a religious encyclopedia, or a compendium of human problems and divine solutions. Nor is the Bible just a collection of stories and their interpretations. Rather, the Bible is *one* story that stretches from cover to cover. Every mini-drama in Scripture is a thread in the cord of the maxi-drama that reaches from cover to cover. The individual threads only make sense when they are understood in the light of the whole cord. If you try to understand individual stories on their own, you will make conclusions that appear to make sense, but will prove to be nonsense when they are seen from the perspective of the whole story.

As God's child, your story is a chapter in his story. The Bible is God's telling of his story so that we can know him, know ourselves, and live in a way that is consistent with his plot. The problem is that not only do we want to occupy center stage (which is reserved for God alone), but we also want to be novelists. We spend a lot of time trying to write our own stories and are often upset and anxious because the plot we have written is not unfolding. Few us of actually live functionally with God's story in view. We get stuck in our own autobiographies. But our stories do not belong to us.

Living with Another Story in View

The purpose of the Bible is to help us get to know the One who is always on center stage so that we can live with a God's-story mentality, deciding and acting in ways that fit within the plot of his story. The Bible wasn't given to solve all of your problems; only eternity will do that. The Bible was given so that the God of the plot would be the God of your heart, and you would live with a deep and personal commitment to the success of his story.

Midlife is the God-ordained collision of two stories. Even though Don didn't realize it, there were two competing stories developing in his life. Both stories could not coexist because both were in direct competition for Don's heart. They defined life, identity, meaning, and purpose in very different ways. They both competed for Don's time, gifts, energy, and allegiance. They both motivated Don with a set of promises and rewards. They both warned Don of what would happen if he got outside of the story. These stories had coexisted for too long, so God, through the vehicle of Don's physical disease, allowed them to collide. This dramatic and painful collision was not God turning his back on Don, but God turning his face *toward* him. It was not an ending, but a God-given new beginning.

To experience this God-given fresh start, Don surrendered his writer's pen and saw the honor and rest found in being a character in the story of the Lord. Don had to move from mourning what he had lost, to celebrating what he had gained. But it was hard. There were many moments when Don was tempted to go back to Egypt, when he felt more ripped off than blessed. There were times when God didn't seem all that good. But Don didn't turn back because he began to live with a God's-story mentality in ways he never had before.

Themes of the Story

Seven prominent threads run through the fabric of God's story. These themes define the God who is at the center, so they are essential to understanding anything you face in your own mini-drama. When the glory of God's story begins to amaze and thrill you, you will never again be seduced by the pseudo-glory of any story you could write for yourself. The themes of God's story become your beacons of wisdom, courage, and hope, exegeting midlife struggles and pointing to the way out of them.

1. ***God's story is a story of suffering.*** It's hard to accept, but one of the most dominant themes in God's story in Scripture is the theme of suffering. It is a sufferer's drama, and if you are inside God's story, there is no way you are going to avoid it. The issue is not *whether* you will suffer; the issue is what you will do *when* you suffer. So making sense out of suffering is a critical part of what it means to live with a God's-story mentality. The suffering of midlife is not an obstacle in the story but an integral part of it.

2. ***God's story is a control story.*** None of us likes our life to be spinning out of control. Most of us tend to lose it even in little moments when things don't go as we planned (a bill we weren't anticipating, a flat tire during a busy morning, the flu on vacation, etc.). We like our worlds to be orderly and predictable. We like to look ahead and have our plans unfold without obstruction. We find it hard to rest under the control of another person. But that is exactly what God's story calls us to do: to surrender control to Another.

3. ***God's story is a worship story.*** Worship is the most important theme in God's story. Worship is the drama inside of every drama in God's story, yet you could easily miss it. When we think of worship we often think of a group of people in nice clothes, standing in rows, hymnbooks in hand, singing to the Lord. That is a formal, corporate act of worship, but it's only a little part of what the Bible means when it talks about worship. Midlife crisis is a crisis of worship. If you can understand this, you are a long way down the road to understanding your struggle and what to do with it.

4. ***God's story is a drama of identity.*** There are few more important questions you can ask than, "Who am I?" Few of us regularly ask this question in a philosophical or abstract way, yet we are always defining our identity and making choices consistent with who we think we are.

5. ***God's story is about values.*** Midlife crisis is about what is really important in life. As we live every day, things that aren't supposed to be so important become important to us,

and things that were meant to be very important hardly get our attention. Every day we seek to obtain the things that are valuable to us and to divest ourselves of what we think has no value. Stories are always built around what is valuable, and only when you have the whole story in hand can you accurately assess what is valuable and what is not. God reveals the beginning and end of his story so that in the middle we will not be confused about what is really important.

6. ***God's story is a story of grace.*** Many people think of the Bible as a book of rules, but it is really a drama of grace. This grace that is on every page of God's story is largely misunderstood, even though it defines who we are, what we need, and what we can look forward to. When you really do see and understand this, you have a whole new way of responding to the pain and disappointment of this period of life.

7. ***God's story is an eternity story.*** You do not have be lost and confused because God in his mercy tells us the end of the story. Every present moment is connected to the future, so today can only be properly understood when it is viewed from the perspective of eternity. Without this eternal perspective, life explodes into the chaos of confounding mini-dramas that lead to nowhere. God's story has a direction and an ending. Because the end defines the middle, the perspectives of eternity are essential for making sense out of the struggles of midlife.

Another Kingdom, a Better King

Every day thousands of Dons get up in the morning and wonder what has happened to their life. Perhaps their first waking thoughts are filled with anger. They worked hard and did what is right, yet they have little to show for their years of perseverance and dedication. Or maybe their minds are flooded with bitter envy. They can't resist scanning the lives of others and wonder why the wrong guys are winning. Perhaps they awake to a body that is talking back to them. They simply feel old, as if life is passing them by and there's nothing they can do about it. They may also be consumed with deep regret. They failed to keep so many promises and left so much potential unfulfilled. Even if they always meant well and tried their hardest, they still feel like failures. Perhaps they wake to a marriage that has long since lost its warmth and vitality, a job that has been devoid of luster for years, or children who haven't become what they had the potential to be. It wasn't supposed to be this way! Maybe, they think, some more youthful clothes and a faster car will help them to deny where they really are in life.

Pastors are leaving churches because they have lost their way. Marriages are breaking up because a husband or wife has lost the way. There are people leaving jobs, relationships, communities, and churches because they have lost their way. Yet many of them are still quite convinced that their biggest problems lie somewhere outside of themselves.

The struggles of midlife do not fall outside of the circle of Scripture's light, nor do they fall outside the boundaries of the Gospel's grace. The presence, power, practicality, and glory of God's grace in Christ Jesus are most evident and effective when we have hit the wall of our own weakness, inability, and sin.

Life in this fallen world is really hard. Things around us and inside of us simply don't work the way they were meant to work. Add to this the fact that it is nearly impossible for you to have perfectly pure motives about anything because of the sin that wages war for control of your heart. And then there are so few things in life that you can actually control. It is scary to face how weak, needy, dependent, and powerless we all are. Maybe that is where midlife bursts with its greatest potential. Midlife doesn't introduce you to a new you; it forces you to admit who you have been all along. In doing so, you are more ready to understand and receive what God has for you in Christ than you have ever been before. Midlife provides a golden opportunity for us to chuck our tendencies toward self-reliance, self-righteousness, and selfishness in order to experience the fullness that can only be found when we live for and rely on Another.

The next few chapters will introduce you to another kingdom. It is vastly more beautiful and rewarding than all the kingdoms that fill our vision and consume our energies. But we will not simply tour the kingdom; we will have an audience with the King. We will be there by his own invitation, written by his hand before this earth was formed. If you are God's child, this kingdom and its righteousness belong to you. Your expenses have been paid, and the cost was death. Come with me. Bring your discouragement, regret, bitterness, anger, and disillusionment. Present them to the King, and see what he will do with them.

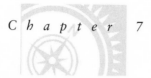

Chapter 7

Painful Faith: God's Story and Suffering

The pain of the mind is worse than the pain of the body.
—Publilius Syrus

A miserable slave is he who makes himself a garment of his pain.
—Gabriele D' Annunzio

It wasn't some heroic feat. I was just getting out of the chair to leave the family room, and I twisted my knee. The brief spike of pain wasn't followed by much more ... until the next morning. My throbbing knee was my alarm clock, and even by readjusting my position, I couldn't turn it off. I woke up saying, "I hate when this happens!" as I hobbled to the bathroom, thinking about what the day would be like with this pain. I soon realized how difficult it was going to be to navigate steps with a stiff and painful knee. Getting into the car took on a whole new meaning, and by the time I got to my destination I was wondering if I really wanted to be up and around at all! I was frustrated and angry that joint pain was going to be my constant companion for days to come.

When I saw her for the first time that day, Luella immediately asked what was wrong. "I twisted my stupid knee," was my happy response as I limped out of the room. I sat in the living room thinking about how much I hate dealing with obstacles like this and how everything would be more difficult in the days to come until my knee got back to normal. It was a full-on midlife moment. My limber-muscled youth is gone. I am not yet ready for a walker, but I will suffer pain and inconvenience that will be with me until I die. It was a very minor circumstance of suffering, but I didn't like it or what it seemed to predict.

Sometimes little moments are the best place to learn significant things. In the big, cataclysmic moments, we are working so hard just to survive that it is hard to learn much in the middle of them. Because the little moments get our attention without being so confounding, they can be better teachers. Such was the case with my throbbing knee, which immediately reminded me of two things.

First, we all tend to hate pain. I know this isn't a life-altering insight for you, but permit me to elaborate. Even though we all know that we are living in a seriously broken world, where things simply do not operate as they were created to, we all tend to live with an expectation that we will be able to avoid life's obstacles. When you plan your day, you don't build in extra time for physical pain, relational difficulty, and situational suffering. And when these things come your way, you, like me, probably tend to respond with much more surprise and dismay than you should, given what you know to be true about the condition of the world in which you live. A subtle expectation of uninterrupted ease, coupled with the thought that the "good" life is the pain-free life, leaves us often frustrated, confused, and angry when suffering comes our way. It's hard for us to "count it all joy" when the pain we are experiencing not only doesn't seem good in itself, but seems like an unnecessary obstacle in the way of obviously good things.

All of this confronts us with the fact that God doesn't evaluate our lives the way we do. His "good" is often radically different from the definition that we carry around in our minds. How is it good for us to have an accident that eats up our time and money on the way to a job that is a God-ordained means of investing our time to make money? How is it good for a young father to die, leaving a wife and children to fend for themselves? How can war and disease be good things? Why would God, who is in complete control and who is the source of all goodness, wisdom, and love, allow any of these things in his world? Why is suffering ever a part of the picture?

These questions are important in the middle of a book on midlife because midlife is a time of suffering. Whether it is the inner-being pain of disappointment and regret or the external pains of weakness, aging, or disease, you won't go through midlife without some kind of suffering. In the throes of unexpected midlife pain, many people try all kinds of things to relieve it that only exacerbate their trouble.

These questions are also important because God's grand story, of which your story is a part, is a suffering story. From the pain of Adam and Eve being thrown out of the garden, to the violent stories of the Old Testament, to the torture and execution of Christ, to the account of the suffering saints weeping their way into glory in Revelation, one of the dominant themes in the great story of redemption is suffering. It is a story of suffering sinners in a suffering world who are given a suffering Savior who will lead them to a place where suffering is no more. A robust and practical theology of suffering is one of the most essential tools for making sense out of the struggles of midlife.

Ian had come into Serena's life in college. She wasn't at all attracted to him at first. He just wasn't her type. He wasn't particularly handsome or athletic, and he surely wasn't as driven as Serena. As Ian continued to pursue Serena, however, her affection for him began to grow. Ian was solid and dependable, a man of character and conviction. He loved God and seemed to be very good with people. He was one of the few men Serena could confide in. She got used to having him around, enjoying his company, and seeking his advice. During college they spent most of their free time together and went to one another's homes for the holidays. Sundays were always special because they would go to worship and then spend a quiet afternoon together.

Between their junior and senior years of college, Ian traveled to Serena's hometown to ask for her hand in marriage. It wasn't one of those wild and memorable proposals; that wasn't Ian's style. It was just a loving request for a life together on a park bench on a summer evening. Serena immediately said "yes" and began to dream of what life would be like with Ian. The problem was that there was another dream inside of Serena that would collide with her Ian dream.

Their senior year of college was so much fun. They both lived within walking distance of the university. They were very busy with classes and part-time jobs but managed to spend lots of time with one another and talk a lot about their future. Serena was a very gifted artist, and she had always dreamed of working for a big-name advertising or design firm. She loved graphic design and was at the top of her class in college, with her professors constantly telling her that she would go far.

Ian was busy the weekend of the job fair, so Serena decided to go alone. "What harm would it do to see what is out there?" she told herself. She had no more than entered the convention center when she saw it; there in the largest booth was the firm of her dreams. She went straight to the table and introduced herself. Forty-five minutes later, Serena was walking home with her head spinning. She had been offered a better job, with better pay than she thought she would ever have. She was guaranteed advancement because she was going to be immediately placed in the executive track. They promised to cover her moving expenses in June and assist her in her search for a home. It was what she had always wanted, the thing for which she had always dreamed.

She greeted Ian with the good news, but it didn't seem like good news to him. She talked as if it was a done deal. He felt as if she had made the decision without him. She felt as if he was unsupportive, threatened by her success and jealous of her dream. He said to her, "But Serena, it's all the way across the country. What about my future job, our life together, and a family?" Serena was angry and defensive; Ian tried to tell her that he wanted her to be happy and successful, but if they were planning a life together then they had to make major decisions together, seeking God's help and wise counsel.

That evening ended with Ian frustrated and Serena in tears. Their relationship was never the same. As much as Ian tried to communicate that he was not jealous or seeking to rob Serena of her dreams, she could not be convinced. In June, instead of Serena and Ian getting married, they ended their engagement and Serena headed for the big city.

Serena is now forty-five and as successful in her career as anyone could imagine, but she is consumed with regret. She has gotten everything she dreamed about, yet she has come up empty. Rehearsing that fateful day has become an obsession. Why did she ever go to that job fair? Why had she made the decision so fast? Why had she been so defensive? Why had she allowed herself to get so bitter that she had broken her engagement? Why had she let her dream get in the way of something wonderful that God had placed in her path? How could she have been so blind, so stupid? She had lost track of Ian until a recent a college reunion. He was now a successful, small-town lawyer with three children and a beautiful wife.

Serena lived every day weighed down with the thought that she had blown her life. Increasingly she wondered why God, if he really cared about her, hadn't stopped her. She was living every day with a pain that nothing seemed to take away. She felt trapped. She had gotten what she dreamed for, but she was increasingly paralyzed with the visions in her brain of what she had forever left behind.

To Understand Suffering, You Must Disagree with Yourself

To have an accurate, biblically balanced view of suffering, you must first say suffering is a bad thing. Its existence points out all the things that are wrong with us and our world. We live in a world that is broken and groaning under the weight of all the damage that the fall has done. We should never look at all of this carnage and think that it is okay that people suffer. Scripture calls us to be a community of compassion, motivated by love, and zealous to relieve or remove suffering whenever and wherever we can. And the Bible promises that there will be a day when all this carnage will forever end, and we will be welcomed to a place totally free of any pain or suffering.

Having said all of this to yourself, you must now turn and say that suffering is a good thing. Suffering is an evil that an all-wise, all-righteous, and all-loving God uses for eternal good. The Bible again and again talks about the good things that only suffering can produce (See Romans 5:1–5, James 1, and 1 Peter 1:3–9). In each of these passages we are faced with the fact that God is sovereign and good, not just over our moments of blessing but over each moment of suffering as well. In saying these things the Bible never downplays the evil of suffering. When you seek to understand suffering biblically, you cannot opt for an easy "either-or." No, you must hold on to two seemingly opposite perspectives. To be right about suffering, you must disagree with yourself. The suffering that we all experience in this fallen world is very, very bad, yet in the hands of God it becomes something that is very, very good. In this instance you not only *can* have it both ways, but in order to be biblical you must.

Both the physical pain of the body and the heart-crushing pain of regret remind us that things are not the way they were meant to be. Bad things happen to good people all the time.

Aging and regret are visible signs of the physical and spiritual death that sin brought into the world. This is not a good thing. But neither are the sufferings of midlife entirely a bad thing. You are in trouble if you think either that your midlife suffering is a sign of God's distance, unfaithfulness, and inattention, or that it is evidence of God somehow being evil. The Bible is so strong in its call for us to see the good God does in the bad, that it calls us to greet our trials with joy! (James 1:2). When is the last time you really rejoiced in your suffering? This balance is both hard for us to understand and difficult for us to live out, so we tend to careen between the two extremes. If it's someone else's suffering, you and I tend to be able to see the "good" that can result, but if it's our own suffering we are tempted not to believe in the love and faithfulness of God.

The Cross, Where Ultimate Evil and Ultimate Good Kiss

There is no better place to learn how to understand and deal with suffering than on the hill of Calvary. It is here that the two disparate perspectives on suffering come together as essential pieces of the ultimate moment of hope. Peter, in his great sermon in Acts 2, gets this essential balance completely right. First, Peter says that Jesus of Nazareth was "handed over to you by God's set purpose and foreknowledge" (v. 23). God was in control of every moment of Christ's suffering. He suffered and died because God had ordained it to happen so that sin would be defeated and redemption would be accomplished. The crucifixion was not a moment where evil was out of control. On the cross, love and righteousness were not being defeated; they were winning. The cross was Satan's moment of greatest victory, but also his most crushing defeat. So, Peter essentially says, "Don't you see, God was in control of all of this, doing something that would result in the salvation of his people." The cross was a very good thing.

But Peter then turns and says something equally important. He says, "You, with the help of wicked men, put him to death by nailing him to the cross" (v. 23). Could there be any more wicked thing to do than to put to death the Messiah? Is it not a very bad thing to make a mockery of a system of justice and the obvious innocence of a man in order to put him to death? Isn't this made even more heinous when you understand that this man was the Son of God? Could there be a more callous act than jamming a crown of thorns onto his head and pounding nails through the holy hands of the Son of Man? Can you think of anything more arrogantly evil than to mock the Messiah while slapping him, spitting on him, and yanking out pieces of his beard? Could anything be more treacherous than to sell the Messiah to his executioners for a few silver coins?

Peter reminds you and me that we cannot look at the cross and simply say that it was a good thing. It was the most horribly evil thing that was ever done in all of human history. We murdered the only One who walked on earth who was worthy of our worship. We condemned the only Person who ever lived without guilt. We exercised capital punishment against the only "criminal" who ever lived who was innocent in every way. The crucifixion of Christ on the cross was a shockingly bad thing. Yet Peter doesn't hold this perspective to the exclusion of the other. They are inseparable to him, as they should be to us.

Consider why this balance is so important to our understanding of the cross. First, it is absolutely necessary that God is in complete control of all things, good and bad, so that he is able to fulfill every redemptive promise he has made to his children. Complete sovereignty is essential to the accomplishment of redemption. God must have the unchallenged power and authority to do whatever is necessary to redeem his children, or his promises mean nothing and there is no hope for us. This means that he is ruling over all things, even those things that we would say are evil, and using them for his good redemptive purpose. We know from the specificity of Old Testament prophecy that God ordained and controlled every evil act that was done to Christ. That Passion Week, God was not taken by surprise or struggling to snatch victory from the jaws of defeat. Peter said that God knew exactly what was coming because he ordained it all. All of the evil done to Christ was part of a very good thing that God was doing, redeeming the world from sin and death. You have to call the cross a good thing.

At the same time, nowhere in the Bible does the sovereignty of God absolve evil people from their responsibility for the evil they have done. That Passion Week, wicked men made evil choices to condemn, torture, and execute the Messiah. Each participant stands guilty for each choice he made and each action he took. No one is able to say, "I didn't have any choice." And no one can look at these choices and call them good.

Recognizing that the crucifixion was a very bad thing done by morally evil people actually highlights the need for the very thing the cross was ordained to accomplish. The world really is this bad. Sin really is this evil. The heart of man really is so dark that it will hate what is good and love what is evil. People really do suffer for wrongs they did not do. Every day people go through heart-wrenching rejection and physical mistreatment. Each act of hatred, injustice, and physical or emotional mistreatment is a violation of God's law, and therefore, evil. Each day people suffer weakness and disease in a world that is no longer a harmlessly beautiful garden. The Bible never calls you to look at this broken, fallen world and say that because God is in control it is okay. The Bible calls us to weep, fight, and pray, pleading for release to a place where evil no longer lives. The circumstances surrounding the death of Jesus prove just why he had to die: because this world is a very bad place in need of redemption.

So, on that hill that fateful day, for God's glory and the good of his people, ultimate evil and ultimate good were made to kiss. When you see and understand the cross biblically, you can begin to have a balanced perspective on the suffering that is so much a part of midlife.

As long as you live in this fallen world you will be pulled by each side of this contradiction. There will be moments when you will encounter hardship that seems unlikely to produce any good. There will be other times when you will be able to see the distinct good that has resulted from a moment of suffering. As you face the trials of midlife, you must become comfortable with disagreeing with yourself, unwilling to live on either side of the contradiction. You must require yourself to experience both the sadness and celebration that can be found in moments of difficulty and pain.

Perhaps this is the reason that we all tend to hate pain. It forces us to deal with things we would rather ignore or avoid. Suffering is like a spiritual dentist. You know that good things can come from his work, but you also know the process is painful and you'd like to avoid it if possible. So you do everything you can to convince yourself that your teeth are okay. In the same way you and I would like to think that we could acquire the things that suffering produces without actually having to go through the painful process.

The One Thing that Gets Everyone's Attention

Pain tends to be the one thing in life that always gets our attention. Isn't it amazing how a little throbbing gash on your finger has the power to break your concentration? Isn't it interesting how hard it is to keep something that has upset you from flooding your mind and dominating your thoughts throughout a day? Isn't it incredible how pain has the power to alter your emotions, shape your decisions, and even define your identity?

We all know that physical pain was designed to be a warning system that things in our physiology are not the way they are supposed to be. Pain announces to us that something is wrong, and therefore, it is dangerous to ignore. Pain exists because the world is in a degraded, fallen state. The world we live in is a house of pain, and we cannot live in it without it touching us. You will never be smart enough to escape its grasp. From the violence of childbirth to cut fingers and scraped knees, from sibling mockery and peer rejection to familial brokenness, suffering is part of every phase of human existence. We enter life through suffering's door and we exit life through suffering's door.

What does this mean for the struggles of midlife? It means that they are not unique. No person passes from stage to stage untouched. The sufferings of midlife are only unique in that they are tied to the situations and relationships of that phase of life. But what should you do with your midlife suffering? Listen to your pain. It is telling you something that you need to hear. Here are some of the things your pain is announcing to you.

1. ***You live in a fallen world.*** This is one of the sad but unavoidable themes of this book. I desperately wish it did not have to be, but it must be. Since that tragic moment of sin and rebellion in the Garden of Eden, the world we live in has limped through history in its crippled condition, staggering through century after century. Only when you are biblically ignorant or spiritually naive will you be surprised at the suffering that inflicts you and those around you. Because of the universality of suffering, our lives are more powerfully shaped by *how* we suffer than they are by the fact *that* we suffer.

Throughout the course of your life, you are shaped and directed by *how* you respond to the pain on your path. We all know that suffering can be the soil in which saints and heroes grow, but it can also be fertile ground for criminals and cowards. How is your life being shaped, not just by what you are suffering, but by how you have chosen to deal with it? More specifically, how is your life being shaped right now by how you are dealing with the pain of physical aging, disappointment, and regret that have greeted you in these midlife years?

2. ***There is something wrong with you.*** It is always important in times of suffering to ask, "What is wrong here?" Midlife disappointment and disillusionment with life may be God's

alarm, pointing you to the fact that your dreams have ruled your heart more than you ever knew. Perhaps, without you ever knowing it, they became functional god-replacements. Or maybe the physical pains and body changes of midlife are a God-given searchlight, revealing how much of your identity and security was placed in your physical health and beauty. Or perhaps during these midlife years you have increasingly struggled with regret. You have tried your best to be happy, content, and thankful, but you seem unable to resist replaying the video of past decisions and actions over and over again. Maybe this inescapable and paralyzing regret is a powerful indicator of an insidious self-righteousness that, over the years, functionally gave you more spiritual comfort than God's forgiveness. Perhaps you felt good because you thought you were good, and the archeology of midlife has uncovered sins of heart, hands, and lips that have decimated your confidence in your own performance.

Think of what you do when a smoke alarm goes off in your house. You don't just sit there and listen to it or get angry that it is going off. No, you are thankful that the alarm has done its job, gotten your attention, and propelled you to action. In his wisdom, God has built warning systems into our lives just like that smoke alarm. The pain of disappointment is meant to warn you and propel you to action. The pain of regret is meant to warn you and spur you to action. The pain of aging is meant to warn you and call you to action.

Are you hearing the squeal of midlife alarms? Are they getting your attention? Are they propelling you to action? Are you thankful that you are being warned and rescued?

3. ***Your suffering is not okay.*** It is very important that you are never "okay" with your suffering. We should all hate all kinds of suffering. Every time anyone anywhere suffers, it reminds us that something terrible has happened that has fundamentally changed the way the world operates. This is the balance to the good side of suffering. Something is very wrong with you if you don't care about, or are even happy with, the

suffering of another. The same should be true of you. You should hate the fact that sin has entered your world and damaged you and everything around you. You should hate the fact that your every thought, motive, word and action is tainted. You should hate the fact that your environment is so fraught with temptation and danger. And you should hate the fact that there is no immediate escape.

The struggles of midlife should make you angry. Not angry because you haven't gotten your way, or because you are no longer young, or because you are not independently righteous, but angry at what sin has done to God's originally good creation. The existence of evil, sorrow, and disease should remind us that we too are broken people. This deep-seated hatred of sin and its effects will drive each of us to seek and celebrate redemption. You don't go to your doctor when you think that things are okay. In the same way, if you are able to look at yourself and your world and not be viscerally moved by sin's effects, you will not daily seek the help of your Savior to deal with your sin and the dangers of life in a world gone bad.

4. *You are not alone.* One of the big mistakes we all tend to make when we suffer is to let ourselves think that we have been singled out. Part of the pain of suffering is that we feel like we have been wrongly targeted. In this way of thinking, we are always able to identify people around us who seem to deserve suffering more than we do (See Psalm 73). So we tend to think that God has gotten the wrong address. In fact, the opposite is true. Suffering is the shared experience of everyone who has ever lived. The kinds of things we suffer vary widely, but no one lives outside the boundaries of suffering.

There are two reasons why we never suffer alone. First, because we all live in the same world. It's like the sidewalk in front of your house. It is no longer smooth and level as it was meant to be. It is cracked and lopsided because of the tree roots growing under it. So you trip and fall as you are walking the dog. In the same way, life in this world is not a smooth walkway. In midlife you come to realize that sin left life cracked and lopsided, and you have scrapes and bruises to show for it. Everyone who has traveled over life's walkway does.

Second, and it is humbling to admit, we bring much of our suffering on ourselves. And even when we didn't cause our suffering, we tend to make it worse by the wrong things we think and do in the middle of it. Because we are sinners, we do things that bring it our way. Think of how much of the suffering in our world is not the result of natural environmental fallenness, but of wrong human decision and action. A community of sinners will be a community of sufferers. The two are inextricably woven together.

In your midlife suffering, you must remind yourself that you are not alone. You have more friends in suffering than you ever knew. More importantly, you have a Friend in suffering that you may be tempted to forget. He is the one friend who is not only with you, but can help you. Your Savior is your brother in suffering (See Hebrews 2:10–11). He knows exactly what you are going through. No, he never sinned himself, but because he lived for thirty-three years in a fallen world and died an unjust and cruel death, he experientially knows the full range of sin's effects. Because he suffered, he is able to come near and help you in your moment of suffering. When you suffer, you are in the best of company. In your suffering you are numbered with the Suffering Savior King, your brother and friend who is uniquely able to help (See Hebrews 4:14–16).

5. ***There is something better to come.*** The pain and disappointment of midlife should not only make you hunger for a better life but also for a better world. God is not done; there is more to come! In each moment of suffering there is a promise of a new and better world, a world where sin, sorrow, and suffering no longer have a place. God will not rest until each of his children has been rescued and the world has been totally restored. You may not get a better life today or tomorrow, but you can rest assured that a better world is coming. The things you have suffered will be like blips on the map compared to

the astounding glories that you will experience for eternity (See Romans 8:18ff).

Sufferers and the Suffering Story

When I read books by other authors, I find myself paying attention to the things they do to make their writing work. There is something I have discovered about good novelists. They never assume that you will remember the plot as you are reading the details of the story, so they find ways of summarizing it for you. Perhaps it is a conversation that looks back to the past, or a dream sequence, or a legal investigation. Each gives the author an opportunity to summarize the plot for you. The Bible, being the world's best story, is dotted with plot summaries. These summaries give us the helicopter view of our lives, a view that we must always keep in place if we are going to live our lives God's way. They usually come just before God gives us a practical set of directions. The commands that follow the summaries are not so much a script, as if God is telling us exactly what to do or say at 10:30 p.m. on Tuesday night, June 3. They are directions on how to live inside of the plot of God's story.

Here's how it works: the summary gives you the information you need to make biblical sense out of what is happening in your life and the directions that follow tell you how to respond to it.

I want to direct you to a story summary that is form-fitted to our topic. It is written to people who are suffering, and it is followed by a very practical set of directions that address the issues of midlife very well. The first Epistle of Peter is probably the Bible's clearest and most concentrated treatise on suffering, so it makes sense that it would start with a summary of God's story of redemption. When you are in the middle of the painful heat of difficulty, it is very hard to keep the big picture in view. It is very easy for your view of life to shrink to the size of the difficulty of the moment. When this happens you begin to live more for survival than with purpose. This often leads to decisions and actions that you later live to regret. So, after a brief greeting, Peter starts with the big picture.

Then-Then-Now

> *Praise be to the God and Father of our Lord Jesus Christ! In his great mercy he has given us new birth into a living hope through the resurrection of Jesus Christ from the dead, and into an inheritance that can never perish, spoil or fade—kept in heaven for you, who through faith are shielded by God's power until the coming of the salvation that is ready to be revealed in the last time. In this you greatly rejoice, though now for a little while you may have had to suffer grief in all kinds of trials. These have come so that your faith—of greater worth than gold, which perishes even though refined by fire—may be proved genuine and may result in praise, glory and honor when Jesus Christ is revealed. Though you have not seen him, you love him; and even though you do not see him now, you believe in him and are filled with an inexpressible and glorious joy, for you are receiving the goal of your faith, the salvation of your souls (1 Peter 1:3–9).*

You won't understand all that Peter has to say about suffering in the rest of his letter unless you understand this amazing story summary. It gives us the helicopter view that makes sense out of everything else Peter will say.

The structure of Peter's summary is quite typical of the summaries throughout the Bible. It is a "then-then-now" summary. Peter begins with the *then of the past*. Verse three summarizes everything God has done in redemptive history up to that point. Peter is saying, "Don't you see that from before the foundation of the earth God has been working on your new birth? From day one he has had a single focus: redemption." Think about what an amazing perspective this is on the Old Testament. When we, as the newborn children of God, read biblical history, we are not reading the dusty accounts of saints long gone. No, we are reading our own biography, because all of it was done with our new birth in mind. Peter wants us to look back through the lens of redemption. What does this mean? It means every situation, every judge and king, every moment of trial and victory, every battle, every prophet, every promise, and every provision was for us! Each was a critical piece of God's carefully planned and orchestrated redemptive plan. Each moment was a step toward the time when the Messiah would come and, by his life, death, and resurrection, purchase new birth for his children. We are redemptively connected to every moment of it. We are spiritually tied to each Old Testament saint. We are brothers and sisters in the same story, that great story of redemption. What a past!

Next Peter looks at the *then of the future*. In verses four and five Peter points us to something that is as equally amazing as what we have just considered. Peter is saying, "Don't you know that because of what Christ has done for you, your future is guaranteed?" He says that we have "an inheritance that can never perish, spoil, or fade." Think about what this means practically. You have a spiritual trust fund that no one can touch. All the things that are really worth living for, no one can take away from you. They are locked safely away in God's celestial vault. No one can take God's love from you. No one can steal his forgiveness. No one can take his Holy Spirit from within you. No one can rob you of his strength or wisdom. No one can take away your justification or adoption. No one can plunder your place at his side for eternity. No one can pilfer your deliverance from the presence and power of sin. The real riches of life that you and I could never earn, which are only obtained as a gift, are never at risk.

They can take your job. They can take your house. They can damage your health. They can reject, oppress, and abuse you. They can rob your possessions and empty your bank account. They can rob you of friends and family. But the most essential and wonderful things in all of life are unassailable. No one can touch them. They are guaranteed. When these are the things you prize, when these are the things that really give shape and direction to your life, you can live with courage and hope. How's that for a good investment?

But there is more! Notice what Peter says next, because it is simply astounding. He says that not only is our inheritance locked away and guaranteed, but we are daily "shielded by God's power" so that when it is time to receive our inheritance, we will be there to receive it. Let me illustrate what this means. Imagine you put your life savings in a local bank, and the bank officer gives you a contract guaranteeing that nothing will ever touch your investment. But imagine further with me that he also says, "To make sure that you are able to enjoy your investment when it fully matures, I have hired the world's best physician, the world's best chef, the world's best physical trainer, and the world's best security service to protect you." This is what Peter is saying. We have a future that is absolutely guaranteed and predictable, because we are being protected by God's power every day so that we will be there to enjoy what God has so faithfully stored away for us. What a future!

Consider how these two "*thens*" can alter the way you view the midlife struggles of the moment. We cannot allow present difficulty to loom so large in our eyes that it blocks out our vision of the past and the future. Even the most significant moment in your life is but one piece of your personal story. Your story stretches from before the foundations of the world were laid down all the way into the distant regions of eternity. No matter what you are going through now, it is vital to remember that God harnessed the forces of nature, controlled the events of human history, and sent and sacrificed his one and only Son in order to give you new birth. No matter how hard the difficulties of the present seem, you need to say to yourself, "This is not *it* for me, because I have a rich and eternal future that has been locked away and guaranteed. Whatever is at stake at this moment cannot rob me of the new life and eternal hope that God has given me, and those are the only things that are really worth living for."

And Now for Now

Although the "*then-then*" perspectives of Peter's summary are exciting, his primary focus is *now*. Peter is answering the question that we so often ask, "What in the world is going on?" A more biblical way to state the question is, "What in the world is God doing?" The way you answer these questions will have a profound effect on the way you deal with the blessings and trials that come your way in midlife.

In defining and explaining what in the world God is doing now, Peter says that "now for a little while you may have had to suffer grief in all kinds of trials." What a description of what is going on now! In this time between the "*then of the past*" and the "*then of the future,*" trials and grief are our unavoidable realities. You and I wish we were smart enough to avoid difficulty and all the grief that goes with it, but we cannot, and Peter tells us why. He says that these trials have come *so that* (purpose clause) your faith may be refined. It's here that we find a powerful metaphor which explains why this "now" period is a time of inescapable trial and grief.

Peter is using a powerful metaphor from the world of metallurgy. When the metallurgist mines the metal, it is in an ore state with a mixture of dross. That means there are inherent corruptions in the metal that rob it of its strength and beauty. In order to bring the metal to its purest state, the metallurgist applies white hot heat until the ore is liquefied and boiling. In this process, the corruptions are boiled out, and it becomes fundamentally stronger and more beautiful than it was before.

What are trials? They are God's boiling pot. When we come to Christ we are dross corrupted Christians. We are carrying around inherent corruptions inside of us that rob us of our strength and beauty. So God, in the grandeur and faithfulness of his redemptive love, boils us. The difficulties that come our way are not a sign of his unfaithfulness and inattention. No, they are an indication of his love. He knows that we are not yet what we were meant to be. He has dug us out of the mine, but we need to be refined.

Now why is this so hard for us to deal with? I am convinced it is because we tend to live with a *destination* mentality. We want life to be as easy, satisfying, and good as it can be, immediately in the here and now. But, this isn't a time of destination. Peter says our destination is guaranteed, but we will not have it now. Now is a time of *preparation*. It is a time of radical personal growth and change, so God applies white hot heat to prepare us for the destination to come.

Think about midlife struggles from this perspective. Why does this stage of life have to be marked by painful trial? Because that is exactly what God designed it to be in order to complete the amazing thing he has begun in us. Your struggle is not taking place because Christianity does not work, or because God's promises aren't trustworthy, or because God is unfaithful. Your struggle is actually a proof of his presence, his faithfulness, and his love. He is near you and he loves you too much to let you stay in your dross state. He is boiling you until you reach that highest state of strength and beauty, the likeness of Christ.

I am deeply convinced that we need to be preaching the theology of *uncomfortable grace* to one another. Peter says that the trials that grieve us are the trials of grace. God is patiently and perseveringly doing exactly what he promised. He is delivering us from sin and forming us into the image of his Son. I am persuaded that many times, as we are wondering where God's grace is and crying out for it, we are actually getting it. The problem is that we are seeking the *grace of release*, when God knows that we need the *grace of refinement*. During this "now" period of preparation, God's grace will come to us again and again in uncomfortable forms.

This is where we tend to have an agenda conflict with our Lord. We don't tend to be very excited about being Christ-like and holy. Instead, we get excited about being around people who love and affirm us. We get excited about children who grow up and do what is right. We get excited about making plans that actually come true. We get excited about physical health. We get excited about investments that have a good return. We get excited about having a safe, successful, stress-free, and predictable life. The problem with all of these things is not that they are wrong to desire. The problem is that we have settled for far too little. And we are surprised, shocked, and disappointed when God shakes them in order to refine us. You see, God has planned more and better things for us than we would want for ourselves. He is not content for us to be content with situational and relational ease. He will settle for nothing less than that we would become partakers of his divine nature (2 Peter 1:4).

How do you assess a good day? Do you tend to celebrate the smooth-running, unobstructed days and curse the days when difficulty has been in your path? How small a trial is able to make you angry? How quick are you to question God and his goodness? How apt are you to lash out at others who seem to have gotten in the way of your plan? How much do you envy the apparent ease of others? How much is your joy and contentment directly tied to comfort and ease? Are you in an agenda-collision with your Lord? Do you live with a destination-mentality, cursing the heat of preparation when it comes your way?

God's Story and Midlife Struggle

You cannot read 1 Peter 1, Romans 5, or James 1 without concluding that there is redemptive purpose to the pain of midlife struggle. Peter states it very clearly in verse 9, "you are receiving the goal of your faith, the salvation of your souls." In those times when you are tempted to see yourself as losing, you are really gaining. In those times when you are tempted to be captivated by what you have not received, you are receiving something of eternal worth. In those moments when it seems like life has passed you by and God has forgotten you, you are actually the object of his focused and productive redemptive love. In those moments when you feel like you've lost your will to fight, God is fighting for your soul. The painful regret, the disappointment of broken dreams, and the scary specter of old age are, in the hands of your Lord, the boiling pots of redemption. He is freeing your soul from bondage to your *own* righteousness, from slavery to your *own* dreams, and from false refuge in physical things that are progressively passing away.

Peter calls you to look beyond the regret and disappointment and embrace the glory of refinement. God loves you so much that it is impossible for him to be satisfied to keep you in your dross state. Yes, you will experience loss and disappointment. Yes, you will look back and be flooded with the pain of regret. Yes, you will long for the return of your youth. But each one of these experiences is meant by God to produce a harvest of good fruit in you. It is not only right to mourn what you have lost, but you also must celebrate the redemption to be found in the middle of it.

If This is What is Going on, How Should You Respond to It?

Sam is a man who felt that so much of his life had been a waste. He loved his wife, but she was pretty distant. He knew that he was a Christian, but Sam also was aware that there was not much life in his relationship with God. For the first time in his life, Sam felt lost. He had no idea where he was going and no idea how to get there.

But Sam had even more trouble. For the first time in his life he was in debt. His three-bay garage was a graveyard of man-toys. The sports car, the motorcycle, and the Jet Ski were a testament to failed attempts to escape his depression and reclaim his youth. And there was trouble on the family front. Sam couldn't let himself admit that he hadn't always been the perfect father, and as his children grew into adulthood and began pointing out his weaknesses and failures, he grew increasingly angry and defensive. As his children pulled away in hurt, Sam got all the more self-righteous and self-protective. Sam was in trouble at work as well. He had always been a model employee, but he had lost his drive. His work was so sporadic and sloppy that he was demoted. Sam thought it was the beginning of being "put out to pasture." In the face of all this, he began to question God. Why would he let this happen? Why would God let him work so long for things to fall apart in the end? Didn't God promise to bless his children? God no longer seemed very loving or kind.

Food and television became Sam's drugs of choice. Food is an instant pathway to pleasure, and Sam took this road with gusto. It wasn't long before his weight was not only impossible to hide but demanded larger clothes. Sam's evenings consisted of a huge supper and then a constant stream of snacks and soda in front of the television until he fell asleep and went up to bed. The food gave Sam comfort, and the television took him away from the reality he has having such a hard time dealing with.

Now deeply in debt, with his job at stake, his family hurt and divided, no life in his relationship with the Lord, and gaining weight every day, Sam was a man lost in the middle of his own life. Not only did Sam not know what to do, but everything he decided to do just made his situation worse.

There are many Sams among us. The details are different, but many men and women try to deal with what is going on inside of them and end up making things much worse. Perhaps you are one of those people. You not only need to understand what in the world God is doing in your life, but also how you are supposed to respond to it. Remember, our suffering is shaped not only by the difficulties that come our way, but also by how we respond to it as well. This is where what Peter writes next is so helpful for us.

Peter follows his *then-then-now* story summary with a set of directives. In doing so he essentially says, "If this is what God is doing, then what follows is the only appropriate way to respond to it." In other words, these directives tell you what it looks like to live inside the plot of God's story in the context of your everyday situations and relationships. Written to suffering people, these directives speak with power and practicality to the pain, difficulty, disappointment, and suffering of midlife:

> *Therefore, prepare your minds for action; be self-controlled; set your hope fully on the grace to be given you when Jesus Christ is revealed. As obedient children, do not conform to the evil desires you had when you lived in ignorance. But just as he who called you is holy, so be holy in all you do; for it is written: "Be holy, because I am holy."*
>
> *Since you call on a Father who judges each man's work impartially, live your lives as strangers here in reverent fear. For you know that it was not with perishable things such as silver or gold that you were redeemed from the empty way of life handed down to you from your forefathers, but with the precious blood of Christ, a lamb without blemish or defect. He was chosen before the creation of the world, but was revealed in these last times for your sake. Through him you believe in God, who raised him from the dead and glorified him, and so your faith and hope are in God.*
>
> *Now that you have purified yourselves by obeying the truth so that you have sincere love for your brothers, love one another deeply, from the heart. For you have been born again, not of perishable seed, but of imperishable, through the living and enduring word of God (1 Peter 1:13–23).*

And Now for a Practical Plan

Perhaps you're saying, "Okay, I get the story, but I don't know how to live inside the plot." In the verses that follow, Peter gives us an "if-this-is-what-is-going-on-then-this-is-what-to-do" plan.

Before we get to his specific directives, let's examine the nature of God's commands in these kinds of passages. The best way to do this is to use a musical illustration. Most of us would like God to give us sheet music, where every note on the page gives us precise counsel about how to live our lives in harmony.

When you are in a musical group, all you have to do is obey every note and you will be okay. In the same way, I think we often wish that God had given us a score, with all of the appropriate words and actions prewritten on the page. This is not, however, what God has given us in his Word. We have not been given sheet music. Rather than being like notes on the page, biblical directives are more like a key signature and a time signature. If you are going to make harmonious music with your Redeemer, you had better be in the right key and keeping the right time.

So you're not told what house and car to buy. You're not told exactly what words to say to your neighbor, boss, parent, child, husband, wife, or friend. You're not told exactly where to live, or exactly what to do with each of your dollars. You are not told how to invest each Tuesday evening or Saturday morning. You're not told exactly what church to attend or what job to seek. You're not told exactly whom to marry or whom to seek as a friend. The Bible does not give you sheet music, but it gives everything that you need to live in harmony with the God who has written the melody.

Perhaps we wish for the sheet music or the script because we really don't want to live in the personal communion of faith with the Messiah. We don't want to have to rely on his wisdom, his provision, his grace, and his strength. We don't want questions, dilemmas, obstacles, and mysteries in our lives. We want our lives to be comfortable and predictable. But what God wants is *us*. He wants us in a living devotion and dependence on him. God is not working on constructing the best life for us; he is working on reconstructing us, so he speaks to us in ways that call us to rely humbly on his active presence and his gracious love.

God's directives speak to every issue of the human experience. I have just studied the Ten Commandments, and I was again astounded, not only at their wisdom, but also at their expansiveness. They really do reach into all of life but in a way that keeps us always reliant on the Lord who gave them to us.

The seven directives that Peter lays out for us are the key signature and the time signature for a harmonious life with God. Here is how you can make harmonious music with the God who is troubling your life by his grace. I've summarized these directives in my own words.

1. ***Be careful what you think (v. 13).*** Much of the trouble we get ourselves into during the midlife years is rooted in poor and unbiblical thinking. We are all interpreters, each day working to make sense out of our lives, and what we do is based on the those interpretations. Because our thoughts precede and determine our actions, the poor choices we make and the poor actions we take are always rooted in poor thinking. The Bible exegetes and interprets life for us. When we hold ourselves to the highest standards of biblical thinking, we place ourselves in the best position to respond to life in the right way. Where have you allowed yourself to think in ways that simply do not accord with what God says is true?

2. ***Be self-controlled (v. 13).*** During times of midlife discouragement and disappointment, you will be hit with powerful emotions and powerful desires. People often make the mistake of going where their emotions and desires are leading them and end up doing things that, for whatever temporary comfort they bring, only produce a harvest of bitter fruit. In our union with Christ, the power of sin over us has been broken, and the Holy Spirit who dwells in us battles with our sinful nature on our behalf. With these great gifts, we can stand in the middle of raging emotion and desire and turn in another direction. Where are you failing to exercise the self-control that is your ability as a child of God?

3. ***Watch where you put your hope (v. 13).*** You are always living in pursuit of some kind of hope. There is always some dream that motivates you and organizes your actions. Midlife is often a time of dashed hopes. It makes sense. As sinners, we tend to place our hopes more in the creation than in the Creator. And because we have placed our hope in things that we cannot control and that are passing away, our hopes disap-

point us again and again. What hope has captured you? Financial ease? Ongoing health? Loving family? Career success? The affirmation and respect of those around you? The list could go on, but the point is that midlife is a wonderful time for hope reassessment. It is a time when we can learn as we never have before to put our hope in the one place where it will never disappoint us: in the Lord.

4. ***Don't give way to wrong desires (v. 14).*** Midlife is rife with temptation. There is the temptation to selfishness. You have lived your life to serve, protect, and provide for other people, and you just want to do a few things for yourself. There is sexual temptation. The person you married simply isn't so young and attractive anymore. Your sexual relationship isn't so exciting. Your relationship with your spouse can be pretty casual and mundane. Suddenly, your eyes see things you hadn't noticed before. There are desires that you have not had in this way before. Or there is the temptation to materialism. You think you can fight inner unrest with outer pleasures. You may have a little more money now, and there are many things that you are tempted to feel that you just have to have. And there is the temptation to doubt God. You look back wondering if following him so faithfully has really been worth it. Midlife is a time when it is vital to fight the war of desire, because what you give your heart to, before long you will give your body to as well. Where is the war of desire raging in your life right now? How well are you fighting?

5. ***Be committed to do what is right, no matter what (v. 15).*** The standard here is the Lord. As a child I went to a German Lutheran school, and in catechism class we were taught this question: "How does God demonstrate his holiness?" Now, perhaps it would seem logical to answer, "By the cross of Jesus Christ," or "By his holy law." But the answer we were taught was more profound than either of these. We were taught to respond, "In everything he does." Think about it. There is nothing that God has ever thought, desired, spoken, or done that is not essentially and absolutely holy! That standard is our

standard for daily living. When you are taking an accounting of your life, and it doesn't seem like it's been worth it, and you are defeated and discouraged, it is very tempting to let down your guard. It is very tempting to quit doing the good and right things that God has called you to do every day. Often the very moment we are being tempted to let down our moral and spiritual guard is the very moment when we need it more than ever before. Where have you let down your guard and let wrong subtly creep back into your life?

6. ***Live here as a stranger (v. 17).*** Perhaps you're thinking, "I understand how all the other directives fit, but this one doesn't make sense." Let me explain. If what we're living in is not a time of destination but of preparation, then we should live here as if we are pilgrims. Scripture says we are supposed to be tent dwellers, to approach our lives like camping. I am convinced that the long-term good of camping is that it causes us to long for and appreciate home. The first few days at the campsite, you love your tent dwelling and the way food cooked over a fire tastes so different. (That's the ash in the food!) By the fifth or sixth day, you're tired of sleeping on the uncomfortable ground, you're tired of eating food with grit in it, and you begin to long for home. You think about your wonderful refrigerator and stove. You fall in love with your mattress all over again. You have a deeper appreciation for your warm shower than you have had in a long time. Camping is doing in your heart exactly what it was meant to do.

Now, it totally misses the point to "camp" in a sixty foot Winnebago, with the kitchen of Emeril Lagasse, a forty-two inch plasma television, and a satellite dish! Your camping site is better than home. So, Peter says, don't spend all of your time and effort seeking to make life as comfortable as it could possibly be. Remember, all of those physical things could never have purchased for you the spiritual life that your life is really about. Live like a stranger. Realize that you are not home and treat this like the journey that it is. Live with one eye on eternity and do all you can to participate in the preparation that

God is putting you through. Midlife can be such a time of disappointment over physical comfort never gained or physical comfort lost. It can be a time where we are tempted to purchase for ourselves all the luxuries we were never able to afford, but now don't actually need. Right now, where are you tending to live more for present comfort than as a pilgrim preparing for home?

7. ***Be devoted to living a life of love (v. 22).*** Life in this fallen world is hard for everyone. It beats away at our perseverance and hope and attacks the borders of our faith. Scripture is very clear that we were never meant to go it alone. Life is a community project. Midlife, a time when people are often less encumbered than they once were and therefore more able to love and serve others, often becomes a time marked by self-focus and self-love. We feel like we've done our time. We've given ourselves to others and we've worked hard and we simply want a little time for ourselves. Yet there are people all around us who could benefit from our experience, who would be helped by our investment of time and who could use the resources that we are blessed with. Who near you is struggling with life in this fallen world? Who is God calling you to love in word and in action? Is your life shaped by a devoted love of others or by devotion to yourself?

God's story of suffering and redemption really does make sense out of the struggles and opportunities of the midlife years. The question is, "Are you living in the middle of your trouble and disappointment in a way that fits well within the plot of God's story?" In the middle of what seem like very bad things, God is doing very good things. Are you making harmonious music with him? Midlife is one of God's most effective boiling pots. God's grace is not only making you uncomfortable, it is refining you. Don't doubt your Father's goodness. Don't question his love. Don't allow yourself to run away from him. Run to him in faith and love and be thankful that he loves you so much that he refuses to walk away until what he started in you is absolutely complete.

Chapter 8

May I Speak to the Manager, Please?

Because something is happening here
But you don't know what it is
Do you, Mister Jones? —Bob Dylan

Where the battle rages, there the loyalty of the soldier is proved, and to be steady on all the battlefield besides, is mere flight and disgrace if he flinches at that point.
—Martin Luther

It was supposed to be a simple family meal at a huge Mexican restaurant where there would surely be plenty of room for our family of six. When we arrived, already tasting the food in our minds, we opened the door of the restaurant to find the lobby packed with people and impossible to negotiate. I told my family to wait outside while I pressed my way through the crowd to see what the scoop was. The crowd in the lobby wasn't very happy, (probably our first clue as to what was to come), but I didn't pick up on it. I finally bumped, squeezed, and excused my way to the reception desk. The girl behind it moaned, "How many?" without looking up. I said, "Six," and she said, "An hour and a half." I couldn't believe it. We were hungry. I knew I couldn't give her my name without consulting with my ravenous family, so I pressed my way through the impatient masses one more time. After a longer-than-necessary family summit, we decided to hang around in hope of a table before the night was over. There was a mall just a parking lot away, and we could go there and kill time.

After an hour and a half of walking through stores, we resisted killing our appetite in the mall food court and traipsed back to the restaurant for our meal.

When we opened the door, we were amazed that the crowd in the lobby didn't seem any smaller. In fact, I think the population had increased! I made it to the desk, gave them my name, and learned that there were several parties in front of us, but that they were seating people quickly. About twenty minutes later our name was called. We had never been so excited to sit down and eat! As we scanned our menus, Hector, our waiter, introduced himself and took our drink order. We salivated our way through our menus, but before long we had made our choices and were all anxious to order. Hector seemed to have fallen off the face of the earth. Not only did he not bring our drinks or take our order, but we could not see him at any other table. The food court was looking better all the time.

I finally got the attention of another waiter who not only looked frazzled but also irritated that I had taken him away from his tables. I explained that somehow we had lost our waiter, and he said that he would see what he could do. About ten minutes later Hector reappeared, carrying our drinks, and mumbling some kind of apology. Not wanting him to leave before we ordered, we told him we were ready and he took our order. We were hoping to ease our hunger with the traditional tortilla chips and salsa, but they never came. In fact, Hector *never* came back! The next person who approached our table was the manager, because we had requested to talk to him. Hector had been gone, without our food, for forty-five minutes. We told our story to a completely frazzled and appropriately apologetic manager. He assured us that our meals would be on our table promptly, and food did arrive quickly. It just didn't happen to be ours.

The manager retook our order, and in less than ten minutes, we were eating. We weren't charged for our meal that night, and the manager begged us to have dessert on the house. We declined, but only because we were afraid that we would be late for work the next day!

Have you ever been in the middle of a situation and wondered who in the world is in charge? Maybe your life seems all too much like our night at the restaurant. Maybe you're tired of having to wait, only to be disappointed in the end. Maybe you're tired of feeling like you're just another name in the line, another hungry face in the crowd. Maybe you look around and see people eating their fill and you wonder why you're still standing around, hoping and hungry. Maybe you've "gone to the mall" and tried to distract yourself, but it only works in the short run. At the end of the day, you are still discouraged and hungry. Maybe you've gotten close enough to your dream to read the menu and smell the cuisine, but you never seem to get the meal, and you're angry because it feels like you've been toyed with. Maybe you gave up hope and went to the "food court," sad that you had to settle for second best. Or maybe you've been waiting all of your life for your name to be called. You've watched the crowd in the lobby dwindle down till you were standing there all alone, and at this point in life, you're pretty convinced it will never be.

Have you ever wanted to stop in the middle of your life and say, "May I talk to the manager, please?" Do things always turn out for you the way you planned, or do you feel like your life is more out of than under control? Midlife is one time of life when the delusion that your life will unfold as you planned quickly evaporates. It is this sense of a loss of control that is one of midlife's most powerful and difficult experiences. Not only has your life not worked as you planned, but you are also dealing with inescapable and potentially life-altering things that you seem to have no control over. This chapter is written to address those moments.

Looking for Who's in Charge

Think about how little of your life you actually control. You did not choose where you would be born, yet the location of your birth shaped the entire story of your life. This impresses me every time I travel abroad. What would my life have been like if I had been born on the violent streets of Belfast, or in the filth of a ghetto in New Delhi, or in a tiny flat in Moscow, or in an apartment in Seoul? You did not choose the family you were born into, but how could any decision be more important than that? You did not choose what period of history you would be born into, yet it has shaped everything you have experienced. Imagine what your life would have been like if you had been born into a peasant family in medieval Europe, or into the family of an ancient Chinese craftsman. Imagine being born on a wagon train heading for a tract of land in the pioneer Northwest, or if you were a slave in Pharaoh's Egypt.

You did not choose the world events that would take place around you, but they have shaped your life nonetheless. Almost every time I go to board a plane, I think about how a group of Middle Eastern men plotted for months to hijack planes and fly them into buildings. I did not know these men and I was not the target of their attack, yet my sense of the world, my personal security, and my habits of travel have been shaped by what they did.

You do not control the progress of science and knowledge, but your life has been shaped by a myriad of discoveries that you had nothing to do with. You will live longer because of penicillin, aspirin, sterilization, the thermometer, the x-ray, and the MRI. You will live safely and in liberty because of the rise of democracy, free elections, and democratic government. You can accomplish more because of electricity, the internal combustion engine, telecommunication technology, the microprocessor, and modern plumbing.

We all need to be humbled by the vast number of things that have impacted our lives over which we exercised no decision and exerted no control. My life is a perfect example. I did not plan to be born in Toledo, Ohio to a man and a woman who had recently come to Christ. I did not plan to have Scriptures read to me every day or to go to church faithfully, Sunday after Sunday. I did not plan how many brothers I would have, or that I would have only one sister. I did not plan where I would be in the order of my siblings. I did not plan what my personal gifts would be. I did not plan what the culture of my home would be like or the blessings and struggles that I would encounter there.

I did not plan what high school I would attend and the massive socio-cultural changes that would take place during those years. I never wanted to attend a Christian college, but my parents required it of me. I did not plan to stay there and graduate. I did not plan to stand in a lunch line in the beginning of my freshman year behind the woman who would later become my wife. I did not plan to be married before I graduated from college or feel called to the ministry during my time there. I did not plan to have the Vietnam War drive me to seminary.

I did not plan to end up in Scranton, Pennsylvania after seminary. I did not plan to be a young pastor with four children in a place where the American dream had faded away decades before. I did not plan to have people with broken lives come to me seeking counsel and wisdom. I did not plan to go, out of a sense of ministry need, back to seminary to study biblical counseling. I did not plan to move to Philadelphia after my counseling studies to start a new phase of ministry that continues to this day.

It is an amazing and humbling thing to admit, but almost none of it was my plan. There was no way that I could have anticipated all the necessary events, locations, people, conversations, problems, and world events that all had to come together for the plan to work. When you stop to consider all the things that had to come together for any one piece of your story to unfold the way it did, it almost melts your brain.

I am now in my fifties. I live in Philadelphia, a city I love and call my own, which was never on my map of potential destinations. I am married to Luella. She is a lovely lady, full of life, bursting with gifts, and in love with the Lord. Had I shopped and planned for decades, I would not have been smart enough to say, "There is this missionary kid from Cuba who lives in South Carolina and I need to find her because she is my ultimate life partner." Yet, in the last thirty-six years, no one has been a dearer friend or had a more profound effect on my life than she. I am part of a ministry that I love, that I feel privileged to be a part of each day, and that makes good use of my gifts. But, had I been shopping for places to invest my prime ministry years, I doubt that I would have ever found this wonderful place to do God's kingdom work. After almost three decades of parenting, we look at the lives of our four children, each unique, and are amazed how their lives have unfolded. As much as we tried to guide them, we could never have planned their lives for them.

One of the most dangerous delusions for each of us is the delusion of our own sovereignty. And one of our most dangerous idols is the idol of control. If we spend our days trying to establish our sovereignty and our control, then we have not yet learned to rest in the Lord's control. In this way midlife is incredibly important spiritually because it tends to explode the myths of personal sovereignty and control. The malaise of discouragement that follows is not an introduction to a world that is out of control, but a God-sent reordering of control that can put you in a better place spiritually than you have ever been. At the precise moment when you face the fact that you are not in charge and never have been, you are finally ready to know and experience what it means to rest in the control of another. Yes, Someone is in charge. Every detail of every minute of your life has been ordered by him. The problem is that in midlife our plans and his plans tend to collide. In the carnage of that midlife intersection, many people lose their way.

God and Surprises

When you read biblical history you can't help concluding that following God brings a life of surprises. Whatever plans God's people made, and however they tried to figure out God's plans, they were inevitably greeted with surprises. There were turns in the story that no one could have anticipated. God's plan consistently included things that would have been left out of the story if his people had been doing the planning. One of the reasons for this is that we human beings tend to focus on outcomes. We want things to go well and turn out all right. Although God surely does care about the end of all things, he is at work in the process as well.

God often requires us to wait. (Remember Abraham and Sarah?) We think of waiting as a waste of time because our focus is on the thing we are waiting for. We think the good stuff only begins when we have finally received it. But God is not only present at the final delivery; he is present in the process as well. The Bible teaches that when God ordains us to go through the trial of waiting, he changes us as we wait. The biblical perspective on waiting is not only about being patient until we receive, but also about what we are becoming as we wait. For example, Romans 4:20 tells us that while Abraham waited for the promised heir, he "was strengthened in his faith and gave glory to God." The father of the faithful was changed by waiting.

The Bible is also very clear about God using trials to mature us. God-ordained trials are not in the way of life but are one of God's primary means for producing and maturing spiritual life in us. Our problem is that when we are experiencing difficulty, we only focus on when it will end, rather than examining the good things that God is doing in us in the middle of it. But God is at work in the process. He surprises us again and again with turns that we could never have anticipated and would never have chosen for ourselves.

We get surprised for another reason. We tend to live with what is good for *us* as our deepest concern. We want our friendships to be happy, our investments to have a good return, our health to be constantly good, our families to be united, and our futures to be secure. Now there is nothing wrong with wanting these things, but if that is all you want, your world is narrower than it was ever meant to be. You see, God isn't entering into your miniscule little kingdom to do everything he can to make it successful. Instead, he has welcomed you out of your personal kingdom allegiance into the history-spanning expansiveness of *his* kingdom, to be part of what he planned not only before your first breath, but also literally before the foundations of the world were laid in place. You were never created to live with your goals and needs as your deepest concerns. You and I were created to know, serve, love, and worship him. This means desiring that his kingdom flourish and his glory to be displayed. Practically, this means being motivated more by the glory of God than by what you think would make you comfortable and happy.

So God will do things that rob you and me of our comfort, that interrupt our plans, and that even bring pain and suffering our way. And he will do this to complete what he has begun in us and in the world. God will take away what has brought us temporary joy in order to drive us toward the greater delights of his kingdom and his righteousness. And as much as we know this to be true, we will continue to be surprised by the turns he ordains our lives to take.

When you read the covenant promises in Genesis, you would not anticipate that a 400-year captivity as slaves in Egypt would be part of God's plan for his people, but it was. When you read the promise of a land reserved for the people of God, you would never think that it would be filled with warring pirate nations who would fight with all their might to drive God's people out. You would never anticipate that Jerusalem would someday be destroyed and that God's people would be taken into exile. With all of your Old Testament knowledge, you too would have been shocked to discover that the Messiah would come from a working-class family in Nazareth, grow up to be a controversial itinerant preacher, and die on a cross like a criminal. You would never have predicted that Jesus' ragtag band of followers would, under the fiercest persecution, spread the good news of saving grace around the world. The history of Scripture is chock full of mystery and surprise because God is in control and people are not.

What does this have to do with midlife? Consider for a moment why midlife is a time of struggle at all. Is it not because what we have planned has not come to be? Beneath the struggles of aging, regret, and disappointment are haunting questions of God's sovereign wisdom, goodness, and love. In those moments when your mind wanders into fantasy and you create worlds of your own making that do your bidding, you are actually expressing a deep dissatisfaction with God's rule and wishing you could have your hand on the cosmic joystick.

As pseudo-sovereigns, we hate waiting, disappointment, obstacles, and failure. We struggle to accept the fact that these things exist in a world that is under the wisest and most benevolent rule possible. C. S. Lewis comments that a hardy belief in the truths of Christianity actually makes your experience of pain more painful. It is bad enough to have to endure pain, but as a believer you must say that it was not an accident and that it was sent by a God who declares himself to be good! To us, God's order looks like disorder, and his wisdom looks like foolishness. God's lovingkindness often seems to be anything but loving, and definitely not kind. All of this has to do with one humbling thing that we all have to admit: as sinners, we want our own way. It is hard to rest in the rulership of the King when our hearts and minds are so preoccupied with the success of our own little kingdoms.

Midlife surprises us with the reality of who is king and how different his will and way are from ours. We have lived for decades in the world of our needs, our wants, and our dreams. For decades we have nurtured the illusion that if God really does love us, he will give these good things to us. We have convinced ourselves that if we obey, God will keep his part of the bargain and send good things our way. We thought that if we parented well, then all of our children would turn out the way we hoped. We thought that if we worked faithfully then we would harvest the seeds of our investments in our later years. We thought that if we kept our bodies under subjection then the Lord would bless us with good health. We thought that if we followed the Lord in personal devotion and public worship and ministry, then our lives would be spiritually rich.

Remember, God's people have always struggled with the shock of his rule. The kingdom of darkness is being destroyed by the kingdom of light, and none of us can escape being affected by the carnage. Deep beneath every midlife struggle is a collision of kingdoms.

Require yourself to be brutally honest in this moment. What is it that you really want out of life? What is the true dream for which you have been working? What were the joys that captivated your eyes and controlled your heart? What is your, "If I only had _____, then I would be happy?" How much have your dreams been personal, earthbound, physical, and here-and-now? Have you been motivated by *your* kingdom more than *God's* Kingdom? How is your present discouragement, disappointment, and grief a window on what has actually captured your heart? Have you really wanted God to be your wise and loving Father who brings into your life what he considers best, or have you wanted him to be a divine waiter, the all-powerful deliverer of your dreams?

Consider Todd. Todd was the ultimate planner, a little sovereign over his own world. He wasn't aggressively controlling or insensitive to the needs of others. It was just that he had a plan, a very clear, prioritized, personal life plan. He even had his life organized in decades. He reasoned that the first two decades would be for education, the second two for career and family development, the third two for enjoying the returns on his investment, and the fourth decades for rest and retreat. Ask him about marriage, and he had a plan. Ask him about parenting, and he had a plan. Ask him about vacations, diet, leisure, investments, or any other practical life topic, and Todd had a plan.

On the surface Todd was a committed Christian with a strong faith in the Lord. He was an outspoken and courageous evangelist. He gave his time and money to support all kinds of Christian causes. He knew his way around the Bible and had his theological ducks in order, but there were indications that there were problems underneath. Todd had real trouble when the people around him messed up, and his impatience degenerated into anger quite quickly. He was a severe disciplinarian at home, and it seemed as if his children feared him more than they respected him. As for his wife, whom he said was his best friend, he seemed more concerned about her maintaining the orderliness of their home and schedule than he did about building a relationship of appreciation, intimacy, and love. He was definitely a successful businessman and was admired for his accomplishments, but he was not loved for his character.

If Todd were a casual acquaintance in your church, you would really look up to him. It seemed like success stuck to him like glue. His personal life, family, and career all looked to be in order. The problem was that Todd was dedicated to *his* plan. Without ever knowing it, Todd was heading for a collision that would forever alter his world.

It was very late on a Saturday night, and Todd was arriving home from one of his high-powered business weekends. As he drove up the long driveway to their six-car garage, it seemed odd that the house was dark. He let himself in, fumbled for the lights, and called to his wife, but there was no answer. He tried the intercom, but there was no response. It was then that he saw the envelope with his name on it, sitting on the kitchen counter. It was from Helen. In it she told Todd of years of dissatisfaction with his selfishness, demands, criticism, and anger. She told him that he had made the whole family slaves to his agenda. She said that he needed to get some help, and she would come back when he had.

Todd was filled with a combination of fear and fury. It was like being in the middle of a nightmare, but he knew he was awake. *All I tried to do was make a nice life for my family*, he told himself. *All I did was work hard and teach my kids to do the same.* "Helen had nothing before she met me," he mumbled to himself as he collapsed into the leather chair in the corner of the breakfast room. He wasn't about to go crawling for forgiveness when he hadn't done anything wrong. He hadn't had any affairs. He hadn't forsaken his faith. He had trained his children well and saw to it that each of them got a good start. He had given away much of what he had made. *Where would they all be without me?* he thought, as he trudged up to the bedroom he had shared with Helen for over a quarter of a century.

Todd woke up angry the next morning. Not angry at Helen but angry at God. *This is not what I signed on for*, he thought. *I'm one of the good guys! What did I do to deserve this?* Todd's plan had never included this. Over the next few weeks, his anger and bitterness spilled over into work. Soon the CEO of his company was suggesting that he take a leave of absence. That first day off was torture for Todd. He didn't know what to do with himself. By the end of the day he had contacted his pastor who in turn contacted me.

Todd was a hard man to counsel, but I'll never forget the day he said to me, "Paul, I know what you're trying to say to me. You're telling me that I have been so busy trying to be God, that I have little time to actually serve God." Todd was shocked and surprised by his midlife harvest because he had been in a war for a very long time. It was a war that he could never win—a war with God over sovereignty.

It's All About Control

This is one of those places where the Bible is so wonderfully helpful. The biblical story is dyed throughout with the theme of sovereignty, and its central character is the Lord Almighty. He is good, powerful, wise, loving, and sovereign; the designer, creator, and controller of all that is. He created a world of awesome and multifaceted beauty and placed man and woman in it. They enjoyed intimate fellowship with God and had their every need supplied. But sadly, they fell for an offer to be free of their submission to God, believing the serpent's promise that they could be like their Creator. It was a horrible moment! They left the best place in the universe, where they could rest in God's sure rule, in order to vie for the most dangerous thing a human being could ever do: to trust his life in his own hands.

This moment was the beginning of the struggle that is chronicled in every period of biblical history. It gets down to one of two lifestyles, and everyone who has ever lived falls into one or the other. We are either resting in the glory of the sovereign rule of the Lord, or we are trying in some way to establish our own rule. This battle can show itself in an obvious and arrogant lifestyle of power and control, or it can live as a subterranean independence that colors every action, reaction, hope, or dream. Adam and Eve were called to trust and obey, but they wanted their own way. The Children of Israel were called to trust and fight, but they went their own way. New Testament Palestine was called to see, listen, and believe, but they sent the Messiah away. The struggle to trust in the Lord, rest in his rule, and faithfully do his will, is what sin is all about. You see, every act of disobedience, whether subtle and secret or public and arrogant, is a direct challenge to the sovereign rule of God. Every time I step outside of the boundaries of *trust* and *obey*, I call into question God's power, wisdom, and rule.

To be a sinner is to want to rule your world. That's why Paul says in 2 Corinthians 5:15 that Jesus "died for all, that those who live should no longer live for themselves but for him who died for them and was raised again." Now if sovereignty really is at the center of our struggle with sin, and if it is true that the most powerful and pervasive of all idols is the idol of self, then it should not shock us that this battle rages at midlife. Midlife is a time when you assess outcomes and survey what future is left for you, so there is a strong temptation to question God's exercise of his rule. In the middle of your life, it is very tempting to conclude that the plan that you had for your life was qualitatively better than God's plan for you.

Yet it is so very hard to look at the disappointing impact of sin on your family, or the decay of long-held dreams, or physical aging, or a thousand other personal harvests, and to rest in the One who has carefully administrated every detail of it. In the middle of a huge sense of loss, inescapable grief, or crushing disappointment, it is so hard to look toward the heavens and say, "You, my Lord, are loving, kind, and good. You are grand in your wisdom and glorious in your grace. You have authority that cannot be challenged and power beyond my imagination. What comes into my life is there because of your wise counsel and your perfect will. All of your ways are right and true. So I rest in your rule. I take refuge in your power. I hide in your wisdom and make your grace my place of retreat." It is hard, but this very death of our claim on our own lives is what turns a midlife moment into a gracious reordering of control, which will in turn deepen our rest, worship, and love for our Lord.

This is a spiritual war. Think with me for a moment about the characteristics of a person's midlife struggle that we examined in chapter two. The dissatisfaction, disorientation, discouragement, dread, disappointment, disinterest, distance, and distraction are all reactions that flow out of our deep struggle with accepting what God has allowed to come into our lives. Perhaps there is no war more important than this one. God is in charge, and we are not. God is intent on seeing his kingdom succeed, not endorsing ours. The people around us are not under our rule, so they will not always do what we wish that they would do. We live in a world that does not belong to us, with people who belong to Another. In fact, we don't even own our own lives. "You are not your own; you were bought at a price" (1 Cor 6:19–20). It is in resting in his rule and committing to his glory that we find the greatest of joys and the highest of personal pleasures. These are the things we were made for.

Characteristics of the Struggle

If the deeper disappointment of midlife is really a disappointment with God, then it is helpful to identify the characteristics of our midlife struggle with God's rule. The following list includes the kinds of things that will characterize a person's life who is struggling with God's sovereignty. No one is likely to have all of these traits in his life, but if there is a cluster of them in you, then it is probably an indication that beneath your struggle with midlife is a more profound and more spiritually debilitating struggle with God.

1. *Cynicism about life.* Believing that God is in complete control of life is the most positive view of life that anyone could have. I will never understand why God ordains many of the things he does, and I know that this belief will not remove mysteries from my life, but I wake up each day to the amazing reality that my life and my world are under the wise control of my Heavenly Father. When a believer has a hopeless, what-difference-does-it-make, I've-tried-that-and-it-didn't-work view of life, he is struggling with the One who holds all circumstances in his hands.

2. *Withholding our worship and service.* In human relationships, when you approve of and appreciate another you are willing to praise them and to demonstrate your thankfulness with acts of service. Disappointment with God is often revealed by a person's lack of enthusiasm for worship and lack of zeal for ministry. A bitter middle-aged man once said to me, "I can barely stand going to church and hearing those hymns. Every time I hear people sing about God's faithfulness, I get

angry and wonder, 'Where was his faithfulness in my life?'" It is very hard to run to the One you think has failed you, joyfully praise the very Person you are questioning, and give yourself in acts of sacrificial service to One you think has done you wrong. Many people in midlife who are struggling with God's plan for their lives have lost their heart for God. They don't completely forsake the faith, but there is a going-through-the-motions lifelessness that characterizes their participation in the community of faith.

There was a time when Serena was present whenever the doors of the church were open. She just couldn't seem to get enough of worship and good preaching. Serena loved her Sunday school class, her women's Bible study, and her home group. She loved to hear and sing the great hymns of the faith. Serena also found great joy in ministry. She was a three time short-term missions veteran and by far the most faithful participant in the ministry to the local women's detention center. But all that seemed long ago. Serena had always thought her gifts would be recognized, and she finally got her chance at full-time ministry. The rejection she got from the mission board stuck in her heart like a lump in her throat. She could barely get herself to church, and she soon found other things to do with the summers she had once dedicated to short-term missions. Now fifty, Serena was still at church almost every Sunday, but she was more of an attendee than a worshiper. It was all a matter of duty now, rather than a matter of the heart.

3. *Anger with the people around you.* The anger I often express toward people and things in my life is often misplaced anger at God. Think about it. When I get angry at my car because it won't start and I say, "Stupid car!" I'm not actually thinking that my car has intentionally plotted against me in order to make my life more difficult. No, the angry words I say to my car are really directed at God for allowing such obstacles in my life. Or when I am angry with someone in my family because they have made me late, I am not simply angry with them. I am angry because my life isn't working according to my plan, and therefore I am angry at the One who controls the plan. In my work with angry people, I have learned that anger with others and with circumstances is often the sign of a much deeper system of anger that sucks the life out of their faith and causes them to run from the only place to ever find help—the Lord.

Jack was known as a "tough" guy, but really he was an angry man. At 48, the man who was once the life of the party was now the fellow who wouldn't hesitate to give you a piece of his mind if you crossed him. His wife Sue was almost afraid to go out with him in public, because Jack would often be dissatisfied with something and make a scene. Jack's kids had been stung by his wrath more than once and had learned to keep their distance. Jack's mantra was, "I've been taken once, and it won't happen to me again." Yes, Jack had his share of disappointment in this fallen world, but not any more than the next person. If you were around Jack for very long, his anger would be targeted at you.

4. ***Craving for power and control.*** Often when I think my life is out of control, I will put a firmer grip on the steering wheel of my life than ever before. My struggle with God's sovereignty results in a quest for my own sovereignty. It's like watching someone paint a wall, and because you don't like how they're doing it, you finally yank the brush out of their hand and say, "Forget it; I'll do it myself!"

5. ***Theological doubts.*** Theological questions in midlife are often more the product of disappointment than they are questions about what the Bible actually teaches. When people are having a hard time reconciling their experience with what Scripture teaches, they are tempted to ease the stress of apparent contradiction by backing away from things they have believed for years. During the powerful struggles of midlife, one of the most significant things you need to decide is whether you are going to let the theology of Scripture exegete and interpret your life, or let life reinterpret your theology. If you allow yourself to doubt a doctrine as central as the sovereignty of God, what

will keep you from doing the same with a host of other doctrines that, in your limited view, do not always seem to be operating in your life?

Mary sat in my office in tears, "Paul, I've never said this to anyone else before, but I'm not sure I believe those things anymore. I mean, look at my life. Years ago, I went into all of this with such faith, hope, and courage. Because of God, I wasn't afraid of anything. But look what happened. Where was God during all of this? I'm here because I know I am in a bad place, and I know that I need help, but, to be honest, the naive faith I once had in the Bible just isn't there anymore, and I don't know how to get it back."

6. ***Impatience with the circumstances.*** This is the person with a short fuse. You know, the person who is quickly irritated, reacting in anger to even the smallest things. Their coffee is too hot, their meal is too cold, the soda machine doesn't have their desired drink, traffic is moving too slowly. Here is a principle that will help you understand what is happening: whenever the size of a person's emotion is bigger than the size of the circumstance, it is an indication that the emotion is coming from somewhere else. People who are easily angered by little things have walked into those little things already irritated with life, and that is why it does not take much for them to explode. Remember, anger with life is always anger with the One who rules it.

7. ***Letting go of godly habits.*** Often when we are discouraged, we quit pursuing the disciplines of godliness that were once our regular habits. Underneath this neglect is a deep disappointment with God. It is a "If this is what happens anyway, then what difference does it make?" way of living. So you quit having personal time with the Lord or attending your small group. You quit pursuing godly friends or giving regularly to your church. You forsake good reading and little acts of self-control. Nothing you do seems to matter. Think about how this reveals what really motivated you for all those years. You had reason to do good things because you were excited about

how your life plan was unfolding. You were excited with the Lord and motivated to do his will because he was giving you your dream, but when the dream went south you had no reason to continue.

Randy and Elaine had once been the picture of Christian discipline. They had firm habits of personal and family worship. They were leaders of their small group and lived with an open home. They nourished their Christian friendships and seemed to thrive on the fellowship. Randy had a group of guys he would regularly pray with and Elaine was constantly reading a new Christian book. For many years their life together was organized by the habits of the faith, but not anymore. As the kids began to grow up and struggle, they progressively began to let go of their good habits. No one thought much about their giving up the small group since they had been doing it for years and probably needed a break. Randy told his prayer group that his job had altered his schedule, and it wasn't possible for him to meet with them anymore. To ease their consciences Randy and Elaine attached a plausible explanation to each habit they forsook. Underneath, they were struggling with God's plan for their lives. When they came to talk with me, they didn't really understand how what was happening in their hearts was shaping the choices they were making.

8. ***Willingness to question God's love.*** What is it that leads a person to question what they have believed and defended for years? What leads to doubts about the very worldview that organized their lives? What leads a person to the place where they actually question the love of God? The answer is rooted in a person's inability to reconcile the contradictions between what has gone on in their lives and what Scripture says about who God is. God declares himself to be the ultimate definition of what love is and what love does. Yet what God brings into our lives doesn't always seem to us to be good and loving. In our finite and biased view of life, we must not let our experiences function as our primary biblical hermeneutic. Whenever

they do, we will inevitably come to question God's goodness and love.

9. ***A willingness to question God's wisdom.*** The Bible says many things to us that on the surface don't appear to be wise, like "turn the other cheek," "do good to those who mistreat you," "a soft answer turns away wrath," "if a man comes to you seven times in a day and repents, forgive him." A person's willingness to live inside of the wisdom boundaries is not typically based on some abstract acceptance of the logic of Scripture. Rather, it is based on trust in the Lord who is the source of all of the wisdom in his Word. When a person begins to doubt the wisdom of the Lord's rule, then it is very hard for him to continue to accept and live within the wisdom of his Word. It is like getting driving directions to the most important meeting of your life from someone you simply don't trust. So it often is with us. When we begin to question the Lord behind the wisdom, we find it much easier to step outside of the wisdom boundaries that he has laid down.

Allen was constantly saying, "I know what the Bible says about this, but it seems to me that..." He had just turned forty and he envied the younger guys around him who had so many years of potential before them. Allen felt like an old man at work. He felt dead-ended in a life he did not like and couldn't get out of. He had worked so hard, taken his decisions seriously, and prayed with faith, yet it all seemed for naught. His life wasn't horrible; it just felt like he had missed the life that was supposed to be his. And as Allen began to harbor fundamental questions about the wisdom of the way God had ordered his life, it became harder and harder for him to hold on to a childlike faith in the wisdom of the Word.

10. ***Weakening of your witness.*** It is quite typical to share with others the things that you are excited about. From the little boy who just got a new bike to the woman who found the store with the great dresses to the man who landed the amazing fish, we all naturally talk with others about those things that are special to us. A Christian's witness to the world is a natural extension of the genuine love, worship, and gratitude in his heart to God. It is when this gratitude begins to degenerate into questions about God's wisdom, faithfulness, and love that this witness begins to wane. Many people in midlife, because they are disappointed at what has happened in their life, are also not motivated to share with others the comfort and glory in resting in the care of the Lord. They are not celebrating God's wisdom, forgiveness, presence, power, faithfulness, and love, but only struggling to hang on to their belief that God is good. This struggle is not the fertile soil of a consistent life of witness to those around them.

11. ***Growing attraction to the world.*** The Bible is very clear that we *do* tend to exchange worship and service of the Creator for a functional worship and service of the creation (See Romans 1:25). There is a war for each of our hearts that is taking place in every circumstance, relationship, and location of daily life. It is a war about what kind of glory will attract my attention, command my affection, and control my behavior. Will my life be shaped by the unsurpassed glory of knowing, loving, and serving God? Or will it be shaped by pursuing the glories of the surrounding world? When I begin to struggle with the Lord's rule in midlife, what is glorious no longer looks glorious, what is wise no longer looks wise, and what is loving doesn't seem loving. Because I am not amazed at God's glory, I will be all the more tempted to find life, peace, happiness, security, pleasure, identity, etc. in the shadow-glories of the world around me. This can mean eating too much or spending too much, or it can mean struggling more than ever before with lust. This can mean buying a sports car or taking a lavish vacation. Or it can mean a subtle migration away from a God-centered life into a functional worldliness. Typically this person will still hold onto the external habits of the faith, but love of the world has replaced love of God as that which gives their life shape and direction.

Tina really did love the Lord. It was evident that this more than anything else was the thing that organized her life. She wanted her life to please him in every way. Tina wasn't legalistic and self-righteous, but she took her relationship with God very seriously, so it factored into every action she took. The sickness that began to inflict Tina at 39 not only introduced a huge physical struggle, but a spiritual one as well. She had faithfully followed the Lord, so she couldn't understand why God would let this happen to her. As much as Tina tried to avoid a struggle with God, that is exactly what it became. Without ever making a conscious decision, Tina began to try to comfort her heart with things. Even though she was sick, she demanded that her husband move them into a lavish new house. She dragged her husband to exotic vacation spots all over the world, even though her weakness robbed her of experiencing much of what these locations had to offer. There was always some material thing that Tina just had to have. She even silently wondered whether having a more sensitive husband would make her life easier. At 46, this woman who once couldn't get enough of the Lord now couldn't get enough of the world. Yet she was still dissatisfied, unhappy, and unaware of the massive shift that had taken place in her heart.

So the war rages. Will I rest or complain? Will I believe or doubt? Will He be my greatest joy, or will my heart be ruled by the joys the earth offers? Will I let pain and disappointment put a wedge between me and my Lord? Will I continue to hold on to my dreams with clenched fists long after they have slipped through my fingers? Will I enviously compare my life to those around me? Will I allow myself to rehearse to myself again and again how my life could have been different? Will I try to drug my disappointed heart with the temporary joys of the surrounding world? Will I let devotion to God give way to questions that can never be answered? Will I begin to walk away from the one place of hope to which I once constantly ran? Will I let my joy ebb away, or will I, in the middle of my disappointment, battle for my heart with all the fight that I can muster? Will I worship a God whom I cannot fully understand?

Will I find joy in him and his love even though I struggle with the difficulty he has brought my way?

There are many people in midlife who quit fighting the fight of faith. They let doubt and bitterness seep into their hearts and begin to eat away at love and worship. They give in to the cancer of envy and they get paralyzed by what could have been. They succumb to a whole catalog of idolatries that only temporarily fill the void once filled by joy in the Lord.

Perhaps you're reading and wondering if you are in a struggle of sovereignty with your Lord. Examine the list above. Are any of these things in your heart and in your life? Go in your mind right now to the thing in your life that is the most difficult for you to accept. Are you able to stare this thing in the face and at the same time celebrate the Lord and his wisdom, power, goodness, and love? Do you struggle to look honestly at your pain and still hold firmly onto a childlike faith in God? If you cannot hold real life in one hand and a firm rest in God's rule in the other, then perhaps the war of control is raging in your heart. Make this moment a moment of fundamental turning. This struggle is not the end, but rather can be a new beginning of a deeper worship and a sturdier faith than you have ever experienced before.

Turning the Corner

There is a passage in Acts that gives us a very different perspective on God's sovereignty than you and I are tempted to have. Often when I hear people debating this important doctrine, it seems as if they are describing God as a cosmic chess player in the sky. He sits off in the distant heavens, stoically and impersonally moving the chess pieces from square to square in any way that gives him pleasure. In this view, you know his fingers are going to be on you any moment, that he is going to move you somewhere you didn't plan to go, and that there is nothing you can do about it. But the Bible never teaches distant and impersonal sovereignty. In fact, it actually teaches the opposite, and Acts 17 is the quintessential example. This passage defines what it means to say that God's story is a control story, and how that can be a tremendous comfort on the rocky roads of midlife:

> *While Paul was waiting for them in Athens, he was greatly distressed to see that the city was full of idols. So he reasoned in the synagogue with the Jews and the God-fearing Greeks, as well as in the marketplace day by day with those who happened to be there. A group of Epicurean and Stoic philosophers began to dispute with him. Some of them asked, "What is this babbler trying to say?" Others remarked, "He seems to be advocating foreign gods." They said this because Paul was preaching the good news about Jesus and the resurrection. Then they took him and brought him to a meeting of the Areopagus, where they said to him, "May we know what this new teaching is that you are presenting? You are bringing some strange ideas to our ears, and we want to know what they mean." (All the Athenians and the foreigners who lived there spent their time doing nothing but talking about and listening to the latest ideas.)*
>
> *Paul then stood up in the meeting of the Areopagus and said: "Men of Athens! I see that in every way you are very religious. For as I walked around and looked carefully at your objects of worship, I even found an altar with this inscription: TO AN UNKNOWN GOD. Now what you worship as something unknown I am going to proclaim to you.*
>
> *The God who made the world and everything in it is the Lord of heaven and earth and does not live in temples built by hands. And he is not served by human hands, as if he needed anything, because he himself gives all men life and breath and everything else. From one man he made every nation of men, that they should inhabit the whole earth; and he determined the times set for them and the exact places where they should live. God did this so that men would seek him and perhaps reach out for him and find him, though he is not far from each one of us. 'For in him we live and move and have our being.' As some of your own poets have said, 'We are his offspring.'" (Acts 17:16–28)*

Not only does Paul's description of God's control over our lives correct the way we tend to think about it, it also provides the basis of personal comfort and rest. Most often when we think of God's sovereignty, we think of it as one of his *transcendent qualities*, the ones we can't share. And it is that. But Paul presents the Athenians and us with a theology of God's *immanent sovereignty*. Rather than our lives being controlled by One who is distant, unknowable, and unreachable, Paul says that it is his control over every detail of life that actually makes God *near*. He isn't off in the distant heavens. He is actively with you in each moment of your life. Whatever we say about the "there-ness" of God's absolute rule over all things, must be balanced by the "here-ness" that Paul is emphasizing in this passage.

What is amazing and encouraging in this passage is what Paul presents as God's purpose behind his sovereign nearness. Verse 27 is a purpose statement: "God did this *so that* men would seek him and perhaps reach out for him and find him, though he is not far from each one of us." Wow! God's purpose in controlling the details of your life (the exact length of it and the locations where you live) is so that at any moment in the middle of your unfolding story, you can reach out and touch him, because his rule makes him very near to every one of us. What each of us really needs in our finite and faltering humanness is not so much the success of our plans, but *God himself*. He administrates our lives in such a way as to be constantly available to us. What we really need is wisdom, strength, grace, forgiveness, peace, and love; all things that can only be found, pure and untainted, in the Lord. He rules in order to be near, so that what we really need will be ours even in the most troubling, confusing, painful, and discouraging moments of life.

The lie that we tend to embrace is that if things could be our way, then we would have what we need and be happy. I have sat with so many people looking back on life and have heard them say in a variety of ways, "If only I had _____ then I would be ______." Our deepest need is to find and rest in the thing for which we were created—a right relationship with God. In surrendering our sovereignty, in confessing that his wisdom is infinitely more wise than our most brilliant thought, and in admitting that no plan could be more perfect than the plan that comes from the mind of the Almighty, we can begin to reach out to the One who is near and find just what we need for the difficult moments that we face.

You and I will never completely understand what God is doing. We will often be confused by what we are experiencing and ask ourselves how it can be "good." Knowing that God is sovereignly near will not make you understand your life, but it is vitally important precisely because you won't understand it. Rest will never be found in having your own way or in figuring it all out. Rest will only be found as you are willing to believe that there is Someone who is controlling the details of your life, not only for his glory, but also for your good.

Maybe you are in one of those episodes in your life where you are tempted to scream, "May I talk to the manager, please?" Perhaps you wonder why God doesn't give you more physical strength, or why it would have been so bad to give you just a little bit of your dream. Maybe you struggle with the fact that you made so many mistakes, and you wonder why God didn't teach you earlier. Whatever the nature of your midlife struggle, you must realize that it is a struggle for control. Receive the comfort of God's sovereign nearness. It really is the only place where rest can be found.

There will be a day when God's story is complete, and we will all be looking back at it. In that day we will "get it." We will finally realize that we did not need to worry or fret. We will know that it was useless to battle for control. We will finally understand that each of our individual stories was but a chapter in the one story that was guaranteed to be successful. Your story is not really *your* story, but part of the amazing fabric of God's wonderful and glorious story. The success of your story does not depend on the success of your plans, but on the success of his. Rest in his rule and celebrate his presence. When you are discouraged or confused, don't run away from him; run *to* him. Though your difficulties cloud your vision, he is right there with you, just as he purposed to be.

Chapter 9

Golden Calves

I just need enough to tide me over until I need more.

—Bill Hoest

He loves too little, who loves anything together with Thee, which he loves not for Thy sake.

—St. Augustine

It is one of those amazing, truth-is-stranger-than-fiction stories that punctuate the biblical narrative. As you read it, it almost takes your breath away. God has dramatically delivered his people from 42 decades of slavery and in the process has plundered the Egyptians, decimated their military, and displayed his own splendor. For the first time in a very long time the Israelites were free. God was their governor, protector, and provider. Before long they would be in the land that had been promised them so long ago. It feels like the end of a great novel. You can almost hear the victorious crescendo. The people of God have survived. The covenant promises will come true. The promised seed has been preserved. God in his glory actually dwells *with* his people!

So God leads his people to the base of Mt. Sinai. Here he will reinforce his covenant and reveal the covenantal obligations that his people must keep. Of all the nations on earth, only Israel is given the law because only Israel is God's treasured possession. This law expresses not only his authority but also his love and mercy.

Then the unthinkable happens. Moses is up on the mountain receiving the law from the very hand of God, and the people get impatient. They gather around Aaron and say, "Come, make us gods who will go before us. As for this fellow Moses who brought us up out of Egypt, we don't know what has happened to him" (Exodus 32:1). Let this sink in for a moment. These people had just experienced the most unbelievable display of divine power that could be seen. God had sent plagues on Egypt that not only proved his power but also mocked the power of Pharaoh's gods and brought Egypt to its knees. The clear message of the plagues was not only that these were God's people and he could lead them wherever he wanted, but also more fundamentally that there is but one God and his name is I AM. God had once and for all demonstrated that the gods of the Egyptians were no gods at all.

How could the Israelites possibly consider, even for a moment, worshiping anything other than this majestic Lord? In their impatience, they press Aaron to provide something concrete and visible for them to worship. What they say about these man-made gods is hard to fit into your brain. They want gods "to go before" them. This phrase is not about the gods' location in respect to the children of Israel, but an idiom denoting rule. To "go before" is to lead, guide, direct, and protect. Essentially the Israelites are asking Aaron to make idols to rule them in the way that God had covenantally promised to do and had actually done as he rescued them from Egypt.

It is important to realize that the Israelites were asking for something more than a ceremonial idol. They were asking for something that would replace the Almighty as the one who would provide them with identity, security, well-being, and purpose. Understanding this makes this request all the more heinous. They were asking Aaron to provide something that would take a place in their lives that only God was meant to occupy. It's so outrageous that it is almost impossible to understand. But there are more shocks to come.

Aaron, who had been handpicked by God and who was a right-hand witness to the glory of God that accompanied Moses' challenge of Pharaoh, does what the Israelites request without hesitation, or protest, or warning. Immediately he begins collecting the gold needed to construct the god-replacement that the people demanded. Have you ever wondered what mental and theological machinations Aaron had to go through to be comfortable and willing to participate in such a thing? The issue was not just his willingness to be an accomplice in outrageous idolatry, but also a direct desecration of his God-appointed office of leadership. Aaron had no trouble collecting enough gold to make the idol calf. Israel had plenty of gold because God had told them to plunder the Egyptians as they were making their escape. Think about it, the very provisions that God had given them for their journey were used to construct the thing that would function as his replacement! But it gets worse.

Aaron collects the gold, melts it down, and uses his tools to form it into something that looks like a calf. What was he thinking as he carved and shaped the metal into a worshipable form? Just when you think you've been shocked as much as you possibly can, something happens that shocks you even more. After Aaron has finished his idolatrous craft, the people begin to chant. It is the content of the chant that blows your mind. As they dance around the calf they say, "These are your gods, O Israel, who brought you up out of Egypt." Not only are they placing their future identity and security in the hands of the idol; they are also creating a revisionist history that attributes to this lifeless beast the glories of their recent redemption. Consider what is happening here. Moses' absence is longer than the people expected, so they replace God with a thing and call it both the lord of their future and the redeemer of their past. Instead of celebrating what only God by his love, mercy, and power could have done, they give the credit to the creation of their own hands.

You would think that when Aaron heard the chant, he would have been shocked into a realization of the horrible thing that he had done, but he was not. Rather, he declares the next day to be a holy day, a festival of sacrifice and celebration to the "Lord." Early the next morning the people made sacrifices to their newly minted "Lord," and then went on to have one wild orgy!

When Moses hears and sees what is going on, he naturally thinks that Aaron must have had his life threatened in order to have participated in such a horrible act. To paraphrase the scene, Moses says, "Aaron, what in the world did these people do to you that you would lead them into such horrible sin?" Aaron tries to deflect the blame saying, "You know how evil these people are. They thought you were gone, and they wanted gods to go before them, so I collected their gold jewelry. Then, Moses, the most amazing thing happened. I just threw the gold in the fire, and lo and behold, out came this calf!" It's hard to imagine that this is what Aaron actually said, but he did. Not only did he take a lead role in Israel's treasonous idolatry, but also he totally denied his complicity in it.

Getting the Point

What does this have to do with your struggle to get beyond the regrets you can't seem to shake, or the physical changes in your body, or the funeral of your long-held hopes and dreams? How can this story help me in a practical way? Let me suggest some ways that this passage can diagnose the heart of what your struggle is actually about.

1. ***Remember, all of Scripture is about midlife.*** Every ministory that is part of the larger biblical story of redemption was written and retained for our help and instruction. Because the whole Bible is about who we are, who God is, and what life is about, there is a way in which every passage is about the struggles of midlife, for every passage reveals something about how sinful human beings operate. Every passage reveals how God rescues us from our deepest and most abiding difficulties. Every passage reveals how we can functionally be part of what God is doing in us and in his world.

The previous passage, though so culturally different from what you and I experience, still focuses on the core struggles of a middle-aged person living in the twenty-first century. Even though cultures constantly change, life in this fallen world is pretty much the same as it always has been. Even in places where the lifestyles of people in Scripture look strikingly different from ours, there are also pointed similarities. Remember, the Bible presents real people in a real world, relating to a real God. This is precisely the perspective on Scriptural history that Paul lays out in 1 Corinthians 10:6–14, in which he teaches that the events of the Old Testament were written as warnings to us to flee idolatry.

The whole Bible is a mirror that helps you to "see" incredibly important things about yourself. If you were looking for a topical insight on midlife, you would quickly pass over Exodus 32. On the surface, passages like this do not address midlife. Yet Paul operates from the assumption that the whole Bible speaks to all of life. Thus it exegetes midlife as much as it does childhood, parenting, and marriage.

2. *The Israelites were people just like us.* The closer you look at the people in Exodus 32 the more familiar they will become. This is because they are people just like us. When you allow yourself to look beyond the huge cultural differences, you will be able to relate to the thoughts, desires, words, and actions of the people you find there. People are people. At the level of the heart, we are all the same. We can relate to Cain's jealousy, Moses' anger, Achan's greed, David's lust, Absalom's disloyalty, Nebuchadnezzar's pride, the Pharisees' self-righteousness, and the depression of Elijah. These are not aliens from a different planet. They are people whose feet have walked the same ground as ours and stumbled in the same ways that we do.

If you open your Bible with humble hands, you will find yourself on every page. You and I would have grumbled about the quasi-tasteless manna of the wilderness. You and I would have questioned Moses' leadership at the Red Sea. You and I would have been attracted to the culture and idolatry of the nations of Palestine. We would have probably failed to recognize that Jesus really was the Messiah. We share identity with the people of Scripture, and because of this, there is no struggle in our lives that the Bible fails to address in some way.

3. ***We are all constantly worshiping something.*** This is the radical epicenter of the anthropology of Scripture. When you grasp that fact, you will no longer live in a bifurcated world of the spiritual and the secular. The Bible tells you that you *are* a worshiper. You are always in pursuit of something and in service of something to provide you with meaning, purpose, and joy. Now, as I have already written, there are only two options in life. These two options are blatantly obvious in Exodus 32. If God isn't the central reason for doing all that I do, then something in the creation will be. It is an insight that is inescapable and profound. Every moment of life is spiritual. Everything I do is theological. There is never a moment—never a word, action, or reaction—that is not somehow shaped by whatever has claimed the allegiance of my heart. There is never a split second when my heart is not claimed by something. There is always some desire that rules me.

Watch closely and you will see that all the biblical stories are about worship. The Fall is a drama of worship, and it is followed by a long string of worship dramas; that is, people allowing their hearts to be kidnapped by the creation and making disastrous choices as a result. Underneath midlife struggles is a drama of worship as well. Midlife crisis is not just about the surface issues of aging, regret, and lost dreams. These things alone would be fairly easy to deal with. No, the real drama of midlife takes place in the heart. What you worship will make a huge difference in how you deal with the things that almost everyone faces during the midlife years. To the degree that your heart has been captured by something in creation, even if you have not realized it, midlife will be extremely difficult for you. You see, it is these very things in creation that tend to slip from our fingers in the midlife years. If you have looked to these things for life, they will start to fail you in the rocky realities of midlife struggle.

4. ***We all tend to substitute the physical for the spiritual.*** I have already said much about this in Chapter 4, but a reminder here won't hurt. As Exodus 32 powerfully illustrates, it is very hard to follow a god that you cannot see, hear, or touch. Notice that when Moses, who functioned as a visible representative of God, was gone longer than the people of Israel thought he should be, they immediately turned to making a visible god that they could worship. Perhaps this migration takes place more often and in many more ways than we think. In subtle ways, midlife reveals that we have replaced spiritual hope with physical hope. We have staked our well-being on things that we *can* see, hear, touch, and quantify. When these things fail us or fade away, it feels like life is leaving us as well.

If you pay attention, you will see this spiritual-to-physical shift all around you. Commitment to spiritual health gives way to a focus on physical health. Desire for physical riches replaces gratitude for spiritual riches. Thankfulness for acceptance with God gives way to an anxious pursuit of approval from people. Physical food gets your attention more than spiritual sustenance. Spiritual character has trouble competing with physical appearance. Daily spiritual gifts from God's hands go unnoticed as we count our physical possessions. God's presence gets taken for granted while we gush over human love. Identity in Christ does not get the attention that physical location and position does. The shift is everywhere around us, and it is a huge issue in midlife. In midlife you tend to assess the return on the investments you have made. It is then that you get hit with the fact that you have invested your well-being in things that decay, can be stolen, or fade with age. Didn't Jesus say something about this?

> *"Do not store up for yourselves treasures on earth, where moth and rust destroy, and where thieves break in and steal. But store up for yourselves treasures in heaven, where moth and rust do not destroy, and where thieves do not break in and steal." (Matthew 6:19–20)*

5. ***We all tend to attribute to the creation things that can only come from the Creator.*** When you read Exodus 32, it's hard to believe that the Israelites, having just seen an awesome display of God's power, would attribute that power to an image they had just finished making, but that's exactly what they did. Maybe it's their speed and brazenness that shocks us, but we should not be shocked. We do it all the time. We attribute our financial well-being to the economy, our happiness to our marriage, our health to good eating, our spirituality to a good church, and our safety to a good security system. As believers we should question this apparent logic. We know that there are many people who are smarter investors than we who have lost their shirts. We know many people who have taken care of their bodies, only to have their vitality sucked away by some disease. We know many people who sought to make wise choices to provide security, yet they found themselves in danger.

What's the problem here? Does God's physical absence tempt us to credit tangible things for giving us what only God can give? He is Lord over our finances, our health, our happiness, our safety and our spirituality. Yes, we are called to make good choices, even as the Israelites were called to do certain things as they were being delivered from the slavery of Egypt. But they could not, by doing all of those things, deliver themselves. This is true of us as well. God calls us to make responsible, godly choices, but unless God is bestowing his gracious favor and sovereign protection on us, we will not be okay.

Again, this is very germane for midlife. Because midlife tends to be a time for assessing our past, we tend to do a lot of giving credit and assigning blame. This is where we get ourselves in trouble, because we tend to make assessments that take ourselves off the hook (blame) and forget God's constant care altogether (credit). One of the most important things that you must require yourself to do in midlife is to look for the hand of God in your life. You and I need to take an accounting of his presence, protection, provision, wisdom, guidance, and grace.

There is something terribly wrong when we can look at our lives and not see God. There is something deeply idolatrous about crediting the creation with what only our loving, wise, and sovereign Lord is able to do. In all the potential disappointments of midlife, it is wonderful to look back over your life and to see it as a story of grace and mercy, love and faithfulness, guidance and protection. Yes, you lived in a fallen world. Yes, there were difficulties and disappointments along the way. No, things didn't turn out exactly as you had planned, but when you look back, you see God's hand again and again, and you are thankful.

6. ***Impatience and idolatry go hand and hand.*** It's Saturday morning and you are standing in line for donuts. There is some delay up front, and you find yourself increasingly impatient. You're thinking, "They're making donuts, not skyscrapers. What can be taking them so long?" You stand there a bit longer, getting more irritated all the time, when all of a sudden you remember that there is a great donut shop about a mile away. So you get in your car and make a mad dash for it. It is your impatience that caused you to go to the second bakery. The same dynamic is operating in Exodus 32. The details of the account are carefully recorded for us, because these details matter. The people were tired of waiting for God's visible ambassador, Moses. They reason that he had been gone for much too long. In fact, they told themselves that something must have happened to him. So, if God is not on site, deliver-

ing what we want when we want it, our confidence in him flags, and we tend to give our hearts to something else.

One of the hardest things for sinners to do is to wait. We have little toleration for delayed gratification, so when we ask God for things, we include our schedule for delivery in the request. But God's sense of timing is infinitely different from ours. Who would have thought that there would be thousands of years between the Fall and the cross? Who would have thought that the world would have to wait so long for Abraham's promised seed? Who would have thought that God would allow his chosen children to be subjugated to slavery in a foreign land for four hundred and twenty years? Who would have thought that the "last days" that Paul talked about would still be continuing? God has a perfect sense of timing. His moment is always the right moment. He never gets his schedule mixed up or gets things out of order. Yet the wait confuses us, because we reason that if the thing is a good thing, then a loving God would deliver it to us with haste.

Here is the midlife connection: In our discouragement with the wait, like Israel at the foot of Mt. Sinai, we began to give ourselves to other things. Maybe it wasn't as brazen as the overt idolatry at the base of the mountain while God, in his love, was dispensing his law, but rather a subtle migration of affection. In ways that we did not realize, we gave up on God and gave our hearts to things that we could see, hear, touch, taste, measure, and quantify. These things became our "Plan B" messiahs. We asked them to give us the things that only God is able to give. We looked to created things, maybe even things that we made for ourselves, to give us meaning and purpose, a sense of identity, hope and security, contentment, and peace. We hoped that houses, cars, careers, experiences, and people would satisfy our hearts. We looked to those things to give us life. We got tired of waiting on God, so we drove to the shop down the street, hoping that it would be able to deliver.

The grief of midlife is not simply that we all collect things to regret, that we all fear getting old, or that we all mourn the demise of our dreams. We mourn the fact that midlife exposes our idols' fundamental inability to deliver. **Think about it:** The idol that Israel said would lead and guide them was made of metal and formed by human hands. It had no mind, emotion, power, or life. It was, in the fullest sense of the term, an inanimate object. It had no ability to do anything but divert the worship of the people who had made it. It could only disappoint. So it always is with created things. They can never fill the void in our hearts; only God can do that.

7. ***We all tend to blame our idolatry on others.*** Look at the "logic" behind Israel's idolatry. The people would say, "Moses and God disappeared and we didn't know if they were coming back, so we made this calf to lead us and make us feel secure. If Moses hadn't been gone so long, this wouldn't have happened." Or think about what Aaron says about his complicity, even leadership in this horrendous idolatry. You can hear him saying, "I gotta tell you, Moses, these are pretty evil people, and it didn't take them very long to turn their back on you. I was a minority of one, so what was I supposed to do when they asked me to make something they could worship?" Aaron even shifts blame from himself to the fire. He essentially says, "Moses, it was the strangest thing. I've never seen anything like it before. I put this gold in the fire, and not only did it melt, but it formed itself into a perfect rendition of a calf. How amazing!"

There is a great temptation in midlife to blame the idols that God is exposing on the people and things around us. The man whose idol was success in his career and who consequently spent most of his time away from his family is tempted to look back and say, "You don't know how much it costs to raise four children and to support a wife in this economy. There just never seemed to be enough money, so I committed myself to advance in my career so I could make more. After all, God called me to be a good provider for my family, didn't he?" Or the wife, who was excessively controlled by the beauty of her home, says, "I know it seems like it took too much of my time and energy, and it seems like I was far too attached to things, but I just wanted to create an environment that our kids would be proud to call home." Or the man who spent far too many of his parenting years angry because his heart was controlled by a desire for respect says, "Yeah, I know it looks like I was a pretty hard-nosed dad, but you don't know what my kids were like. Things aren't like they were when I was growing up. Kids were much more respectful in those days. I just didn't want my kids to leave home without learning to live under authority."

What does each person have in common? Each of them is making an assessment of his life. Each has had to face the deficiencies of the legacy that he has left behind, but none of them have really admitted that their legacy is directly tied to the desires that ruled their hearts. In fact, each one has shifted the blame for their idolatry to something or someone else.

8. ***We all use the things God has provided to build our own personal golden calves.*** Remember where these recently released slaves had gotten all their gold? It had come from Egypt. As God was slaying the firstborn sons of the Egyptians, he told the Israelites to ask for silver and gold from their captors. Now maybe you're thinking, "If I were an Egyptian and these slaves had caused all this trouble, the last thing I would do is give them my valuables to take with them!" But Exodus 11:3 explains that God made the Egyptians favorably disposed to their soon-to-be-liberated slaves. The gold they took with them into the wilderness was directly provided by the hand of God. Consider what this means. The very valuables that were meant to visibly testify to God's covenantal commitment were then used to build an idol to replace the God who had provided those valuables in the first place!

This is spiritually important. In midlife you are faced with the fact that you have used the very things God provided for your welfare and good to functionally replace him. Those things that were supposed to be a visible reminder of the glory of his presence in our lives became the replacement glories that wooed us away from him. For example, he provided us with the gold of friendship, and we came to crave the acceptance of people more than the love of God. He provided us with the gold of marriage and family, but marital bliss became more important to us than pleasing him. He provided us with the gold of work, and we let this means of provision become the thing that controlled us. He gave us the gold of material ease, but we came to live more for things than we did for him. Much of the harvest that is so hard to accept in midlife is directly attached to the fact that we failed to keep things in their rightful place.

9. ***God is jealous for our worship and will do what it takes to get it.*** It is hard to accept, but three thousand people died because of the construction and worship of the golden calf. There are two ways to think about this. One would be to see it as sure proof that God is not loving, merciful, or kind. The other way is more biblical. If God really loved Israel, there was no way that he could accept their giving the love that belonged to him to an inanimate object! Wouldn't you agree that true love is always appropriately jealous? If I plop down on our couch and tell my wife that she was one of many women I loved very much, how do you think she would respond? If she has any love for me at all, she would be jealous and outraged. The only way she would accept it would be if she had no real love for me in her heart at all. Likewise, God finds Israel's idolatry unacceptable. It cannot fit within his plan. It has no place in the kind of loving relationship that he has covenanted with his people.

There is something else here. God is willing to sacrifice what is important to us in order to reclaim our hearts. God loves Israel so much that he is willing to lose three thousand Israelites in order to turn the hearts of the whole nation back to him. The one thing God is unwilling to share is our hearts. So he uses everything at his disposal to reclaim our affection, adoration, and worship. God's reclaiming actions are often devastating, but they are at the same time a sure sign of the depth and faithfulness of his love. He will not stop fighting for our hearts. He will not share us with another. He will battle to be the center of our personal universe until we are with him in eternity.

Much of the loss that tends to take our breath away has to do with God's jealous love. God is willing to have our dreams crumble, our plans fail, and our hopes erode in order to win back the love of our hearts. He could not love us and let our job, house, friend, spouse, child, or position replace him. His love is beautifully intolerant. He is willing to be severe in order not to lose us. He is willing to do drastic things in order to free us from slavery to things that were never meant to rule us. Do not let the losses of midlife allow you to question his presence and love. They actually prove the opposite. God has been battling for your heart even if that means taking away things that have become precious to you.

10. ***All of us need to ask, "Where are my golden calves?"*** As sinners who tend to exchange the Creator for the creation (Romans 1:25), all of us have somehow taken the "gold" that God provided for us, formed it into our own calf, and served it more than we served him. Maybe it was your children. When they left home, you felt like your life was over, and you didn't know what to do with yourself. Perhaps it was your job. It got you up in the morning and kept you motivated day after day, but its control over your heart has left a painful legacy in your personal life, your family, and your relationship with God. Maybe it was your physical health or physical appearance. You got more identity from being beautiful or fit than you ever realized, and the changes of old age have been a bitter pill to swallow. Maybe it was financial success and material ease that hooked you. Your life became more about acquiring things as an end rather than as a means to help you live your life. Now that you are getting older, the big house leaves you empty, the fine furniture doesn't mean as much, and the luxurious cars don't excite you like they once did.

Maybe your golden calves are still in place and you still don't see them. If I watched a video of your week, what would I see that you are living for? One of the saddest things is to hear from people who are going through a midlife struggle, assessing their life, yet failing to learn their lessons. It is sad when God has been battling for your heart for years, and you are still fighting to hang on to your idols. Have you seen your calf-construction tendencies? Have you learned your lessons? Are you fighting for your golden calf at the very same time that God is fighting for your heart? What in your life right now tends to get out of its rightful place? Are you still melting down your gold and silver because you don't know what God is doing and feel that you can't wait anymore?

Building a Golden Calf

Life started out hard for little Kristi. Born to a very troubled single mom, she was passed from foster home to foster home. By God's grace, when she was seven years old, Kristi landed in a very solid home and was eventually adopted. Kristi's parents weren't Christians, but her father was a hard worker, her mother was a committed homemaker, and they were both dedicated parents. Though every other member considered her to be a part of the family, Kristi was always very aware that this was not her home, and no home ever would be. She was very attuned to issues of identity and acceptance. Under the watchful eye of her parents, Kristi did very well in school and got accepted at a very good college.

The college years were life-transforming for Kristi. In her freshman year she shared a room with a believer. At first Kristi thought her roommate was strange, and she was skeptical about her beliefs. At the same time Kristi was attracted to the joy and surety with which her roommate lived. With a little bit of fear, Kristi went to her first campus ministry social with her roommate. To her surprise, Kristi enjoyed herself and the people she met there. Two weeks later she reluctantly accepted an invitation to a Bible study. Kristi had no idea what she would encounter that evening, but she found herself strangely interested in what she heard. After three or four Bible studies, Kristi decided she would read the Bible on her own. Over the next three months, what started out as an exercise in skeptical investigation became a personal journey of faith. God made himself known to Kristi, and her skepticism morphed into love and worship. With the help of her campus ministry leader she gave her heart to Christ.

For the first time in her life, Kristi felt like she really belonged. She was deeply touched by the fact that she had a heavenly father. She loved the fact that the body of Christ was also called the family of God. She was excited that suddenly she had acquired a worldwide network of brothers and sisters. Kristi was filled with more joy and hope than she had ever had before. She had experienced her own personal exodus. Her next year was spent at the foot of her own personal Mt. Sinai, learning the faith to which she had committed her heart. She listened carefully and read voraciously, and other things were taking place as well.

Kristi talked to Freddy for the first time when the Bible study divided into smaller groups for prayer. After the study they chatted briefly and walked across campus to the dorms together. A week later, Freddy called Kristi and asked her to a movie. The idea made Kristi uncomfortable for some reason, so she made up an excuse and declined, but Freddy was not about to give up so easily. After about a month of Freddy's persistence, Kristi agreed to a night at the movies. She couldn't believe how easy their conversation was, how relaxed she felt with him, and how much fun the evening had been. Freddy felt the same, and the two began to spend a lot of time together. Kristi thought that life couldn't get any better. She had her newfound relationship with the Lord, and now she had a real-life boyfriend.

In all her thankfulness and joy, however, there was something else going on. The more she gave her heart to Freddy, the more insecure she became. She was very aware of how he responded to other girls, she was very demanding of his time and attention, and she flooded him with questions about how he spent his time when they were apart. Again and again Freddy assured Kristi of his love and did things to demonstrate his affection. With all of this happening, Kristi and Freddy began to discuss their future. They went to their campus ministry leader for some pre-engagement counsel. After a few weeks of talking with him, they got engaged.

Kristi had one year left of college and an engagement ring on her finger. She couldn't believe it. She'd had a vague idea that she would end up single, in a big city with a good career, but her life had taken an amazing and wonderful turn. She just couldn't wait to get married and to begin to have a family of her own. Kristi and Freddy graduated together, got married and settled down together. Freddy had a good job and they found a solid church to attend. Kristi was not interested in working because she really wanted to begin a family.

Kristi was a high-maintenance wife. She had to know where Freddy was all of the time. Kristi would melt away into silence whenever she thought Freddy had not given her enough attention, or when she thought he had given too much to someone else. Each time Freddy would draw her out, but increasingly it irritated him that he always seemed to have to prove his love. Freddy thought that starting a family would help Kristi, and he was sure it would make his relationship with her easier. At the end of the first year of their marriage, Kristi got pregnant. They were both very excited, but Kristi was fearful and determined. She did not want her child to experience any of what she had in her younger years, so she was determined to make her home the most wonderful home a child could ever live in.

Kristi and Freddy ended up having three children, which was both very wonderful and very hard. Each of them was thankful for their relationship and for their children, but Kristi was never satisfied. No matter how nice the house looked, it could always look better. No matter how well she cooked, she always thought she could do better. No matter how well Freddy provided, Kristi always thought they needed more. No matter how well the children behaved and achieved, Kristi was convinced that they could do better. She was both a doting and demanding mother. Several times a day Kristi would assure her children that she loved them and then ask, "Do you love mommy? Tell mommy how much." She also was driven by their success. Kristi stood over the children as they did their homework and was obsessed with their grades. Swimming lessons, music lessons, library reading club, ballet, and gymnastics filled every free moment of their days.

Freddy was more and more frustrated about his relationship with Kristi. It seemed that he could never love her enough and was incapable of doing anything right. He constantly had to explain himself, and he didn't understand why he still had to prove his love after all these years. He was tired of the "silent treatment" and irritated that he could barely have a conversation with another woman without Kristi getting angry. The children were now in high school, and they, too, found their relationship with their mother hard. Satisfying their mom was like an ever-moving target that they were never able to hit. It also seemed like their loyalty and love were always being tested. If they didn't verbalize their love for Kristi every day, she would act hurt and depressed. And as they got older, it felt like Kristi wanted to be too much a part of their lives.

All three of her children went away to college, got married, and moved quite a distance away from their home. Kristi was hurt that none of her children wanted to be near her after all she had done for them, and she was very lonely. At the same time, her relationship with Freddy was not good. Over the years, Freddy had finally given up trying to prove his love to Kristi and had withdrawn into his own world. Kristi was angry that she was stuck with a cold and distant man and wondered why she had ever married him. She occupied herself with writing weekly letters to each of the children, baking regular care packages for them, and weekly phone calls. But the children did not reciprocate. She and Freddy did things together, but their relationship wasn't what it once had been.

Kristi became increasingly depressed and angry. She was not quite fifty, but she felt like her life was over. She looked back over the years and felt ripped off. It wasn't supposed to be this way. She had always dreamed of having a big inviting house that her kids would love to come home to. She dreamed of close relationships with each of her grown children. She had dreamed of lunches and shopping together and being the always-available grandmother-babysitter. She couldn't believe that her children were scattered across the country and made contact with her so infrequently. Just when she and Freddy could spend some fun years together, it seemed as if they had little relationship left.

Beneath all of this, Kristi was disillusioned with God. She couldn't understand why he had let all of this happen. After all, she had done all the things a good Christian mom was supposed to do. She had worked hard, given her love to her children, and had made sure that each of them was prepared to face life as an adult. And what had she gotten for all of this? She got a husband who didn't seem to love her and children who forgot what she had done for them the minute they left home.

Each day Kristi withdrew further, and not just from her husband and her activities, but from her Lord as well. The Bible didn't seem to mean anything to her anymore. The hymns she once loved no longer gave her hope and encouragement. Kristi was lost in the middle of her own story, and she didn't know how she got there. Many days when she was at home alone, she would fantasize about leaving Freddy and moving closer to one of her children. Many times when she was out with Freddy, she would find herself wishing that she could find another man who would really love her enough to want to spend the rest of his life with her. Kristi had quit living her life because the thing for which she had lived all these years had been taken away. This one thing had ruled her heart, shaping almost every decision she made, determining her words, and conditioning her reactions to what had gone on around her.

Without ever knowing it, Kristi had taken the gold that God had provided for her deliverance and had used it to make her own personal golden calf. God had made himself known to her and had redeemed her from her slavery to sin. He had given her the world's best and biggest family, the family of God. He had provided for Kristi many of the things she had never known. Yet Kristi put these things that God had provided at the center of her life, the one place where only God was to reside. Marriage and family had become Kristi's golden calf, but it was such a plausible idolatry that she never saw it. God had created marriage and family, and he had called Kristi to be committed to her role in both. It seemed like she was doing what was right, but there was a problem. The item of provision had become the object of worship. Remember the biblical principle of idolatry, *desire for a good thing becomes a bad thing when that desire becomes a ruling thing.* In ways that she failed to see, Kristi had taken the God-given gold of marriage and family and melted it into the calf that she worshiped every day.

At forty-nine, Kristi was reaping her own harvest. It was hard to face. She had smothered her children for years. She hadn't joyfully received their natural love; she had demanded it. She hadn't been happy and encouraged with their achievement but expected it and always required more. Nor had Kristi ever relaxed and accepted Freddy's love. She had demanded his attention and affection, tested his love and loyalty every day, and punished him in various ways every time he disappointed her. Kristi's heart was a battlefield of redemption. She had given her heart to a jealous Savior who loved her with an everlasting love, and he was unwilling to share her heart. All the carnage was not because God had forgotten and forsaken her, but because once again he was actively wooing her heart. In melting her golden calf, grinding it to powder, and letting her drink its bitter consequences, God wasn't ending Kristi's life, but welcoming her to a whole new beginning with himself at the center and all that he provided in its proper place.

It was in the middle of a Sunday sermon that Kristi's eyes were opened. Her pastor asked this question: "If someone wrote the history of your life, what would be the one thing that they would say you lived for?" The question haunted Kristi like a ghost in her heart until she finally understood. The one thing she had lived for was family. Her family had been her god! God had given Kristi himself, but she had replaced him with all the other things that he had provided. That's why she had been so insecure and demanding. That's why she had been so prickly with Freddy. That's why her kids had been driven away. In a moment of amazing grace, it all became clear.

Kristi couldn't believe what the Lord was showing her. She began to take on a whole new way of thinking about her life. As she did her midlife archeological digging, she uncovered the pottery shards of her idolatry everywhere she looked. Though it filled her with grief, she had such a sense of God's love that she was more convinced than ever that her life was not over. Neither Freddy nor Kristi will forget the night she asked him to reserve an evening so they could talk. With humility, remorse, love, and wisdom Kristi walked Freddy through her golden calf years. He couldn't believe what he was hearing. Not only was Freddy ready to forgive Kristi, but he also realized that night that he loved her more than he ever had before. They didn't experience marital bliss immediately, because God's work of heart-and-life change is more a process than an event. Yet they were on the right trajectory for the first time in years. They experienced not only a deep affection for one another, but also a heartfelt gratitude for God and his rescuing grace.

The relationship-mending process with the children was harder because they were hurt, skeptical, and afraid. But Kristi was learning to trust the Lord, to be willing to wait, and to be committed to do the good things that he had called her to do. Each of the children came to learn by personal experience that Kristi's confession was genuine. Not only was she a changed woman, but she was also committed to build relationships with them that were very different. Slowly the children began to reciprocate as Freddy helped Kristi to keep the gold that God had provided in its proper place.

In the midst of all this, God's Word had opened up in a new way to Kristi. She began to understand that the biblical story was her story, and there was heart-revealing, God-revealing, and grace-revealing insight in every passage. She began to see the theme of idolatry and external worship everywhere. She began to realize how much Christ had given her, not just for eternity, but for the struggles of living as a sinner in a terribly broken world. She began to understand that her early childhood experiences did not cause her to turn her family into her own personal golden calf. She was born with the propensity to worship and serve the creation more than the Creator, and her early experiences simply established the tracks on which her idolatry would run. It was all very humbling, yet liberating, to realize that her greatest problem in life was inside and not outside of her. And it was tremendously encouraging to grasp the fact that Jesus had come so that she would no longer live for herself but would be freed to live for him (2 Corinthians 2:14–15).

Kristi's love for the Word, for public worship and preaching, and for the fellowship of God's people began to return. She loved the correction and encouragement that she received from the great songs of the faith. As she listened to her pastor preach, it often seemed as if he had been in her home that week. She also enjoyed how much she learned from the honesty of sharing personal struggles and biblical insights in her small group. She was encouraged by the gracious perseverance she had received from Freddy over many hard years. In all of this there was one passage that Kristi came back to constantly. It was more to her than a piece of Scripture. It had become her God-given friend. It meant so much because it not only described her struggle, but also gave her the daily hope that she needed to fight the temptation to once again turn her God-provided gold into another golden calf. That passage was 1 Corinthians 10:6-14:

Now these things occurred as examples to keep us from setting our hearts on evil things as they did. Do not be idolaters, as some of them were; as it is written: "The people sat down to eat and drink and got up to indulge in pagan revelry." We should not commit sexual immorality, as some of them did—and in one day twenty-three thousand of them died. We should not test the Lord, as some of them did—and were killed by snakes. And do not grumble, as some of them did—and were killed by the destroying angel.

These things happened to them as examples and were written down as warnings for us, on whom the fulfillment of the ages has come. So, if you think you are standing firm, be careful that you don't fall! No temptation has seized you except what is common to man. And God is faithful; he will not let you be tempted beyond what you can bear. But when you are tempted, he will also provide a way out so that you can stand up under it.

Therefore, my dear friends, flee from idolatry.

Melting Down Your Golden Calves

Let's consider why this passage was so helpful to Kristi as she lost her way in midlife and struggled to find her way back.

1. ***She began to realize how helpful the history of the Old Testament was.*** Kristi now saw that those people were part of the same story of which she is a part, and that they were people who thought, desired, acted, and spoke just like she did. When she examined why they did what they did in response to what God was doing, she learned much about herself. Kristi was amazed at what an accurate mirror the Word of God was. In account after account, she not only found God actively redeeming his people, but also she was gaining rich insight into the labyrinthine corridors of the thoughts and motives of her own heart. She began to realize that these things were written for her example, instruction, and rescue. She now knew what the Bible meant when it said that the heart is deceitful (See Jeremiah 17:9). It was hard to understand just how blind she had been and how long she had been that way.

She was grateful for the mirror of God's Word and the rescue of his grace.

2. ***This passage helped her to face her laziness and pride.*** None of us tends to think of ourselves as lazy, and few of us have recognized the full degree of our pride. That is why we tend to be so critical of biblical characters like David, Peter, or the Pharisees. We feel free to be hard on them because we do not think we are like them. We assume that if we had been in the same situations, we would have responded quite differently. But this perspective is more about our inflated view of ourselves than an accurate estimation of these men. Such subtle self-righteousness will prevent our benefiting from the history of God's unfolding story.

This is why verse 12 says, "So, if you think you are standing firm, be careful that you don't fall!" This warning is a call to recognize humbly that we are just like the people of Scripture. We are not only prone to fall into temptation but also to be blind to the instances where we have fallen. When we scan our own stories, we tend to see a lot more about the difficulties of life and the failures of others than we see our own weaknesses of heart and hands. When you forget the war that is going on for control of your heart, there is no way to benefit from the insight and rescue that the Bible provides. Kristi learned that there was never a moment in the day when she wasn't a person in need of help. Her admission of ongoing spiritual neediness radically changed her study of Scripture, and it began to bear fruit in her heart and life.

3. ***She realized that we all struggle with essentially the same temptations.*** There is a commonality to our struggles and a sameness to our temptations. If you look at verses 7 and 14, it becomes very clear what this common temptation is. It is the war of wars taking place in our hearts. The Bible calls it *idolatry*. Worship is that for which we were made and that which gets us into the most trouble. It lies underneath all of our difficulty with people, places, and circumstances. All of us are attracted to an endless buffet table of God-replacements, and

although what attracts you on the buffet may be different than what attracts me, we share the susceptibility to replace God.

This insight helped Kristi because she had felt that her childhood had set her up for spiritual disaster. She felt singled out and disadvantaged. She struggled with feeling that life was unfair, and if it was, then how could the God who controlled it be any different? She wished she could have someone else's life story, and the more she allowed herself to envy others, the more she felt she needed more than the Gospel provided. Now she knew that she was just like everyone else. Sure, her story was unique, and it contributed to the uniqueness of her relational struggles, but the heart that she brought to her story was exactly what Jesus had empowered her to deal with.

4. ***She realized that her struggle revealed God's faithfulness.*** In the middle of the war for our hearts, when we are experiencing the pain of difficulty and loss, we are most tempted to question the faithfulness of God. This passage reminds us of just the opposite: God is actively working to deliver us from what has enslaved us. Consider Exodus 32 again. If God really did love the Israelites, would he be content to free them from their physical bondage to slavery only to watch them become spiritually enslaved? For the believer, pain, difficulty, and loss are never disconnected from God's work of redemption. They are intertwined threads in his overall zeal to own us completely and unchallenged.

5. ***She was comforted that God would not push her beyond what she could handle.*** "He will not let you be tempted beyond what you can bear" (v. 13) is a beautifully comforting statement. God knows you better than you know yourself. He knows your spiritual IQ and the size of your spiritual muscles. He knows how much you have learned from experience and how much you haven't. He knows exactly how functionally blind you actually are. He knows how big the gap is between your confessional theology and your functional theology. So, he knows exactly how much heat to apply. He knows when to send trial your way and when to provide release. He knows

the difference between refining you and incinerating you. He knows just how to boil out your pride while he is building your courage. He knows just what resources to send your way and exactly when they are needed. Kristi found comfort in the truth that the God who knew her this well was at the same time in control of the difficulties that came her way.

6. ***She realized that no matter how fierce the temptation or how painful the process, God would give her the ability to stand.*** There is a theological honesty to this promise. You see, as long as we still have sin dwelling inside of us, our biggest temptation is to replace God at the center of what we think, desire, and do. There is no complete situational or relational escape this side of glory. God promises to provide exactly what we need. We need the ability to stand in a world of idols and keep God central. We need the ability to trust God in moments when we don't understand what he is doing. We need the ability to be patient when God is requiring us to wait. We need the ability to cling to God when we are tempted to worship the good things he has provided. We need the ability to be content when we are tempted to be envious of others. Until we reach the other side, God will give us the power to stand against the powerful temptation to replace him with some other glory that attempts to claim our hearts.

Kristi felt empowered and encouraged by this promise. She knew that she was in for a long battle, but she realized that in Christ she had what she needed to stand, even in those moments when it seemed impossible to do so.

Locating Midlife Trouble

If all you had to do in midlife was to admit that you had failed along the way, or to let go of some of your dreams, or accept that you were getting older, this period of time would not be so difficult. But the biggest problems of midlife are problems of the heart. We all tend to melt God-given gold into calves for our worship. We constantly attribute to our idols what only

God can do. This struggle, which is evident in every period of our lives, tends to rage during the midlife years.

While midlife is certainly filled with disappointment and remorse, it is vital to see it as a period of rescue and reconciliation. A jealous God is fighting for your heart. He is unwilling to share your affection and adoration. He will do what is necessary to reclaim your worship. In those moments in midlife where you feel lost and alone, you must remember that you are not alone. Much of the pain that you feel is the pain of grace. You are being freed from things that held you fast. You are being loved and taken to the one place where the deepest joy and rest can be found. It would be unbelievably crass and uncaring for him to let us take the things that he provided and turn them into objects of worship. His love for us is appropriately intolerant. It makes no room for other lovers. Your Lord will fight for you until there are no lords that challenge his loving rule.

So, what should you do? Sing with the writer of the old hymn, "O Love that will not let me go, I rest my weary soul in Thee." In this time of difficulty, don't run from the Lord; run to him. Run to him in confession, laying your golden calves at his feet. Run to him in thankfulness, celebrating his jealous love and rescue. Run to him in worship, making him your reason, your purpose, your goal, and your hope. Finally, run to him for the strength you need to stand. Yes, you are facing things that weren't in your plan, but you are not facing them alone. God is with you. He is for you. He loves you. This moment of painful grace is sure evidence of his presence.

Chapter 10

Finding the Real You

Note that shattering conclusion: we become like what we worship. —Vinoth Ramachandra

Talk to a man about himself and he will listen for hours. —Benjamin Disraeli

It was the hardest thing I had faced in my young life, but I had no idea why it was so hard. The struggle was deeply emotional and more profoundly spiritual than I had the capacity to understand. I was surrounded by people who tried to give me comfort and rest, but there was none. I was told what to do and what not to do, but it didn't seem to help. I was given promises of changes to come, but they failed to brighten my perspective. I carried this dark feeling with me wherever I went. Finally I ended up with a bleeding ulcer and a doctor who told me that I had better deal with what was going on inside of me or I was going to be a very sick young man.

The problem was that I didn't know what "dealing with it" meant. It felt like I had died, and the problem was that I was still alive. Not only did I have to live through my own death, but I had to find a new life on the other side of it. It all seemed unfair, overwhelming, and impossible. I had been robbed of my identity, and I didn't know how to get it back.

I was reared in a family where sports were important. My father, an accomplished ballplayer, worked for an upscale sporting goods store. He pushed us toward athletics and would tease us for "throwing like girls." Along the way, I began to set my heart on playing football. I played some summer league baseball and ran track, but football was my first love. I will never forget getting my football gear in my freshman year of high school. I couldn't believe it was happening. I looked forward to every practice. I did not mind any of those insanely repetitive drills. We would run up and down the stands of our football stadium in full gear, but I didn't mind. I was on the football team! I was a football player! I loved the team meetings, the two-a-day practices during the summer, the playbook, and watching grainy films of previous games. I loved the macho locker room banter. There were many nights when I would take all my gear home, put it on, stand in front of a mirror, and bask in the glory of it all.

I didn't play much my freshman year, but I thrived on every game. I told myself I was paying my dues and that my time would come. I ran in the summer to keep in shape and began to work on my kicking skills just to ensure my place on the team. My sophomore year was unremarkable. I played a little more, but not as much as I wanted. I was convinced that my junior year would be my breakthrough year, even though I was not gaining the size that I had hoped.

I went into my junior year full of hope. I couldn't wait for summer practice to begin. I was an upperclassman, and I was a football player; it just didn't get any better than that. Then at the end of the summer practice sessions I sustained a severe knee injury. I actually heard my muscles tear and immediately experienced fierce pain. I was quickly rushed to the hospital and went through knee reconstruction surgery the next day. I awoke to a numb leg that was bandaged from thigh to toe. I immediately knew what it meant: my short football career was over. The doctor informed me that sports were not even a consideration; he only hoped I would be able to walk. I lay in the hospital room feeling like I was in someone else's life. It didn't feel real. I thought I would soon wake up from this twisted dream and go to my next practice, but I didn't. All the football practices I would ever be involved in were behind me.

No matter how well I did with recovery and therapy, I was not recovering inside. The further I got from the day of my injury, the worse I became. What I had lost was more than a period of sports involvement or an exciting extracurricular activity. I didn't know it then, but in that moment of injury, I lost my identity. Football had morphed from being something that I did into being who I was. It was not just that I played football; I *was* a football player. When my injury took it all away, it felt as if I had died with it. I knew I would never get football back, but I didn't know how to get *me* back. I could have lost many things in my life at that time and it wouldn't have been such a huge struggle. Football had defined me, giving me position, pride, a community, a reason to get up in the morning, meaning, and goals. There seemed to be no life possible without it. I was angry, and I didn't know how to get beyond what I was feeling.

Who Do You Think You Are?

You and I are always living out of some sense of identity. The way we answer the "who am I?" question will have a huge influence over all that we say and do. It should not surprise us that high school athletic activities would morph into identity issues. Nor should it surprise us that the struggles of midlife are struggles of identity as well. When you begin to understand this, it becomes enormously helpful in finding your way out of that dense midlife fog. Think about how much of the drama of the biblical story is tied to identity. There is a real way in which the fall of Adam and Eve was about forgetting who they were. They were creatures of God who attempted to take on a whole new identity. Much of the drama of the Old Testament is focused on whether the Israelites would live inside of their identity as the children of God. Would they be wooed by other identities and end up worshiping the idols of the surrounding nations? In the same way, the drama of the later New Testament is about whether the church of Jesus Christ would understand and live out what it means to be "in Christ," in the middle of a world that trumpets many other identities.

The biblical story is a story of identity given, identity lost, and identity restored. God wants you to know who you are and to live out the practical implications of the identity he has given you in him. That is why Scripture is constantly telling us who we are. As sinners we all tend to suffer from some form of *identity amnesia*. This is what Peter describes in 2 Peter 1:8–9. He says that there are people who know the Lord but are *ineffective and unproductive* in their knowledge of the Lord. Such a person is "nearsighted and blind, and has forgotten that he has been cleansed from his past sins." Peter is coupling this blind unfruitfulness with the issue of identity, essentially saying, "Your lives are not productive because you have forgotten who you are." I am persuaded that identity amnesia in the body of Christ is doing much more damage than we might assume.

The problem with identity amnesia is that it gives way to something even more dangerous: *identity replacement*. If I have forgotten who I truly am, that identity will fail to shape my response to the people and situations that I encounter, and I will fill the identity void with something else. My "made to worship and serve the Creator" identity of the Garden of Eden gives way to the "I can be like God" identity of the serpent's offer. No one ever lives without an identity. The problem is that you probably won't be aware that an identity migration has taken place in your heart. It's not as if you wake up in the morning and say to yourself, "You know, I'm tired of the identity that I have been lugging around for years. I think today I'll find myself a newer, better identity." It really is an *amnesia-replacement* dynamic that operates in all of us. Let's look at biblical history for some case studies.

Real People, False Identities

Let's return to Adam and Eve. Think about what would have happened if they had been saying to themselves, "We are God's creatures. We were created to worship and obey him. In him we find everything that we need. Because we are his creatures, we must not listen to any counsel that calls his words into question. To step outside of our relationship with him would relegate us to a subhuman condition." Sadly, they did not do that. In fact, they succumbed to the offer of another identity, a vain promise of freedom from dependence and subservience to the Creator. If they had been thinking from the vantage point of their creation identity, they would have known right away that the serpent was offering a fantasy, utterly devoid of any roots in reality.

Think of the children of Israel in the wilderness as they are actually contemplating going back to Egypt. How could they possibly consider that response if they saw themselves as the miraculously redeemed, sustained, and guided children of the covenant? Could they seriously contemplate, even for a moment, a return to the very place of slavery from which God had graciously rescued them? Imagine the difference it would make during the hardships of the wilderness to say, "Yes, this circumstance if difficult, and no, we don't always know what God is doing. But there is one thing we know. We are the children of God. He gave us his covenant promises, he redeemed us out of slavery, he revealed to us his law, and he has guided and provided for us. Because we are his children, we are never alone. The God who delivered us from Egypt will be with us, even in this tough moment. Our only hope is to remain with him, and any other option would mean denying our very identity as the children of the Most High God."

Or think of the Israelite army on the battle line in the Valley of Elah (1 Samuel 17). Do you think they would have responded as they did if they had been looking at their situation in the light of their identity as the children of the Lord of Hosts? For forty days the Israelite army would draw up their battle lines to meet the Philistines, and for forty days Goliath would come out to challenge them. Every time Goliath appeared and made his taunts, the soldiers from Israel ran in fear back to their tents. What a picture of identity amnesia! If you walked out into that battle with a full and clear sense that you were covenantally connected to the General of generals, Almighty God, the Lord of Hosts, would you run away in fear just because you are faced with a soldier who was measurably bigger than you? If you had your true identity in place, it wouldn't make any difference how your size compared to the champion from Gath. You would know that God, who promised to deliver the occupying nations of Palestine into your hands, was the champion of Israel that Goliath had to face in that valley. And if you began to compare the size, ability, and power of Goliath with the Lord, there would be no question in your mind who was going to win.

When David comes on the scene to fight Goliath, it is not because he is a worthy opponent or because he has an over-inflated view of himself. He knows he is a child of God, so he is not afraid of this man's size or taunts. David's question reveals his understanding of his position as a child of God. He asks, "Who is this uncircumcised Philistine that he should defy the armies of the living God?" Then he goes on to say, "The Lord who delivered me from the paw of the lion and the paw of the bear will deliver me from the hand of this Philistine." David knew what God had promised to do, so he responded very differently to the big man from Gath than did the professional soldiers.

In the New Testament, there is an interesting confrontation between Paul and Peter that illustrates this issue as well. Peter had felt quite free to eat with the new Gentile believers until certain Jews, who came from James, arrived in Galatia. Once they were on the scene, Peter separated himself from the Gentile believers, and the record in Galatians tells us why: he was afraid of what the Jews would think about his open fellowship with these uncircumcised believers. Once again, Peter could not possibly have been responding to this situation out of his true identity as a child of God. The bright news of the cross was that it had destroyed the wall of separation between Jew and Gentile. The cross made it quite clear that no one is made right with God because of his ethnic heritage or his observance of the law.

All of the normal identity distinctions that define and divide people were demolished by the cross. The only hope for Jew and Gentile is the grace of God that is ours through the person and work of the Lord Jesus Christ. At the cross, we are all the same—sinners in desperate need of the forgiving grace of God.

When you are living in the amazing glory and freedom of being "in Christ" and, therefore, being an heir to the promises of God, you don't look for your identity in people, giving way to their demands and fearing their responses. Here was a golden moment for Peter not only to live out of his identity in Christ, but also to encourage the Jewish believers around him to do the same. But like us, Peter is an identity amnesiac, so his behavior directly contradicted the very gospel he was called to communicate.

We could multiply story after story from the pages of Scripture where the wrong responses of the people of God are directly tied to identity amnesia and identity replacement. God's story is about calling a people to be his very own, making a covenant with them, and inviting them to have the success of his kingdom become their meaning and purpose. It is also the honest account of how easily sinners forget who they are, how easily they are seduced by other identities, and how much trouble ensues when they step outside of an identity rooted in the Lord.

The more I counsel with people who have lost their way in midlife, the more I am convinced that this issue of identity is not only one of the most important themes in the biblical story, but is also a significant ingredient in the midlife struggle. The midlife struggle is inextricably connected to identity demise and identity replacement. We have been seduced by false identities that will always fail us, and when they do, it feels like we have lost ourselves. We thought we knew who we were, but all of a sudden it is no longer clear. In this moment, we are much like Adam and Eve, the wandering Israelites, the Israelite army, and Peter in Galatia.

The Diary of an Amnesiac

Joanna never thought she would be at such an exciting place in her life. She had been reared in a home with no faith of any kind. Although she loved her mom and dad very much, they were spiritually unaware people who passed the same down to their children. Joanna had no idea what she was getting herself into when she let a friend at work drag her to a free concert at her church. Something about that experience intrigued Joanna, and in two weeks she called her friend asking if she could go to a service with her to "scope out the scene." Joanna was captivated by the crowd of young and old who obviously took their faith very seriously and enjoyed participating in worship. She was intrigued enough to keep going back, and within six months she had given her life to Christ. She couldn't believe it; she was part of God's family. A year ago she hadn't even believed that God existed! She could not get enough of her new found faith, and she was overcome with gratitude for her new identity in Christ. Joanna really did feel like a brand new creature.

This new identity changed the way Joanna approached everything in her life. At work she saw herself as there to represent her Father. She was much more relaxed with her friends because the acceptance she once craved paled in comparison to the acceptance she now had with God. Her new identity gave her a whole new way of thinking about her past and her future. It really felt like old things had passed away and everything had become brand new. Joanna began and ended each day with a prayer of thanks for being accepted into God's family.

It was on a church-wide retreat that Joanna met Darrell. They sat on the dock at the lake and talked for most of that first afternoon, decided to meet for tennis the next day, and by the time they were going home, they had decided to get together again. The love between Joanna and Darrell quickly blossomed, and within eighteen months they were married. Again, Joanna was so excited. First, she had been welcomed into God's family, and now he had made a way for her to have a family of her own. Joanna couldn't wait to have children because she finally felt ready to rear them the right way.

Although they tried for some time, Joanna and Darrell were unable to conceive. Two years passed, and Joanna became increasingly depressed at being childless. After consulting with three or four different physicians, she was told by one doctor that she probably wouldn't ever conceive. The news would have devastated Joanna had it not been for her sense of identity in Christ and her belief that God had a perfect plan for her. Very soon after the visit to the last doctor, Joanna and Darrell began to investigate and pursue adoption. They were ideal prospects, and within three years Joanna and Darrell had a baby boy and a baby girl. Joanna was determined to be the best mother ever, and she was committed to doing everything she could to make up for her children's hard start. She was a zealous and persevering mother, giving her babies every advantage she could. Then, when her adopted children were three and four, Joanna was greeted with a major surprise. She was pregnant.

There was something magical about this little girl from the time she came out of the womb. She was the baby that was never supposed to be. Once again, Joanna looked into the face of the precious little one with a solid commitment to do everything she could to prepare her to be a successful adult. But there was trouble brewing on the horizon. Jimmy, her adopted son, had become a sullen and defiant little boy. Only four years old, he had gained the ability to completely control the scene. When he threw a full-blown fit, he would leave Joanna and Darrell sad and scared. They tried everything, but conditions with Jimmy only worsened. Joanna tried everything she could to keep the girls from being affected, but it was impossible. You could not live in their home and escape Jimmy's dramatic fits.

Joanna saw herself as a mom's mom, and she lived vicariously through every one of her children's ups and downs. By his teen years, Jimmy became uncontrollable and finally ended up in jail. The girls had lived in Jimmy's troubled shadow and weren't well prepared for life at all. As the girls made their rocky launch into adulthood, Joanna felt anxious and guilty. She couldn't help but feel ripped off. As she watched the girls flounder, she struggled to feel good about herself and her life. Her home was now empty, her parental years seemed largely unsuccessful, and the future seemed only to be filled with loneliness and grief. There were days when she was just sad, days when she was filled with anger, and days when she didn't want to get out of bed. She was mortified when people asked her about her children, and she was convinced that people looked down on her when she told them.

Joanna continued her downward slide. She never wanted to leave the house, and she was barely able to get herself to church. Though she had always cared about her appearance, she let that go as well. She hated facing the day because she didn't know what to do with herself, and she hated answering the phone because she feared it would be about some disaster the children had gotten themselves into. She hated talking to those mothers with successful children who were at the beginning of bright careers. She abandoned most of the housework and refused most invitations to go out with friends. Joanna told me on more than one occasion that it was not just that the kids were doing poorly; she felt like she had died somewhere along the way. She felt empty, isolated, and hopeless, and she didn't know what to do about it.

Why had Joanna so completely shut down? Of course, it would be hard for any of us to go through what she did, but there was more going on inside her. Why had this parental disappointment resulted in her totally caving in? Why was she unable to face reality and move on? The longer I talked with Joanna, the more I became convinced that her downward slide had more to do with Joanna than it had to do with her kids. You see, there was an unseen shift that had taken place in Joanna that had altered her perspective on everything in her world. No one around her knew it had taken place; not even Darrell. This shift took place in the shadowy corridors of her heart, yet its results showed up in bright detail in the everyday moments of her life.

Somewhere along the way, this woman who had so vibrantly celebrated her identity in Christ in the early days of her faith had become an identity amnesiac. She was never aware of moving away from the Lord. In fact, Joanna thought that she had grown in her faith. The problem was that she had forgotten who she was, and it was not long before her identity in Christ was replaced by another identity. Joanna's children became her new identity. They gave her meaning and purpose, and they really did give her hope and joy. The problem was that they were not sent by God to do any of that. Joanna lived vicariously through them, and the more she did, the more she became obsessed with their success. Although Joanna was just as faithful in her personal devotions and public worship, God was no longer at the center of who she was.

All it took was Jimmy to mess it all up. With all his inner turmoil, Jimmy didn't make a very good trophy. Being with him often meant unexpected confrontations and public embarrassment. The girls were forced to live in the wings of Jimmy's drama and they didn't turn out to be trophy children either.

Now that they were adults, Joanna was lost in the middle of her own story. She was paralyzed by what had happened to them, not just because she loved them so much, but more importantly because of what their struggle took away from her. In their tumultuous launch into adulthood, the kids not only broke Joanna's heart, but they also robbed her of her identity. She felt like it had all been for naught. When she looked in the mirror, she felt like she didn't know the person she saw there.

While all this was happening, however, Joanna's true identity lived on. She was still who she had always been. The problem was that she had fundamentally forgotten who that was and getting it back wasn't going to be easy.

A Community of Amnesiacs

There are many people in the middle of what our culture calls a midlife crisis who have no idea that their disappointment is the result of the identity they carried into these dynamic midlife experiences. Long before they entered their midlife years, a seismic shift had taken place in their identity, and it was just a matter of time before it caused problems. Now they mourn, but not just because they are aging or will never realize their dreams or have reason to regret, but because they took on experiences, relationships, or accomplishments as their identity. Sinners tend to move away from defining themselves in relationship to their Creator and begin defining themselves in relationship to the creation. But the creation cannot bear the weight of defining us. It will always come up short. It is bound to happen, and when it does, a moment of disappointment can quickly turn into a fundamental loss of self.

Replacement Parts

When I was in junior high, I became obsessed with cars. It was a silly thing. I was far too young to drive and probably too young even to know what made a good car good, but I still read car magazines and racing novels. I remember the first time I put my hand on a Whitney auto parts catalog. It was a small, black-and-white catalog with grainy pictures of auto parts. What impressed me about the catalog was it sheer size. Page after page was filled with replacement parts for any car that might still be on the road. The catalog excited me because it was a sure testament of just how big the world of cars actually was. I would go slowly through the catalog, pretending that I owned a car and carefully choosing the things I would add to "soup it up."

Just like the Whitney catalog, our fallen world offers an endless catalog of identity replacements. None of us is free from their seduction. Each of us will turn a page of life and find one that is attractive to us. Like a catalog that is organized into auto parts categories, identity replacements tend to fall into four major clusters. Let's look at them together.

1. ***I am my success: Identity in achievement.*** God calls us to be fruitful and productive. We should be concerned about our harvest and the return on our investments. But the minute we take on our achievements as an identity, we become slaves to a never-ending stream of potential successes. This is the profile of a workaholic. He gets his meaning and purpose from the next notch on his belt, so he is unable to say no and unable to slow down. Take away his ability to build toward the next success, and he will be irritated and discouraged. This replacement identity will also distort your decisions. You will tend to go after the things where you think you can succeed, rather than going after them because they are in line with biblical priorities. You will also be more excited about what these opportunities and successes do for *you*, than how they fit inside of the plot of God's story.

What does this have to do with midlife? During this period of time, one of three things can be happening. First, maybe you are beginning to be sidelined. Perhaps your children have grown up, and you can no longer claim that area of achievement. Perhaps major career responsibilities are being shifted to younger people where you work. Maybe there is no more remodeling or landscaping work to do on your property. Or, second, the very opposite could be happening to you. Perhaps you are being given more opportunities to achieve than you have ever had in your life. You are finally becoming a decision maker at work, or you have finally reached a place in ministry where you are so respected that people hang on your every word. You feel really alive, and you find it very hard to say no.

Here is the point: If achievement has become their identity, both the person who is losing his ability to achieve and the person who has more opportunity to achieve are in a dangerous place. The first will feel depressed and discouraged because the thing that defined him has been taken out of his hands. The second person will become enslaved to achievement, making bad choices and staying too busy, because success is where he finds his meaning and purpose.

There are many people in midlife in these two categories. Some are feeling that the best of life is behind them, and some are so enslaved to success that they fail to see the damage that their drivenness is doing to themselves, to their marriages and families, and to their relationship with God. Achievement was never meant to give us identity, and when it replaces our true biblical identity, it will leave a harvest of bad fruit.

But there is a third midlife person to consider here. This is the person who is looking back on his life with great remorse at how achievement drove him. He realizes that his relationship with his wife is distant and cold, and he would love to take back all those parenting years when he was too busy to be the kind of parent God called him to be. Moreover, he feels the same distance from God as he does from others because for years, achievement lived at the core of his life where only God should be.

Does personal achievement mean more to you than it should? Could it be that you have looked to it to provide identity, meaning, and purpose? As you stand in midlife and take an accounting, is there recognizable fruit of this false identity in your life? As we go through these identity replacement clusters, notice how each of them is rooted in something good.

2. ***I am my relationships: Identity in acceptance.*** God created us to be social beings. His plan, from day one, was for us to live in meaningful community with one another. It is one of the primary ways that we image him. Have you ever considered that God himself *is* a community? He is the only being in the universe who can say that. Our relationships are so important to God that he positioned the command for us to love one another as second only to the call to love him (See Matthew 23:37–39). We are called to live in productive community with others, and those relationships must be a very high priority as we make our daily decisions.

Yet, in our sin, many of us look to other people to do the one thing they were never designed to do; give us identity. If we are parents, we tend to try to get our identity from our children. Their love, appreciation, and success become the things that give us a reason to get up in the morning. We begin to live vicariously through them, as if their successes are our successes. And when we need the success of our children in order to feel good about ourselves, we will do anything possible to make them succeed. We tell ourselves that it is for them, but in reality, it is for us. We become smothering, domineering, success-obsessed parents, but we are blind to it because we are always able to say that it is good for them.

Then the day comes when our children begin to leave home, and we do not know what to do with ourselves. The loss we feel is much bigger than the reality that they will no longer live with us; it is a loss of identity. It feels like we're losing our reason for living. We've done everything we can to hold on to them because we need them in order to feel good about ourselves.

Our children were never given to us to be trophies on the mantel of our identity. If anything, their success is a hymn of praise to another Father who provided everything they need to be where they are and to do what they are doing. As parents we are never more than instruments in his redemptive hands.

Perhaps your marriage is the place where you seek identity. You live for the next shot of acceptance and appreciation, and the love of your spouse is the thing that makes you feel most alive. When you seek to get your identity from your marriage, you will tend to turn your husband or your wife into your own personal messiah. You will feel alive and well when they notice your efforts and seek your company, but your joy will come crashing down when you feel ignored or taken for granted.

This is all very dangerous. No sinner can ever be your rock and fortress. No sinner can give you a consistent reason for hope. Sooner or later, everyone around you will fail you. There is, however, an even greater danger here. As you look to this person for identity, you are not really loving them; you are loving *you*. You have turned the second great commandment on its ear. Instead of serving people because you love them, you are willing to serve them so that they will love you. This kind of parasitic relationship is never healthy. Only as you keep the first great commandment will you have any hope of keeping the second.

There are many people in midlife who are now harvesting the bitter fruit of this kind of relationship. What seemed like a giving and serving relationship was actually very selfish and demanding. And when you get to midlife, you are hit with the fact that your marriage lacks tenderness, warmth, and affection. When your marriage has not turned out like you dreamed it would, it is very important to understand why. Often identity replacement lies at the bottom of it all. We looked to people to give us what only God could give. We asked our marriages to give us life, contentment, happiness, and joy. We asked them to give us identity and, like anything other than the Creator, they failed us.

3. ***I am my righteousness: Identity in performance.*** In the early days of his faith, Joe was overwhelmed by the desper-

ateness of his need for God's grace. He was seeing his sin everywhere, and he was constantly thankful for the daily mercy and patience of the Redeemer. Joe was also patient with the people around him who were struggling. He knew that they were essentially no different from him, and that he was only kept by God's grace. Joe lived with that healthy combination of a deep sense of his own need and a lively gratitude for the never-ending supply of God's grace.

As Joe continued to grow, however, something began to change in his heart. He began to feel as though he *deserved* to belong in the community of God's children. He was proud of his theological knowledge and had little patience for Christians who were "just too lazy" to really know their faith. He looked down on brothers and sisters who struggled faithfully to participate in public worship and small groups. When he put his check in the offering plate on Sunday, he scanned the sanctuary wondering who was getting a "free ride." He loved to show people the photo albums of the many short-term missions trips he had been on, and he didn't understand why some people were never willing to give up one week to serve God. The tender, grateful Joe had given way to a hard and self-assured man.

Joe approached every Christian activity as an opportunity to put another notch in his belt of righteousness. He was active and involved, but there was little sense of gratitude because he had little sense of need, and he showed little grace or patience with those around him. Joe had once been a man who had found his identity in Christ; now he was a man who got his identity from his own performance. Joe was constantly debating points of doctrine and increasingly known to be critical and judgmental. Although he could not see it, Joe was much like the Pharisee Jesus describes in Luke 18. The Pharisee was supposedly praying, but in reality he was comparing himself to those around him (including the tax collector beside him), and concluding that he was more righteous than all of them.

His "prayer" was essentially a declaration that he didn't need God.

Although Joe was in church every time the doors were open, there was little true love and worship in what he did. The bottom line was that Joe was doing it all for Joe. The praise always went to Joe, while judgment went to anyone who was unable to live up to his righteous standard. Joe was in the middle of his life, but he had lost the joy of his salvation. He was a sullen and critical Christian with little heartfelt excitement for his faith.

It is often in midlife that one's harvest of self-righteousness comes in. You are faced with the coldness of your relationship with God and you realize that it has been there for years. In moments of midlife regret, you begin to see that while you thought you were serving God, you were actually serving yourself. It is a hard pill to swallow when you have left a Pharisee's legacy. But there is another very important dynamic that troubles the midlife years. Some of us have lived so long, blinded by our own righteousness, that it is very hard to look back and take an accurate accounting. The harvest of our adult years may be disappointing, yet in our self-righteousness, we deny that it belongs to us. In our denial, we then lay the blame at the feet of those around us and maybe even at the feet of God.

How much of your midlife trouble is self-righteousness trouble? Could it be that the massive identity shift that took place in Joe also took place in you? Is there a chance that you replaced the joy of identity in Christ with the pride of identity in your own righteousness? Is it possible that you were more critical and judgmental toward the people around you than you ever were about criticizing yourself? Ask yourself, "Do I feel today like I need Christ's grace as much as the first day I believed?"

4. ***I am my possessions: Identity in physical things.*** Let's face it: Physical things are seductive precisely because they are physical. We can feel their texture, see their shape and beauty, and smell their aroma. Biblically, we know that the most important things in life are unseen, yet physical things are stiff com-

petition when it comes to what gets our attention and shapes our living. It is very tempting for all of us to define ourselves by the size of our pile of stuff. We all know that American culture tends to define success by the size of your bank account, house, and car, not to mention the size of your pool, deck, television, family room, kitchen and vacation home. Someone once said that the highest value in Western culture is not possessing, but acquiring. Our culture assumes that something is wrong with you if you *are* content with all of your things and not looking for ways to go further upscale. So most of us possess more clothes than we could ever wear and more toys than we could ever enjoy.

We may not even realize the extent to which we define ourselves by the pleasures of the physical world. The three big ones here are food, sex, and leisure. Some of us are always trolling for the next best restaurant, continually being seduced by the "more and different" draw of sexual temptation, or willing to spend far too much time and money planning and buying a vacation.

Physical appearance can also control and define us. As we noted earlier, we live in a culture that has institutionalized the practice of being defined by our appearance. No matter how nonchalant we may think we are about the way we look, none of us has escaped this influence. Isn't it true that most of us spend far more time in a given week caring for and adorning our bodies than we do nurturing our souls? We are the kind of people who will fret over exactly the right outfit to wear to a service of worship (think about the contradiction there), or attach career success, not just to the quality of our work but to the cut of our suit.

The material world provides a powerful and seductive replacement for true identity. A big house isn't just nice to look at and live in; if it is yours, it makes you feel good about yourself. A luxurious car is not simply a reliable source of transportation; it functions also as an identity marker. Why do so many professionals drive BMWs? Because the car projects the very identity they are trying to nurture. Beautiful clothes have the power to make you feel differently about yourself. Physical fitness and beauty make you feel self-confident and alive. A gourmet meal not only fills your stomach, but for that temporary moment, it also makes you feel good about yourself.

You don't have to look very far to see that these things have defined us. The average American is living in a house that is much bigger than he really needs; and often much more costly than he can actually afford. Many of us have eaten ourselves into poor health. Most of us are carrying around too much debt. The highest paid members of our society are not the people who teach us, heal us, or lead us in worship; the people we are willing to award with inordinate sums of money are the people who entertain us. The evidence is persuasive and the conclusion is clear: We tend to let the physical things of this world define us.

This identity replacement causes havoc for us during the midlife years. Three words capture the chaos: *delusion*, *disappointment*, and *emptiness*. Identity in things *is* a delusion. True identity is never a matter of the physical but a matter of the heart. Think of what happens to the person in midlife who has tried to define herself by her appearance. First, because she has put her focus and invested her efforts on the physical, she didn't invest as much as she should have on the spiritual things of the heart. And this sets up the crushing disappointment of realizing that what she *has* invested in simply won't remain. No matter what lies the body-reconstruction industry tells us, you can only fight physical aging for so long. Your body will inevitably change its shape, weaken, wrinkle, and malfunction. Your body will die. Midlife is a time when physical appearance and health begin to fail us, and if they have defined you, you are a person in trouble.

Other people in midlife struggle more with disappointment. They feel like life has been unfair because they *haven't* ever been able to acquire and enjoy the physical things that so many other people enjoy. They kept telling themselves that their potential was still there and that material success was just around the corner. But it never came, and now in midlife it seems unlikely that it ever will. Though they possessed few of the physical things of this world, those things still defined their identity. Now they sit in silent moments of disappointment and feel ripped off because they were as dedicated and persevering as their materially successful neighbors, yet they have little to show for it. They wonder why God would single them out for this kind of treatment. Notice the value system behind these conclusions. They define the "good" life as one that is rich in physical things rather than spiritual glories.

Still more people in midlife have a deeper struggle with God than they actually recognize. They have taken him into the court of their judgment and found him unfaithful and unfair. They have been passed by in God's distribution of stuff, and there doesn't seem to be much they can do about it at this stage of their life.

The final group of people in midlife experiences the emptiness that identity in physical things will always end up producing. Should it surprise us that physical things are devoid of any power to satisfy spiritually? In its broadest sense, the biblical truth that "man shall not live by bread alone," means that we were never constructed to subsist only on the physical. We are spiritual beings who need spiritual sustenance in order to be truly healthy and happy. In fact, what we were wired to "feed" on is the Lord himself! He is to be our meat and drink; he is the one who gives us identity and meaning. He alone is able to satisfy our deepest hungers and our most pervasive thirsts—our need to live in a humble relationship of joyful submission to him. Many people in midlife are experiencing an atrophy of the heart from seeking satisfaction where it simply cannot be found. They have defined themselves by a delusion and fed themselves with what can't satisfy.

What is your midlife harvest telling you about your relationship to the world of physical things? Is your harvest a heap of delusion, disappointment, or emptiness? Have you judged

God as unfair and unfaithful because your pile of stuff is far smaller than you think it should be? Are you still buying the delusion? Are you still on the acquisition treadmill, even though it is already quite clear that things have never been able to satisfy you? Over the years, what important things have suffered from your lack of attention and investment? Did your children suffer because of your drivenness and inattention? Did your marriage falter? Has your relationship with the Lord withered? Here is an opportunity to take an accounting, to make honest confession, and to begin walking on a new and better pathway.

Getting Identity Right

Justin was about four years old when he came to me, a bright little boy with a world of questions. We sat down on the edge of the couch together, and he shared with me his dream for his future, "When I grow up, Daddy, I want to be a lion," he said. *Well, who wouldn't*, I thought, *with all that "king of the jungle" stuff we hear so much about?* His mother had been reading him a book about the animals of Africa, and he was enthralled. He was in that time of life when you come across a book that you want read to you over and over again. After at least five hundred readings, he was completely settled on what he wanted to do with his future. He wanted to be a lion.

After he shared why he had chosen this future at the top of the feline world, I launched into a little lesson on biblical anthropology. He sat wide-eyed and attentive as I laboriously attempted to help him understand the doctrine of creation and its specific implications for the identity of human beings. He *seemed* interested as I did everything I could to distinguish animals from people. As I droned on, I noticed that he was getting fidgety and was no longer looking at me with rapt attention, but I thought he was still taking it all in. I wrapped up my identity-of-human-beings monologue and asked him if he understood what his daddy was trying to say.

He looked up at me quite confidently and said, "Yes, I do, Daddy. When I grow up, I am going to be a giraffe!" I ended my failed attempt at early childhood theological education, gave him a big hug, and off he ran.

Little Justin is like all of us. We know that identity influences our thinking, our choices, and our behavior, but we have a hard time getting identity right. This issue is a huge part of the midlife struggle. Identity amnesia, misunderstanding, and replacement make the surface issues of disappointment, aging, and regret all the more powerful and potentially destructive. **Here is the critical issue:** When you have defined yourself horizontally ("I *am* my family, job, marriage, children, possessions, appearance, friendships, career, successes, or position") you are in big trouble. When you enter the stage of life where those things, or your plans for acquiring them, are taken away, you become lost in identity confusion. We are always heading for trouble when we try to define ourselves horizontally instead of vertically.

What we need in midlife is not a world that is utterly free of disappointment, aging, or regret. We need to get our identity right in order to survive these powerful experiences. When you define your identity vertically, you will be able to stand even when the things around you are passing away. Perhaps you are thinking, "Okay, but what does it mean to define myself vertically?" It means that *true identity is always rooted in worship*. In fact, the Bible tells us that a true understanding of anything starts with acknowledging God. As the great Christian thinker John Calvin taught, there is no knowing that does not begin with knowing God. It is only when you have God in his proper place and are celebrating who he is that you can ever truly know yourself. The theological principle is that knowledge of the Creator is fundamental to understanding the creation. The identity struggles that rear their ugly heads during the tumult of midlife are really struggles of worship. To the degree that we have failed to worship God for who he is and what he has done, we will take unseen identity confusion into the issues of midlife, making what is already difficult much worse.

There are three pillars of worship that support a true biblical sense of identity.

1. ***True identity is rooted in worshiping God as Creator.*** To have a sense of identity that will not fail you when you are buffeted by the sure-to-come storms of life, you must start at the beginning. This first means fully and completely recognizing that you were made *by* him. David captures it so well in Psalm 139.

For you created my inmost being;
you knit me together in my mother's womb.
I praise you because I am fearfully and wonderfully made;
your works are wonderful,
I know that full well.
My frame was not hidden from you
when I was made in the secret place.
When I was woven together in the depths of the earth,
your eyes saw my unformed body (Psalm 139:13–16a).

What powerful and amazing words! Every part of the fabric of your personhood was carefully knit together by God's creative hands. There was no part of you that was hidden from him. He carefully examined every aspect of your unformed body before you were born. There were no accidents, no glitches, no thoughtless moments. Just like David, you too were "fearfully and wonderfully" made. The color of your eyes, the shape of your body, your intellectual and physical gifts, your hair, your voice, your personality, the color of your skin, the size of your feet, etc.—all of your hardwiring is the result of God's glorious creative ability. The "package" that created *you* comes from his hand.

Now, as familiar as all of this is, it is nonetheless important. I am deeply persuaded that while many of us worship God as Creator on Sunday, we curse his work during the week. Most of us harbor dissatisfaction with who God made us to be. The short ones want to be tall; the tall ones want to be shorter. The intellectuals secretly wish to be athletic; the mechanically minded people secretly wish they could be more musical. The serious person wishes, just for once, that he could be the life of the party, and the guy who was given the gift to think and to teach wishes he could have been more administrative. There are times in all of our lives when we secretly wish we could rise to the throne of creation and remake ourselves in the image of what we would like to be.

Often this refusal to accept your legacy in midlife is really a refusal to accept your identity. Sam was wired to be bald young and gray early. By forty-two he had little hair left, and what was there was almost white. He felt cursed and did everything he could to prove that he was still young. He was cursing the Creator he had committed himself to worshiping. Justina had been wired by God to be a nurturer, and she made a wonderful mom. Now, with her kids all gone, she had worked herself to the bone for something that left her empty and alone. She was angry that she hadn't been more career-conscious. She was angry at her Creator, and she didn't even know it.

What about you? Are your midlife struggles connected to your failure to celebrate whom the Creator wired you to be?

Worshiping God as Creator also means recognizing that I was made *for* him. If I compose and paint a painting, it belongs to me as a testament to my artistic ability. The same is true of us. If God made us, then we belong to him as a testament to his creative glory. The fact is that you and I were never meant to live for our own success and glory. Every day we are meant to live like our lives belonged to another. This "I belong to another" lifestyle was meant to shape our marriages, parenting, friendship, and careers. It was meant to shape the way we approach position and possessions. As a creature, your life belongs to Another, and so your life is part of *his* dream.

So much of midlife struggle is because we haven't gotten our own way. We have lived as if we belonged to ourselves, when really we belonged to him. While we were supposed to be living for his glory, we set our hearts on other glories that failed us. So, my marriage was never meant as a means for my glory, but as a workroom for his. My kids never belonged to me; they belong to him. My job never belonged to me; it was his all along to use as he wished for the realization of his glorious purposes in and through me.

Have you taken life as your own? Have the normal disappointments of midlife paralyzed you because you went into them forgetting who you are? You haven't been able to say, "The LORD gave and the LORD has taken away; may the name of the LORD be praised" (Job 1:21), because you thought your life was your own.

Worshiping God as Creator also means that we exist *through* him. As Creator, he alone is the giver of life. True life cannot be found outside of him. Paul says, "he himself gives all men life and breath and everything else" (See Acts 17:25, 28). If he is our Creator, then he is also our Sustainer, our constant life source and incessant provider of everything we need. In midlife, we are prone, despite our better knowledge, to look for life outside of him; when you do, you will become enslaved to the very thing you think will give life to you. There are many people in midlife who have had successful families and careers but are lost and empty on the inside, simply because they sought life where it could not be found.

Look back over your adult years. What has tended to enslave you? Have you forgotten that you exist by the Lord, for the Lord, and through the Lord?

2. *True identity is rooted in worshiping God as Sovereign.* As we have already examined in Chapter 8, the midlife struggle is often the result of a collision between your plans and God's. Although you knew exactly what you wanted to accomplish and those things that you determined to avoid, your life didn't unfold as you planned. It is vital to go into the middle years with your biblical identity screwed on straight. You must rest in the fact that every situation, circumstance, location, experience, and relationship of your life has been under the wise and careful administration of the Lord Almighty. He has known from the beginning exactly what he was going to do and exactly why he did it. From his vantage point there are no slip-ups, no oversights, no accidents, no misunderstandings, and no mistakes. Nothing has fallen through the cracks. David captures this comforting fact in Psalm 139:16b:

All the days ordained for me
were written in your book
before one of them came to be.

Wow! It is a view of human identity that takes your breath away. I *do not* write my own story; it has been written for me. My job is to live inside of the plot that God has written for me in the way I have been called by him to live.

There is a direct connection between delusions of personal sovereignty and the crushing disappointments that grip us in midlife. We forgot who we were and began to believe that our hands were really the hands on the joystick. We worked with dedication and perseverance, but we worked like little sovereigns, rather than resting in the One who is sovereign.

Do you question God's administration of your story? Do you wish that you had been able to write your own plot? Do you fall into thinking that if you had been in charge, you would have made better and wiser choices? Do you worship God as sovereign on Sunday and curse his sovereignty on Tuesday? As you look back on your life, is it more a picture of resting in his control or of a quest for control?

God is sovereign. You and I are not. This is not just theology; it is our identity. God is in absolute control, and he is infinitely good.

3. *True identity is rooted in worshiping God as Savior.* When you recognize that God is not only your Sovereign Creator, but also your Savior, you have grasped another essential element of your identity. He is Savior because we are sinners. Worshiping God as Savior means that the most significant drama in my life is not what will happen to my marriage, children, possessions, or career, but what will happen to my sin. It means that the most wonderful thing that could ever happen in my life is my salvation. It means that the most wonderful thing that I could be called is not boss, or husband, or father, or friend, but "child of God."

This identity defines your deepest, most pervasive problem. It is the thing that you most desperately need help with. We don't actually need the vast majority of possessions that we think we cannot live without. The Bible says it very clearly: because we are sinners, God is focused on delivering us "from such a deadly peril," rescuing us "from the dominion of darkness," conforming us "to the likeness of his Son," allowing us to "participate in his divine nature," purifying us "from all unrighteousness," to "purify for himself a people that are his very own, eager to do what is good" (2 Cor. 1:10; Col. 1:13; Rom. 8:29; 2 Peter 1:4; 1 John 1:9; Titus 2:14). Phrase after phrase reminds us of our true identity, and therefore, what we truly need.

We want our lives to be comfortable, successful, and predictable. God is willing to compromise all of these in order to deal with our deepest difficulty, our own sin. When you have failed to worship God as Savior, forgetting your identity as a sinner, you will be completely confused during the midlife years. To the degree that you recognize your identity as sinner, life will begin to make sense to you. God has not forgotten you. He has not singled you out for particular abuse. He is near and he is active. In love he is working on your biggest problem, and he will not stop working until the job is done.

Chapter 11

Last Chapter, First Values

Whoever does not have some foretaste of the heavenly banquet will never partake of it.

—JOHANN TAULER

Our plans miscarry because they have no aim. When a man does not know what harbor he is making for, no wind is the right wind. —SENECA

It was a crime-solving game like "Clue," and our kids could not get enough of it. The secret was kept in a magic envelope at the center of the game. In it were three cards that told you who did it, how they did it, and where they did it. You had to try to uncover what was in the envelope by the process of elimination. This took patience and a willingness to keep track of a lot of details, but if you did that, you could come to a point where you were absolutely sure of what was in that all-important envelope. It was always an exciting moment when someone said they were ready to solve the crime.

The point of the game was that the details don't make sense until you have the whole story in hand. The players were in a race to see who could get to the last chapter first. The game was very similar to reading a novel. In the middle of the story, you don't really understand the plot, the characters' motivations, or how it all will resolve. Only in the final chapter do all the confusing details suddenly make perfect sense. There are times when the details are so confusing that it drives you crazy, and you can't resist jumping ahead and reading the last chapter first. Once you have been let in on the secret, you are able to relax and enjoy the unfolding drama.

Life is much like being in the middle of a novel. Every day you are faced with things that were not part of your plan, and at some moments you wonder what is going on. It may be that you awake with a nagging pain in your abdomen and wonder whether you just slept on it wrong or something is seriously wrong with you. Or you get wind that there are going to be massive changes in the company you work for, and you wonder whether you will be one of the long-term employees to be furloughed. Or you are watching one of your grown children make a rather chaotic launch into adulthood. You did everything you could to help him make a smooth transition, but you wonder every day if he will be okay. Or you sit with your wife and wonder what you could have done to make your marriage more loving, intimate, and unified.

We don't need to read mystery novels; our own lives are mysteries to us. Even with all of our planning, each of us is amazed by the details of his or her own story. None of us can say that we got where we are by careful planning and a disciplined administration of the plan. The details of our own story tend to confound us all, and we wish we could be let in on the secret. We want to get to the last chapter first so that we will know where this whole thing is going. Perhaps you sit in midlife looking back on your life and you are thinking, "If I had only known ... what would happen to the economy ... what kind of church this would turn out to be ... that I would have this problem with my boss ... or the effect this decision would have on my wife ... the impact of the move on my family. If I had only known!"

We all tend to think that if we only had known the last chapter first, we would have dealt a lot better with what was on our plate. We all carry around questions about what will happen, and at various points in our lives we all struggle to accept the actual outcome. What most Christians fail to understand is that God has let us in on the secret. In the Bible, we are given the last chapter. The end of it all is laid out for us. God invites each of us to eavesdrop on eternity and then to look back on our lives with the unique perspective that only eternity can give us. God's story only makes sense from the vantage point of eternity, and your life will only make sense when you view it from that perspective.

The Essential Ingredient

The Apostle Paul wrote two of his longest letters to the church in Corinth. It was a pretty messed-up church. Divided by personality cults, damaged by overt sexual sin, and discouraged by doctrinal controversies, this church, you would think, showed little genuine promise. That is not the way Paul saw it. After confronting the critical problems that the Corinthians needed to deal with, Paul in Chapter 15 lays out a paradigm for making sense out of the Christian life. His logic is as follows.

1. The Gospel is what makes sense out of our lives.
2. You cannot make sense out of the Gospel without the resurrection.
3. The important thing about the resurrection is that it guarantees us eternity.
4. If there is no eternity, our faith has been useless.

Now I know that some of you are thinking, "I just want help for this struggle that I never thought I'd be experiencing. Why do I need to understand Paul's paradigm for the Christian life?" We need to discuss this question at the very outset. Remember that the people in Scripture were people just like us. The questions raised by the Corinthian church were very much like the questions we tend to ask as we do the personal archeological work of the midlife years. You are in a stage when you are taking an accounting. You look back on a myriad of tough decisions. You have dealt with unexpected successes and crushing disappointments. You have had reason both to celebrate and to mourn. You wonder why you weren't given more of your dreams and why you were selected for particular trials. There are many things you would like to take back or do over. There are words that you wish you had never spoken, decisions that you wished you had never made, and reactions that you have lived to regret. You wonder what it would have been like if only you had made a different choice, moved to the other location, or put your trust in another person.

Like the Corinthians, you need a reliable lens through which to look at your life. It is hard to be either objective or accurate in the middle of it all. Your archeological work tends to flow out of two questions that occur to us at some time or another. First, you will ask yourself, *Why did things turn out the way they did?* Second, you will ask, *Was it all worth it*? This is where Paul's paradigm is so helpful for us, because these are precisely the questions that he is answering.

Here's what Paul says to us: "You can't really understand midlife unless you first eavesdrop on eternity." You can't stand in the middle of your story and try to make sense of it any more than you can be reading the middle of a novel and have everything make sense to you. The big problem with the midlife assessments is that we are trying to make them in *middle* of our life. You and I just don't have a wide enough perspective. That is exactly why God invited us to look into eternity and then to look back.

Paul says it very powerfully in 1 Corinthians 15:13–19.

> *If there is no resurrection of the dead, then not even Christ has been raised. And if Christ has not been raised, our preaching is useless and so is your faith. More than that, we are then found to be false witnesses about God, for we have testified about God that he raised Christ from the dead. But he did not raise him if in fact the dead are not raised. For if the dead are not raised, then Christ has not been raised either. And if Christ has not been raised, your faith is futile; you are still in your sins. Then those also who have fallen asleep in Christ are lost. If only for this life we have hope in Christ, we are to be pitied more than all men.*

Paul is arguing that there has to be more to life than this moment. If this is all that there is, and if all of the faith that we have placed in Christ only purchases a better life for us in the here and now, then we are people to be pitied. Paul's argument is powerful. The only way you can make sense out of life is to look at it from the vantage point of eternity. Eternity defines, motivates, and clarifies the life that God has called us to.

Those of us who are lost in the middle of our own stories need more than a lecture on how we should be thankful. We need more than an exhortation to get up once more and follow the Lord by faith. We need more than practical insight on the typical things that people struggle with during the midlife years. We need more than compassion and encouragement. What we need is the big picture. We need to be able to see the issues of midlife in the context of the sure-to-come realities of eternity.

We get blinded by our successes and failures. We get distracted by the drama of the moment. Our ability to think clearly gets clouded by powerful emotions and powerful desires. We become proud or paralyzed by our own legacy. And even if all of these things were not true, our vision would be unreliable for the simple fact that we are finite human beings and, therefore, only capable of seeing one slice of life at a time. Eternity, however, gives us the wide-angle view. It allows us to eavesdrop on the conversations and confessions of those who have passed over to the other side. Eternity really does have the power to dispel our confusion and clarify our values.

Values Clarification

Rodney felt like he had worked hard all his life, but he didn't have much to show for it. Now, in midlife, he was tired of being poor. He hadn't been given much of a start as a child. Being the oldest child in the family, he was thrust into the workplace a couple of months after his dad left. He was only fourteen years old, and he grew up fast. Because he was the primary breadwinner, he was wasn't able to pay much attention to school and never graduated. It was not long before Rodney was married, and the opportunities for him to go back to school seemed to be a thing of his distant past.

Rodney knew the Lord and loved him. He dedicated himself to be a good father to his four children and a godly husband to his wife. But Rodney was poor. He worked long hours as a laborer for a major manufacturing firm and took all the overtime he was offered, but there never seemed to be enough money. Rodney's home was a happy place with lots of love. Family worship punctuated every supper, and Sunday was a day reserved for worship of the Lord. But Rodney was poor. As the children got older, it was quite clear that their house was too tiny to meet their needs. The family never took a real vacation and never enjoyed a lavish Christmas. Rodney wasn't a leader in his church, and he never got the respect that his life of faithful obedience would seem to merit.

Yet Rodney got up every morning and faithfully went to work. He didn't complain his way through his day, and he taught his children to be thankful for everything they had. Although Rodney couldn't teach very well, he determined he would serve the Lord the best way he could—with his hands. He was always fixing something for an elderly person or for missionaries on furlough. But Rodney was poor. He never went on a men's retreat because he couldn't afford to give up the Saturday overtime, and he never went on a short-term missions trip because he didn't have the time to raise the money needed and he certainly couldn't pay for it out of his pocket.

Rodney was humble, loving, and always willing to serve. But at forty-nine, he felt like a failure. He looked around at others his age in his church. He noticed the big houses and the nice cars. He heard the stories of the empty-nester couples who had spent their winter vacation in Hawaii. He and his wife had never even taken a weekend away together. He saw the men who had worked their way up the corporate ladder and was embarrassed that he still worked as a laborer. He hated the fact that there was always dark grease embedded in the lines of his hands and under his fingernails, no matter how vigorously he scrubbed them. Rodney hated church suppers when people would share what was going on in their lives. He hated being asked about investments or vacations because he had neither.

The older Rodney got, the more discouraged he became. They still lived in their little rabbit warren of a house. He still worked in the same job. They still did not have enough money to pay their bills. He hated his house. He hated his job. He hated his cheap clothes. He hated the fact that Shirley, his wife, looked older than she should because of all of her hard labor. He hated driving a car that was unattractive and unreliable. And beneath all of this angst was an even more depressing reality: there was nothing he could do about it. He felt trapped in the middle of a story that he didn't choose.

It became harder and harder for Rodney to get up in the morning. It became harder for him to sing with joy about God's goodness and love. His home was no longer a place of retreat but a physical monument to how unsuccessful his life had become. Shirley felt the weight of it as well. She was aware that Rodney could not provide very well for her, and she tried her best to make do. But she was always asking Rodney for something he could not afford, and with every request he seemed to get more and more depressed.

Now, in the middle of his life, Rodney had just about completely lost his way. He hadn't left Shirley or forsaken the Lord, but if he continued on this downward spiral, he would be strongly tempted to do both.

How would you help Rodney find his way? If you could take him to God's Word, where would you start? How would you bring him comfort and give him guidance?

Robert looked out of his window at the ornamental fruit trees that the landscapers had planted a year ago. Each one was unique and beautiful. It was the final touch of beauty to the three acres where he and Rose had built their dream house. He thought back on that first house they had purchased in the city. It was a tiny little twin with no real front or back yard, but Robert didn't mind because he was never home. On the road all the time, Robert was determined to make it one way or another. Rose was quiet about his constant travel, but she seemed supportive.

The kids grew up with all of the material things they could ever want. They lived in the tiny house for just three years before they made their first move up. The second house was followed by two more, each bigger and better than the other. It wasn't long before Robert was the CEO of his company. His family used to joke that he didn't live there anymore, that his home and office were at the same address.

From a distance they looked like a great Christian family. They were very involved with a good church, and Robert went with them whenever he was home. As the three kids grew up, so many youthful milestones came and went. Rose was always there and had gotten quite skilled at making excuses for Robert. He was a good man. In many ways he did have a very strong faith. He did seem to love his family. He was a wonderful provider. He was an outspoken proponent of corporate morality and was never hesitant to share his faith. He gave liberally to his church and to several key ministries. He was theologically knowledgeable and biblically literate, but he was never home. Everybody who met Robert loved him, and he was constantly held up as the quintessential Christian businessman.

As Robert looked out the window at his little trees, he thought of the kids. It had been some time since he had heard from any of them. They came for Christmas and would call occasionally, but conversations with them were strangely distant. Ever since the kids left home, Rose seemed far away, too. Robert stood examining the fruit of his success, but there was a twinge of doubt inside of him. On one hand he was convinced that he had made the right choices. *Look at the life I've given my children*, he would tell himself. Look how much he was able to support ministries that wouldn't have made it otherwise. Look at the colleges his kids had gone to. He had made the right choice, and someday all of them would recognize it.

But when Robert looked in the mirror, he didn't see the young buck he used to see. For all his self-congratulation, he was nagged by questions that wouldn't leave him alone. Had he really made the right choices all along? He wished his kids would call and visit more. He wished that he and Rose had the wonderful friendship that they once enjoyed.

What would you say to Robert? He's not as discouraged as Rodney, but there are doubts in his heart. Where would you go in God's Word to help Robert find his way? How would you help Robert evaluate his success? What would you suggest that Robert do?

As you scan the stories of these two men, you are hit with the fact that life is fundamentally shaped by the values you carry around with you. Everything you do is an expression of those values. We are purpose-oriented, value-driven beings. Whether or not you have deliberately thought about your values, everything you do in life is somehow your attempt to get what is important to you. The word the Bible uses to capture this concept is *treasure*. It is a wonderful word.

A treasure is something that does not necessarily have intrinsic value. Most often, the value of a treasure is assigned value. That is why one man's trash is another man's treasure. If something is a treasure to you, you will live to gain it, keep it, maintain it, and enjoy it. Your treasure will begin to capture your heart, and whatever captures your heart will control your behavior (See Matthew 6:19ff). Because of these biblical treasure principles, the personal archeology of midlife is a dig for buried treasure. You are looking back at the things you assigned value to and assessing what kind of return you got on your investment. It is often the case that what seemed valuable in your younger adult years isn't a treasure to you anymore.

Whether your treasure was career success, the love and respect of your friends, your appearance, the continual upgrading of your possessions, or some dream of an idyllic future, the crucible of midlife eventually reveals its real value. Your treasures were fool's gold, not really worth anything in the end.

Midlife is all about the values that grip your heart, organize your life, and control your behavior. This is where eternity can help us. As Paul would tell us, eternity is the best values-clarification tool you could ever want, and the value assessments you make during midlife will determine both what you do about the past and what you will do in the future.

Eavesdropping on Eternity

The book of Revelation opens the doors of eternity and invites us to stop, look, and listen while allowing you to sit in the corner of glory and watch angelic celebrations, pronouncements from the throne of God, and the cascading carols of the saints. Their words give hope, encouragement, and guidance to those of us who find ourselves right in the middle of the story. It's almost like there is a sign on the door to eternity that says, "Do you want to know what's really important? Eavesdrop on eternity. Do you want to evaluate the life investments that you have made? Eavesdrop on eternity. Do you want to construct a life that really fits with what God is doing? Eavesdrop on eternity." Eternity is the compass that orients every aspect of a Christian's lifestyle, so it is absolutely essential for understanding the struggles of midlife.

There is a magnificent scene Revelation 5 that puts all of life in its proper perspective. It is one of the most amazing scenes of unbridled and unfettered worship anywhere in Scripture.

> *Then I saw a Lamb, looking as if it had been slain, standing in the center of the throne, encircled by the four living creatures and the elders. He had seven horns and seven eyes, which are the seven spirits of God sent out into all the earth. He came and took the scroll from the right hand of him who sat on the throne. And when he had taken it, the four living creatures and the twenty-four elders fell down before the Lamb. Each one had a harp and they were holding golden bowls full of incense, which are the prayers of the saints. And they sang a new song:*
>
> *"You are worthy to take the scroll*
> *and to open its seals,*
> *because you were slain,*
> *and with your blood you purchased men for God*
> *from every tribe and language and people and nation.*
> *You have made them to be a kingdom and priests to serve our God,*
> *and they will reign on the earth."*
> *Then I looked and heard the voice of many angels, numbering thousands upon thousands, and ten thousand times ten thousand. They encircled the throne and the living creatures and the elders. In a loud voice they sang:*
> *"Worthy is the Lamb, who was slain,*
> *to receive power and wealth and wisdom and strength and honor and glory and praise!"*

Then I heard every creature in heaven and on earth and under the earth and on the sea, and all that is in them, singing:
"To him who sits on the throne and to the Lamb
be praise and honor and glory and power, for ever and ever!"
The four living creatures said, "Amen," and the elders fell down and worshiped (Revelation 5:6–14).

In this scene, someone asks who will open the great scroll. The scroll is God's plan for the ages. John weeps because there seems to be no one worthy to open the scroll. Then one of the elders says, "Don't weep; the Lion of Judah is able to open the scroll." At this point, the Lamb, still looking as if he had been slain, stands up, walks to the throne, and takes the scroll from the hand of God.

Now understand the scene. The three members of the Trinity are at the throne, and the Lamb, the Lion of Judah, is holding God's plan for the ages. It is the plan that foreordained everything that has ever happened from before the foundation of the earth into the reaches of eternity. He holds the Great Story that contains the stories of everyone who ever lived, and in the center of that Great Story is the story of the Redeemed. It is a moment of intense symbolism. We see the triune Lord of the Ages, the God who has won the victory. We see the Spirit who gave birth to everyone who ever believed, the one who illumined their faith and empowered their obedience. We see the Lamb, still carrying around the scars of his willing sacrifice for the salvation of his children. And this Lamb holds the plot of the ages in his hand. God has won! His purposes have prevailed! He has accomplished what he has promised. The Trinity, the Author and Finisher of the plan, now holds it before his creatures in glory and triumph.

At the sight of this magnificent scene, the four creatures and the twenty-four elders bow down before the throne, with harps and golden bowls in their hands, and begin to praise the Lord. The bowls are the collected prayers of all the saints who have ever prayed. The content of their praise should get our attention and begin to clarify our values. They don't sing, "You are worthy to open the scroll, because you always gave your children everything they ever asked for. You gave them nice houses and good jobs; you gave them good children and great vacations; you gave them career success and material ease; you gave them the appreciation of peers and predictability of schedule; you gave them physical strength and freedom from disease." Now, to the degree that God has given us any of these things, it is right to praise him. But in this majestic moment, when the twenty-four beings around the throne are holding the prayers of the saints and looking back, those are not the things that flood their minds.

The overwhelming theme of their song of praise to the Lamb is this: "You are worthy to open the scroll because you *did it*. You shed your precious blood so that you could purchase the redemption of people from every tribe, language, and nation. And you made them a kingdom of priests, to reign with you forever. You won! You defeated sin! You gave them freedom from the one thing they could never escape! You broke the power and dominion of darkness! Before the foundations of creation were laid down, you devised a plan, and you executed every detail of it. You harnessed nature and exercised authority over every single thing in human history with one goal in mind, the salvation of your people. You did it! You saved each one of your children from sin!"

From the perspective of the completed story, this overwhelming fact dominates their praise: the success of redemption. In eternity, many of the things that seem to matter so much don't matter anymore. The size and luxury of your house doesn't matter anymore. Your physical strength or beauty doesn't matter anymore. Family vacations, cars, clothes, and bank accounts *do not matter* anymore.

Redemption is what matters. God has entered this horribly sin-broken world to redeem lost, rebellious, and self-absorbed people from their slavery to everything else but him. And he has welcomed them into citizenship in his kingdom of glory forever and ever. *This* is what matters! If you are one of God's children, *this* is what he has been working on all along. It is the project that God has always been unwilling to leave incomplete. It is the one thing for which this fallen world has groaned for century after century.

As the twenty-eight beings begin to sing their newly composed song of redemption, the angels join in a crescendo of praise that rises like one the universe has never heard before. The angels arise and begin circling the throne with the four creatures and the twenty-four elders. John records the number as ten thousand times ten thousand. One hundred million and twenty-eight beings are now circling God's throne and singing new songs of praise for the Lamb and his salvation. But the crescendo is still building. As the hundred million angels begin to sing, they awaken every creature on earth, under the earth, and in the sea, and they, too, join this thunder of celebration for the Lamb. Now the heavens are rattling with the loudest hymn of redemption that has ever been sung.

It's all clear now. The beings of heaven understand what God has been working on all along. They see the miraculous glory of what he has done. He has defeated every dark thing that ever was thought, said, or done. He has conquered every enemy of what was good, right, and true. He has exposed every lie, pretense, deceit, and heresy. He has done battle with the evil forces of darkness, and he has won. He has softened the hearts of rebels. He has drawn praise from the proud. He caused the disobedient to serve him. He has taken evil captive and given freedom to his children. He is the victorious Lamb. He has won!

Human language is not elastic enough to stretch around the glory of this scene. It is, however, still a very practical scene. God decided to invite us into the halls of eternity because we need this perspective as we face the difficulties and disappointments of living in the here and now. It is so hard for us to keep things in perspective. We get so confused about what is really important. We set our hearts on things that we are convinced we cannot live without, and when they are taken out of our hands, we panic. We tend to love what is temporary and forget what is eternal. With tight fists, we hold on to physical things that by their very nature are passing away. We build what will not last and invest in what will soon decay, while we regretfully forget the things that will never, ever, pass away.

As you examine the return on your life investments, it is tempting to conclude that you have been an unmitigated failure, and God has been shockingly unfaithful. As you do your midlife archeological work, sifting through the sands of your own decisions and uncovering the pottery shards that are left, it is tempting to wonder if it has all been worth it. It is in these moments that you most need the value-clarifying perspectives of Revelation 5.

Listen to the elders and angels in eternity. Listen to the creatures of the earth. They would say it has all been worth it, because the one war that was absolutely vital to win has been won on your behalf. As you were working, praying, hoping, deciding, planning, and doing, God was carefully accomplishing his plan. No act of faith was ever in vain. No choice for what was right was ever useless. Yes, many of your dreams evaporated before they came to be. Many of the people you thought you could trust failed you in the end. With all of your work to fight aging, your body and your beauty continue to age. There are many mysteries still hidden and many things for which to mourn. But, from the perspective of eternity, this one thing is true: God is awesome in his wisdom, power, and grace. He will do every last thing he has promised. There will be a day when you are not just eavesdropping, but singing in the chorus with every angel and saint and beast, "He won! He won! He won!"

This scene of hope speaks within your moment of midlife lostness. For all of its otherworldly glory, it is intensely practical. It speaks with power and clarity concerning midlife struggles about what to hope in. Stop for a moment and scan your midlife disappointments, regrets, and fears. Ask yourself what you have been hoping in. What is really worth celebrating? What is really worth mourning? Force yourself to use the values of eternity as your measuring tool for the here and now. Let eternity argue with the values of the surrounding culture, which says life is all about youth, appearance, success, material ease, power, and control. Resist an eternity-less evaluation that makes the physical, situational, and relational successes of the present moment more important than they actually are.

If you listen to eternity, you can stand in the middle of midlife regret and celebrate. Yes, you did many things that you should not have done. And, yes, you failed to do many good things that you should have done. But in the midst of it all God was still working. He was freeing you all along from the one dark, horrible thing that was your biggest problem all along: your sin. He was delivering something to you that was far better than anything you could have ever conceived for yourself: a place in his eternal kingdom. All of our most crushing disappointments are but blips on the map when viewed from the perspective of the never-ending glory of eternity. With the loud songs of eternity in your ears, stand in the middle of your loss of youth and your fears of aging and celebrate. You have been given a seat in the place where you will live forever, where there will be no weakness or wrinkles, and where you will never again suffer at the hands of a disease. You cannot accurately evaluate midlife unless you read the last chapter first.

But there is more.

From Tears to Eternity

You not only need the values clarification of Revelation 5, but also of Revelation 7 as well. Although the scene is similar to Chapter 5, it adds elements that are crucial for answering the typical questions we ask in the lostness of our midlife archeology. Let's eavesdrop on this scene as well.

> *After this I looked and there before me was a great multitude that no one could count, from every nation, tribe, people and language, standing before the throne and in front of the Lamb. They were wearing white robes and were holding palm branches in their hands. And they cried out in a loud voice:*
>
> *"Salvation belongs to our God,*
> *who sits on the throne,*
> *and to the Lamb."*
>
> *All the angels were standing around the throne and around the elders and the four living creatures. They fell down on their faces before the throne and worshiped God, saying:*
>
> *"Amen!"*
> *Praise and glory*
> *and wisdom and thanks and honor*
> *and power and strength*
> *be to our God for ever and ever.*
> *Amen!"*
>
> *Then one of the elders asked me,*
>
> *"These in white robes—who are they, and where did they come from?"*
> *I answered, "Sir, you know."*
>
> *And he said, "These are they who have come out of the great tribulation; they have washed their robes and made them white in the blood of the Lamb. Therefore,*
>
> *"they are before the throne of God*
> *and serve him day and night in his temple;*
> *and he who sits on the throne will spread his tent over them.*
> *Never again will they hunger;*
> *never again will they thirst.*
> *The sun will not beat upon them,*
> *nor any scorching heat.*

For the Lamb at the center of the throne will be their shepherd;
he will lead them to springs of living water.
And God will wipe away every tear from their eyes."
(Revelation 7:9-17)

The scene also takes place at the throne, but this time it focuses on the children of God who have ended their journey and have finally arrived at home. Revelation puts us in a time capsule and rockets us forward. It is a scene not to be missed because it further clarifies the values we need on hand in midlife. The book of Revelation was given to you by God not so that you could figure out the exact moment of his return, but so that you could properly understand the here and now.

This time the worship before the throne is led by the multitude of the redeemed, who are so populous that they defy numbering. In the multitude are people of every nation, tribe, people, and language. They are dressed in white robes that represent their cleansing from sin, and each one is holding a palm branch in his hand. (Remember Christ's triumphant entry into Jerusalem?) In unison, the crowd is chanting praise. Again, it is a chant of salvation. This is the only thing they are interested in celebrating. "Salvation belongs to God and to the Lamb!" Here is the final celebration of people, who are now at the journey's end and who are now looking back. God was faithful to every one of his promises. He defeated sin. He destroyed the enemy. He made the sacrifice that atoned for sin. He continued his work in his peoples' hearts until that work was completed. "We are redeemed!" is the shout of his people on the other side.

At this point one of the elders asks who these people in white robes are. They are identified as those who have come out of the "great tribulation." Now, because some people have viewed these passages as a map for the future rather than a lens on the present, it is easy to misunderstand what is being said. What is this great tribulation? Is it some defined period of time connected to the second coming of Christ? The context makes it clear that this is not what John is describing. What is the great tribulation experienced by every person who has ever believed, no matter when and where they've lived? The answer is exactly what Paul talks about when he says, "The creation waits in eager expectation for the sons of God to be revealed" (Romans 8:19). It is here that this amazing scene speaks directly to your midlife struggle.

The fact of the matter is that even though you have been redeemed by Christ's blood, even though the Holy Spirit lives inside of you, and even though God's grace works in your life every day, you still live in a fallen world. When you and I come to Christ we aren't immediately transported into eternity. No, God keeps us right where we have been living, in order to deal with the effects of the fall by living in us.

This fallen world is a place of great tribulation. It is inescapable, even for those of us who have been redeemed. Everything in life is more complicated, more difficult, and more dangerous because the world we live in is still waiting for redemption. You cannot live in this broken world and escape the tribulation.

So this is what the tribulation is. It is the period when God's redeemed people trudge their way through the trials of life in a fallen world until they finally make it to the other side. No matter how hard your life is right now, there is another side. There will be a day when all that you find so personally painful will be fully and completely finished. God is going to do two things that become an incredibly sweet ending to his redemptive work on your behalf.

First, he is going to spread his tent over you. In other words, he is finally going to welcome you out of the heat of temptation, disease, conflict, disloyalty, aging, physical weakness, and a host of other human experiences that beat upon our souls. What is the "heat" that burns on you right now? Is it the heat of dreams that have evaporated like shallow puddles in the summer sun? Is it fear of the future and the prospects of retirement and aging? Is it the heat of temptations that dog you wherever you go and that seem to rob you of any hope of present contentment? Be comforted; you will be welcomed out of the heat into the cool shade of the Lord's tent, never to step into the harsh sun again!

There is a second sweet thing that your Lord is going to do. It's so hard to wrap human words around this sweetness that there is nothing like it anywhere else in God's Word. Remember the scene. The innumerable crowd of suffering saints (all of us), walk broken and weary into eternity. Their suffering follows the crowd right to eternity's door. They walk into glory tired, hungry, and thirsty because the heat has beaten on them with every step.

At this moment, an amazing thing happens. God rises from his throne and he begins to make his way through the crowd, personally drying every one of their tears! Let your mind imagine the scene. Person by person, the God who has finally won the last battle, lifts his hand to the eyes of his weary and weeping children and dries their tears. You can almost hear him saying, "You needn't cry anymore. It is over. I have won. You are finally free. There will be no more heat. Never again will you be hungry or thirsty. You will have no cause to cry ever again." The final act of redemption is this final act of comfort and victory. Because the battle has been won, this uncountable company will live in an inconceivable paradise with their Lord. Remember, you are part of that host. And when you are there and when you look back, the seemingly unbearable tribulations of this moment will seem trivial at best.

Like Revelation 5, this scene is given to clarify our values and strengthen our hope. Let this scene speak into your heart. What do you really want from God right now? Is your lostness so profound or your pain so deep that you would give up all the wonders of eternity for present comfort and personal ease? It is so tempting to let the pain of the moment totally dominate your thinking and your desires. It has been said that you can get a truly hungry person to do just about anything if you offer them food. Could it be that you are so focused on escaping the struggle of the moment that you have made yourself unnecessarily susceptible to temptation's offer of escape?

There are many well-known midlife escapes, most of which only aggravate the trouble you were trying to escape. We spend far too much on remodeling the house, or we buy a new motorcycle, boat, sports car, or SUV. We buy clothes that are much too expensive and far too youthful. Or we go to expensive restaurants and take lavish vacations. Although we may not know it, we aren't really attracted to these things. No, they hook us because we think they can provide escape from our struggles.

Others try to find escape in people. We are tempted to think that the people around us can be our personal messiahs and save us from the struggles that trouble our hearts. But people don't make reliable saviors, and we can easily slide from being ruled by another's acceptance to unfaithfulness and adultery. Or maybe we look to position and power as our means of escape. We become achievement junkies, more enslaved than we have ever been to the advancement of our careers.

Here is the point: These escapes ultimately make midlife more difficult, and we get ourselves incredibly lost. Revelation 7 addresses this pain-escape dynamic. It asks each of us to look inside and to ask what we are really living for. Is a pain-free existence really *the* thing you want from God? The white-robed crowd was unwilling to cut and run, taking the first road that appeared to offer escape. Because they lived with one eye on eternity, they kept marching forward, no matter what was going on inside and outside of them.

Do you live with both eyes on the present, all too aware of how much better this moment could be and too frequently wondering why God doesn't provide you with some relief? Or, are you magnetized by eternity? Can you see it in the distance and so keep marching forward? Yes, you still feel the pain that leaves you tired and discouraged, but you really believe that everything you are going through now will seem insignificant on the other side. What shapes your response to your midlife struggles—your dreams of what it could be like *now,* or God's promises of what it will be like *then*?

This passage offers both bad news and good news. The bad news is that we will all weep our way into eternity. For now, your Lord has left you in this fallen world, and you will feel its heat. The good news is that you have been guaranteed a day when all of this will end. What you will experience in eternity will far outweigh the pain you went through in the present.

Think of how important this is. If you get deceived into putting all the eggs of your happiness and hope in today's basket, today's suffering will hit you like a basket of bricks. If your joy is fundamentally attached to a lack of difficulty in the here and now, you are going to struggle all the more when difficulty comes your way. In that struggle, you will be all the more tempted to run after false escapes. If you understand, however, that this part of the journey is hard, then you are neither shocked nor surprised when the scorching heat comes your way, and you will not be tempted by false ways of escape. Your only hope is to keep marching forward.

You have been given a place in the most amazing celebration in the universe, as every creature on earth sings to the glory of the One who provided your forgiveness and eternal freedom. But, between his calling you to himself and welcoming you into eternity, the way will be hard. When the scorching heat hits you, do not feel forgotten or forsaken; it is to remind you that your journey is not over. Remember that those supposed paths of escape will never provide it; they only make your journey more painful. And remember, the God who will wipe that last tear from your eye is with you every step of your journey, offering the comfort, wisdom, and strength that only he can give.

God's story is an eternity story, and in Revelation he has invited you to take a peek at the last chapter. It is tempting to forget that there is an eternity or to think that it doesn't make any difference in the present. Paul says just the opposite to the Corinthians; that if you only have Christ in this life, you are a person to be pitied. Eternity is the only thing that can give you a reason to continue.

No matter what is on your plate right now, if you are God's child, there is one sure thing to cling to: you have a bright future. It is brighter than anything you could grab hold of today. It is brighter than anything you can wrap your brain around. God is going to wipe away your final tear, and you won't have to journey anymore. The only real reason to stay on the pathway is that someday it will end, and in the cool shadows of the Lord's tent you will rest forever. If all that you are facing *now* didn't have a *then*, then nothing you do, no matter how successful or comfortable, would be worth anything anyway. God lets you look into *then*, so that as you face the trials of *now* you will have hope that is stronger than your disappointment, encouragement that overwhelms your regret, and a dream to motivate you that is better than any dream you could have conjured up for yourself.

Chapter 12

Grace That is Greater

In life as in the dance: Grace glides on blistered feet.

—Alice Abrams

Heaven have mercy on us all—Presbyterian and Pagans alike—for we are all somehow dreadfully cracked about the head, and sadly in need of mending.

—Herman Melville

Midlife is about real people, that is why I have introduced you to Bill, Don, Serena, Todd, Kristi, Joanna, Rodney and the rest. Real people, caught in the middle of their own midlife drama. Each person's story is unique and different. Each person is struggling in his or her own way. Every one of them is shocked by the details of their own story. All are overwhelmed by their own struggle, but each needs the big picture in order to make sense of it all. None of them knows for sure what to do next and some of them are already doing things that add more trouble to the trouble that they are already finding difficult. None of them expected to be lost in the middle. None of them thought it would be this way. They have so much in common, but not everything in common.

Midlife crisis is not at all about stereotypical experiences and reactions. No, all of the people that we have looked at found themselves lost in the middle of the details of their own very unique story. No two stories are the same and no two people have responded in exactly the same way. This is what is so helpful about looking at people's midlife stories from the viewpoint of the one story that can make sense of it all, the grand redemption story of Scripture. The biblical story is huge enough, in its origin-to-destiny scope, to make sense literally of the life of every person who has ever lived. You can't squeeze the midlife struggle into a few functional categories, and whatever themes there are must be handled in a way that doesn't ignore the uniqueness of each person's story. The best way to capture what we need to do as we examine human experiences, like the midlife struggle, is summarized by the steps below.

1. ***We need to stop, look, and listen and examine the themes.*** Now the word *theme* is very important here. When we examine human experiences, looking for struggles and reactions that come up again and again, we are not establishing scientific categories, rather we are endeavoring to be wise. The purpose of the themes is not to come up with categories that we then try to squeeze people into, but to have terms available to us that help us get more quickly on board with what people are going through. Yes, midlife tends to be a time when people experience dissatisfaction with life, but Freddy's struggle with dissatisfaction is very different than Serena's. Midlife is often a time when people feel disoriented in the middle of their own stories. Sally felt this way but not at all like John did. Midlife is a time when people grapple with powerful and often unexpected discouragement. John was surely discouraged, but his experience didn't look at all like Benny's. Many people carry a load of dread with them through the midlife years, like an anchor on the heart. Sally's experience was like that, but not in a way that duplicated anyone else's. Peter was a disappointed man but in a way that was qualitatively different from Tim. A lack of interest in life often results from the midlife struggle, but the way that it hit Jim was unique. Most people who are in the throes of the midlife struggle want to distance themselves from their pain and lostness, but Todd and Mary looked to distance themselves in very different ways. John was looking for distraction but not in the same way as Alex.

The themes that you will observe as you examine this period of life are not absolute categories but one tool to use in seeking to get on board with your own experience and that of others. In this book, we have attempted to do that with the midlife struggle.

2. ***We must examine the themes from the vantage point of Scripture.*** One of the main functions of the Word of God is that it exegetes life for us. We are meaning makers. We never leave our lives alone. We are always turning our story over and over in our hands, seeking to understand what we are going through and why we are responding to it in the way that we are. It is as impossible, however, to stand in the middle of your story and make sense of all of its details as it is to read your way into the middle of a novel and know exactly the plot's resolution. So, in the Bible, God has given us one huge, overarching story that can make sense out of our stories. This story not only answers the foundational questions of the human existence, it also gives us an agenda for facing what is on our plate. When the biblical narrative becomes your lens for examining life, things begin to make sense that never made sense for you before, even things about which the Bible seems to say nothing.

In this book we have observed that the biblical story gives us many very helpful windows from which to examine the midlife struggle. The windows of suffering, control, worship, identity, values, and eternity all provide practical insight into the midlife struggles that not only help us to understand why we struggle as we do but also what to do when those struggles come our way.

3. ***We need to own the struggles of heart that the Lord, in his love, reveals.*** It is humbling to admit, but true for each of us, midlife struggles are heart struggles. People don't just lose their way because their dreams die, or they are beginning to show the signs of aging, or they look back and find things that they regret. No, we get lost in the middle of our own stories because of the way our hearts interact with the typical problems that all of us will tend to face during the midlife years. Our struggles are not caused by situations, locations, and relationships. No, those are the locations where the midlife struggle exists, but it is fundamentally a struggle of the heart. What does this mean? Well, first it means that midlife struggles are often rooted in wrong ways of thinking. Perhaps you thought that if you carefully obeyed God's law, that God would endorse your dream. Or maybe you thought that because you are God's child that you would somehow escape the trials of life in this fallen world. Or maybe you thought that God had promised you things that he had never promised or that you had a right to things that were not your God-given right. So much of midlife struggle is rooted in our susceptibility to believe the plausible and seductive lies of the enemy. Adam and Eve did exactly that, and all of us have been paying the price ever since.

During the midlife years, your heart doesn't radically change. You've carried the thoughts of your heart into the midlife struggle. Those thoughts shaped the way that you have responded to the typical dynamics and experiences of this period of your life. What midlife often does that can be personally and extremely helpful is to reveal patterns of false and unbiblical thinking that have been with you for years. The previous chapters can greatly aid you as you seek to correct and hone your thinking.

Midlife struggles are also rooted in the motives, desires, and purposes of the heart. As the Bible makes so blatantly clear, all of us are living for something all the time. The midlife struggle is not about the fact that I have had to deal with difficult and disappointing things, but that these difficult things have stood directly in the way of what I have set my heart on. It's not just that you are getting older, but that age is robbing you of the identity and security that you have been getting out of your experience. It is not just that you have been sidelined in your career, but that this experience has taken the power for which you were living out of your hands. It's not just that you look back and regret the things you did or failed to do, but that honest regret has robbed you of your visions of personal success that gave you a reason to get up in the morning. **Here is the point:** We struggle in midlife not because of aging, disappointment, and regret, but because these experiences rob us of the things for which we have been living.

I am more and more persuaded than I have ever been before, that with all the harsh realities of life in this horribly broken world, the struggle of midlife is fundamentally rooted in the idolatries of the heart. We tend to lose our way during this period of life because the things that have functioned as our god-replacements, that is, those functional pseudo-messiahs that seemed to be life giving, but never are, either fail us or are taken away. And because they are, if feels like we have been robbed of life itself. These idols are so powerfully seductive that there is a way in which they trap us all. We all are seduced by power, success, acceptance, appreciation, possessions, position, respect, performance, control, comfort, or personal happiness in some way. Our decisions and reactions during midlife are not controlled by the situational, relational, or physical struggles that come our way, but by the heart that we bring to these things. To the degree that our hearts are more controlled by worship and service of the creation than of the Creator, to that degree the midlife years will be tumultuous and difficult. There is one thing that you can be sure of; midlife will rob you of your idols, and when it does you are either in great danger or on the edge of one of life's biggest opportunities. Where is God calling you to new patterns of thinking? Where is he calling you away from the service of things that have functionally replaced him?

4. ***We need to own the bad fruit that exists in our lives.*** This tendency is found in all of us, and it keeps us from gaining ground. With more creativity and perseverance than any of us would like to admit, we all tend to deny our own harvest. In moments of subtle, yet shocking, self-righteousness, we are all able to convince ourselves that the bitter harvest in our lives in reality belongs to someone else. The parents point to the children, convinced that the harvest of familial distance belongs to them. The husband is convinced that the harvest of relational coldness belongs to his wife, while his wife is convinced that the intimacy lacking in their marriage is the fault of her husband. The boss attributes the harvest of a negative work environment to seeds planted by his employees, while they are convinced that the seeds belong to him. It is a universally human thing to do. It is one of the ways sinners deal with life. We convince ourselves that the weeds we are forced to live with did not come from the seeds of word, thought, motive, and action that we daily planted.

Because midlife is the time when your life's crops begin to come in, it is also a time when living with a harvest mentality is essential. What can you learn about the seeds you have planted over the years, from the fruit that you are now harvesting? One of the essential ingredients of lasting change of heart and behavior is the willingness to own your own harvest. People who do this grow and change, while people who don't tend to get trapped in the cul-de-sac of their own denial.

5. ***We need to ask the Lord where he is calling us to a harvest of new fruit.*** The good news is that you can change your harvest. My mother was an excellent gardener. Whenever we would move, we would examine what the yard produced, and then she would give herself to the production of a whole new harvest. The plain and weedy yard became a place that was rich with the color, shape, and texture of new blossoms. Yes, you are in midlife, but you can have the beautiful colors of the blossoms of new life as your daily harvest. You are not trapped by your past or imprisoned in the present. The biblical promise of

a new heart brings with it the promise of a new harvest in your life. Relationships that were once broken can live again with new color and texture. The dreams that disappointed you can give way to the flowering of God's new and better dreams. The fruit of new purpose can live where the weeds of regret once covered the soil. The thorns of having our identity wrapped up in appearance or achievement can give way to a new rest in a zeal for the Lord. Where is God calling you to whole new harvest of good fruit?

Midlife is not a time to panic and cave in. It is a time to look up, to look within, and to then move out. It is a time where you can come to know God more fully and yourself more clearly. It is a time when you are not glued to the past, but rather welcomed to the future, with more wisdom and personal insight than you have ever had before. But it is also a time when it is very tempting to give way to the paralysis of disappointment and regret and in so doing add to the trouble that is already troubling you.

Bitter Harvest, Beautiful New Fruit

Calvin had always been able to convince himself that it was not he. No matter what bitter harvest grew in the fields of his life or family, Calvin was always able to argue that it came from someone else's seeds. Year after year the harvests kept coming in, and with every new crop, he was able to tell himself that the cause was somewhere outside of him. Calvin was a slow learner. He and his family ate the bitter fruit of financial and familial difficulty again and again. There seemed to be no stopping it. Yet with all the tumult and chaos, Calvin was sturdily self-righteous. He was always willing to point the finger, and he always knew at whom to point it. Even though Calvin didn't like the trouble that seemed constantly to assault his life, he went to bed each night comforting himself that he was not at fault. And with each new harvest, Calvin became more and more convinced that the seeds did not belong to him.

However, God loved Calvin too much to let him continue to live in his planter's denial. Even though he had no idea that he was doing it, Calvin always lived as a man in pursuit of a dream. He had the picture down pat. From about twenty-five on Calvin carried the vision with him. He had a clear picture of the corner office with floor-to-ceiling windows and that huge executive desk that announces to you that you are in the office of the CEO. In his mind he had designed and redesigned his country mansion, with the rose garden and the natural stone pool. He dreamed of three beautiful children and a wonderful wife, who would also embrace the dream. The vacation home at the shore and the family vacations to the best destinations around the world were all part of the dream.

Calvin wanted to get up every day. He had a reason for living and for dealing with all the problems that come when one is trying to make something of himself. He would not be deterred. He knew where he was going and how he would get there. He started every day reading his Bible and praying for God's blessing, which for Calvin, was a request for God to endorse his dream. He did meet the woman of his dream, they did have three wonderful children, and Calvin got everything he had dreamed about. But, the pool didn't seem so amazing and the roses didn't seem so beautiful. Calvin couldn't believe it; his dream had come up pretty empty.

In order to fight his way up the corporate ladder, Calvin had to make hard choices. He told his kids that he really did love them and wanted the best for them, but that he was going to have to work long hours. He apologized every time he was about to take a trip that would make him miss one of his children's events. He gave Georgia, his wife, everything a woman could want, except companionship. Georgia said it very well, "Calvin's job is his best friend, and I have had to learn to be okay with that." They finally sold the vacation home, because they found so little time to actually enjoy it. In Calvin's absence, Georgia had forged her own life. She had a very successful natural foods store and the children were located around the country pursuing their adult lives.

Sitting in the huge chair by the fireplace, positioned just as he had envisioned, Calvin was left holding his vacuous dream. It was amazing to him that he had done it all, and yet it meant just about nothing. In the chair he was flooded with disappointment and regret. He wanted to convince himself that everything really was better than it looked. He wanted to find away to distract himself. He wanted to run away. But he didn't give in to either impulse. Calvin called his pastor.

The first morning when they met for breakfast, Calvin was strangely nervous. He was never nervous when he met someone for a meal; as the ultimate schmoozer, Calvin was normally at his best in this kind of situation, but not this morning. He knew why he was so ill at ease. Instead of talking about a product or a business deal, Calvin was there to talk about himself. He hadn't really looked at himself for years. He wondered if he ever had examined his heart. This was a whole new experience, and Calvin found it to be quite intimidating. But he wasn't about to back out. He knew his family was hurting, and he knew he couldn't keep on living this way. He also knew that beneath the accoutrements of wealth was a financial mess that sooner or later would come unglued.

Calvin's pastor was very gracious and kind, skillfully drawing him out and giving him an opportunity to tell his story in detail in a way he never had before. As Calvin laid out his struggle, his pastor helped him begin to own the heart behind it. It was remarkable to Calvin that he had been able to live so blind for so long. As he faced the subtlety of his idolatry, Calvin even began to be thankful that God had let it all turn to dust. "I don't think I would have ever seen how far I actually was from where God wanted me to be, if I hadn't found myself lost in the middle of it all," Calvin said. He faced the fact that the values that had shaped his time, money, and energy investments were all about personal success and material ease. Without ever forsaking the faith, Calvin had lived for himself and had come to pay the price. But Calvin was not dead, nor was anyone in his family. So, Calvin committed himself to a harvest of new fruit. He and Georgia sold the mansion and moved into a wonderful townhouse near one of their daughters. He sold stock, which combined with the house sale, helped him alleviate most of his debt. And he began to do everything he could to restore his relationship with his wife and his children.

It was hard. Calvin swung from powerful regret to the fear that he was doing the wrong thing in walking away from what he had worked on for so long. His children were cold at first; they had seen him make many mini-reformations only to realize that he was trying to rein them in to follow his agenda. It wasn't long, however, before they began to realize that this time was different, that their dad really had changed. Calvin did a lot of tearful confessing and made new commitments to a brand new way of approaching those relationships. At the same time, Calvin began to see that his church needed someone with his business acumen. He began to volunteer to help with the many "business issues" that are so much a part of the growing ministry of a church in these modern times.

One Thursday night Calvin got a call from his pastor; he asked him if he could meet him for breakfast the next morning. Calvin drove to the restaurant with a little bit of trepidation, but it proved not to be necessary. That morning he was asked to consider becoming the full-time business and financial officer for his church. Calvin was a bit dizzy all the rest of that day, but after much thought and prayer with Georgia and the children, he took an offer that a few years before he would have immediately refused.

Georgia and Calvin had to watch their finances in a way that they had not been accustomed to for years, but they had no regrets whatsoever. In his heart, Calvin knew that he had been a man in desperate need of rescue and that that was exactly what God had done for him. It was a painful rescue, but Calvin was now free of things that had held him for many years and was now living with a harvest of new fruit in almost every area of his life.

Recognizing Grace, Responding to Rescue

Could it be, that in the middle of your midlife struggle, you are failing to recognize the most important thing in your life? No, it's not the state of your finances or career. It's not the state of your emotions. No, it's not the condition of your relationship to your spouse or your family. It's not your physical condition or the realities of aging. No, it isn't the dreams that have turned to so much dust in your hands. Could it be that what you are failing to recognize in all of this is *grace*? Could it be that what you are living through, what you are finding so painful, and what you have tried your best to deny and avoid has been sent your way by a loving Heavenly Father as an act of rescue? Could it be that in this moment, when you are tempted to doubt your Lord's faithfulness and love, that he is, in fact, graciously near and lovingly active? Could it be that the losses around you have blinded your eyes to the presence and grace of the Redeemer? Could it be that what feels like being forsaken, is, in reality, the rescuing grace of the One who promised never to leave and never forsake?

The grand story of Scripture is a grace story. Again and again, as God's people lose their way or turn away, God provides the grace of rescue that is needed. Immediately after Adam and Eve's rebellion in the Garden, God announces that he is going to provide a once-and-for-all rescue for fallen humanity. Again and again, as wilderness-journeying Israel responds to God with grumbling rebellion, God provides rescue. David commits adultery and murder, but God provides the grace of rescue. Lot wants his own way, but God provides rescue. Peter denies his Lord, but God provides rescue. It is one of the most dominant themes of the story; where sin abounds, grace abounds even more.

Nowhere is this theme of rescuing grace more obvious than in a largely unknown passage in Amos 4. Amos was a farm boy from Judah who was sent to the big cities of Israel to do a very hard thing—announce God's judgment. You would think that this would mean that God was tired of dealing with the constant rebellion and idolatry of Israel, but when you get to chapter 4, you realize that God is actually after something very different:

"I gave you empty stomachs in every city
and lack of bread in every town,
yet you have not returned to me," declares the Lord.

"I also withheld rain from you
when the harvest was still three months away.
I sent rain on one town,
but withheld it from another.
One field had rain;
another had none and dried up.
People staggered from town to town for water
but did not get enough to drink,
yet you have not returned to me," declares the Lord.

"Many times I struck your gardens and vineyards,
I struck them with blight and mildew.
Locusts devoured your fig and olive trees,
yet you have not returned to me," declares the Lord.

"I sent plagues among you
as I did to Egypt.
I killed your young men with the sword,
Along with your captured horses.
I filled your nostrils with the stench of your camps,
yet you have not returned to me," declares the Lord.

"I overthrew some of you
as I overthrew Sodom and Gomorrah.
You were like a burning stick snatched from the fire,
yet you have not returned to me," declares the Lord.

"Therefore this is what I will do to you, Israel,
and because I will do this to you,
prepare to meet your God, O Israel" (Amos 4:6-12).

These are hard words to read but to be understood require close inspection. What hits you first is God's violence against his own people. It is a sobering thing to read. He sent starvation, drought, failed crops, life-sapping thirst, blighted gardens and vineyards, tree-destroying insects, disease, and death by the sword. At first glance, you would have to wonder how a good and loving God could do such a thing to his people. You want to think that maybe these things just happen to fall on Israel as natural consequences of life in a fallen world, but this is not what the passage says. God clearly says to the Israelites, "All of the hard and painful things that you have been going through, all the things that you would tend to think would never happen to the children of God, and all the things that you would expect that I would do to the unbelieving nations around you, I have sent to you. They have come from my hand." Imagine being in Israel during the ministry of Amos and hearing these words! On the surface, it just doesn't seem like these things could come from the hand of a God who declared that he is a God of faithful covenant-keeping love. This is why this passage begs closer examination.

You see, it is very tempting for you too to stand in the middle of your midlife struggle with all of its discouraging fruit and say to yourself, "This stuff simply could not be from God." Because what you are going through does not seem like grace, it is very tempting to conclude that you have been forgotten or forsaken by the Lord. It is very tempting to conclude that God is not near and that he is not active in your life, and when you do this your struggle becomes all the more powerful.

What is going on in Amos 4? Why would God do such things to his people? What can we learn about the struggles in our own life from this startling passage? It is the refrain that begins to completely change the way this passage feels. Each section of the passage is punctuated by this phrase, "yet you have not returned to me." As you read, it is possible to gloss over the phrase because of the power of what God has done to Israel. Yet this is what everything God has been doing is all about.

Israel had been pursuing their own selfish way. In their affluence and material ease, they had forsaken the One who was the source of it all. They no longer cared about morality or social justice. They were no longer moved by the suffering of others. They would sin their way to the temple, then brag about the offerings they had made. The physical blessings that God had provided, Israel had turned into the very idols that replaced him. God could not be loving and good and let this go on. So God sent hardship to Israel, not as an act of *punishment*, but as the *grace of rescue*. His purpose was not punitive but restorative. These devastating things were acts of love, sent to provide the very rescue that was needed.

And what was God rescuing Israel from? Again, at close inspection that answer is quite clear. God was graciously rescuing Israel from Israel! More than from the surrounding nations, more than from false religions, more than from the general hardships of life in a fallen world, the children of Israel needed to be rescued from themselves. And this is exactly where you and I share identity with them. We are so easily self-absorbed. We so much want our own way and wander away. We so easily turn the blessings that God has given us into the idols that enslave us. We so easily absorb our selfish and sinful way into our Christianity, not even aware of how much we have drifted from where God, in his grace, has called us to be. No longer is our relationship with God the causal center of everything we do. Now it rests on the periphery of our hearts and lives. Yes, we still call ourselves Christians and we still participate in the life of the Christian community, but what was once a matter of the heart, so often gets reduced to an externalism that has nothing to do with the heart at all.

Could it be that in this moment of midlife difficulty the pain and lostness that you are experiencing are actually the work of God, acting to rescue you from the one thing you can't escape on your own—you? Could it be that the things that have caused you to doubt the Lord are in your life as a result of his love? Are the difficult things that you are facing, rather than demonstrating God's unfaithfulness, proof that you are the object of his rescuing grace and restoring love? Don't be too quick to doubt the Lord. Don't be too quick to question his love. Don't be too quick to give in and give up. God is near and he is active, as he always is with his children. He is in the middle of your midlife struggles with painful yet powerful rescuing grace. Even though it feels like the opposite, you are being loved. Even though it feels like you are being rejected, you are being rescued. God has plotted to produce your return, even before you had any idea whatsoever that you had wandered.

The Provision of Grace

What often keeps us from recognizing the grace of God is that we long for a *different kind of grace*. In the middle of difficulty we long for the *grace of relief*, while what God is bestowing us with is the *grace of rescue*. We want the trial to end because we don't like pain, while God wants the trial to remain in our lives until it has completed its work in us. We don't rejoice in suffering like Paul did in Romans 5 because we would rather have a comfortable life than the character that God-sent difficulty can produce. Yet God loves us too much to relent. He didn't shed the blood of his one and only Son to leave us to ourselves. He didn't reveal his truth to us only to have us lost and confused in the middle of our own story. He didn't give us the Holy Spirit to have us paralyzed and unable to deal with the significant struggles that come our way. No, we have been and are being rescued by an activist Redeemer. He does not get discouraged, he does not get tired, and he is never distracted. He is intently focused on finishing what he has started in us. So, if it's the heat of rescue that we need, he will not provide relief until the redemptive heat of difficulty has done its work.

It is very important in the darkness of these midlife struggles to recognize the grace of God. If our definition of that grace is too narrow, and if what we expect that grace to offer is too limited, we will be crying out for grace at the very time it is being showered on us. It is quite possible to be the focus of divine love and rescue and at the same time be interpreting what is happening in our life in a very different way. Perhaps the cross is the quintessential example of this. If you had been there on the day that they tortured and killed the Messiah, you probably would have interpreted it as the ultimate defeat. It would have been extremely difficult to gaze up at Christ hanging on the cross between two thieves and see it as a good moment that would result in good things. They had killed the Promised One, the Hope of Israel. You would see him hanging there, seemingly unable to help himself, and you would think that it was a horrible failure of what is good, true, and beautiful. You would have left the hill of Golgotha with a sick feeling in the pit of your stomach, and you would wake up the next day not really able to believe that you just watched Jesus die. And you would be confused, not knowing what to think or do next.

But we know that the cross was not a defeat. It was, as we said in earlier chapters, the victory of victories. No one captures this fact better than Paul in Colossians 2:13-15:

> *When you were dead in your sins and in the uncircumcision of your sinful nature, God made you alive with Christ. He forgave us all our sins, having canceled the written code, with its regulations, that was against us and that stood opposed to us; he took it away, nailing it to the cross. And having disarmed the powers and authorities, he made a public spectacle of them,* ***triumphing over them by the cross*** *(emphasis mine).*

The cross was not a moment of defeat that was later turned into a victory. The cross was not a failure that was overturned by the resurrection. Paul states it very clearly. This moment, which on the surface looked so much like a defeat, was actually history's greatest moment of triumph. The Promised One, the Hope of Israel, was not taking the failure-inducing death blows of the enemy. No, this was the Messiah's moment of greatest power. The cross was the place where he showed just what he was able to do. No one was taking his life from him. No one was snatching victory out of his hand. No one was undoing all of the gracious good he had done. No one was robbing his followers of their life and their future. He was on the cross because that is exactly where he wanted to be. He hung in torture because he knew that that was precisely what was needed if there ever was going to be any hope for those who would believe in him. He did not hang in defeat. He hung in triumph. That afternoon on Golgotha wasn't a demonstration of the power of the enemies of Christ. Paul declares the opposite. Christ was making a public spectacle of their total lack of power and control. They threw everything they had at him, but they were simply unable to keep him from providing redemption for his people. With all of their twisted justice and angry violence, they could not stop him.

The cross publicly mocked their powerlessness. Jesus hung there because he wanted to. He showed divine love and control as he willingly submitted to ridicule and torture, because he knew what he had come to do, and nothing was going to get in his way. What looked like a crushing defeated was an unadulterated triumph. Things are not always what they seem.

It is quite possible, at the moment of their unfolding, for God's processes of grace to look like the enemy's actions of triumph. The loss of a job, the breakup of a relationship, the struggle with a sickness, the death of a dream, the presence of financial burden, or the failure of an accomplishment can all look like evil has triumphed over good. And if you are only looking for the grace of relief and expecting it to produce the fruit of release, you will tend to credit the enemy with far too much power and tend to think of your Lord as being much too distant and weak. That is why the "things are not always the way they seem" perspective on grace is so important for us.

What we have to do is let the goal of grace define our expectation of what the process of grace will look like. When we do this we will become much better at recognizing the grace of God as it operates in, around, and through us. Paul's words to Titus are helpful for us in this regard, because he sets for Titus the goal of recognizing God's grace:

> *For the grace of God that brings salvation has appeared to all men. It teaches us to say "No" to ungodliness and worldly passions, and to live self-controlled, upright and godly lives in this present age, while we wait for the blessed hope—the glorious appearing of our great God and Savior, Jesus Christ, who gave himself for us to redeem us from all wickedness and to purify for himself a people that are his very own, eager to do what is good (Titus 2:11-14).*

When you are in the middle of a struggle, being pummeled by disappointment or weighted down with regret, it is very hard to focus on the goal of God's grace, but it is vital that we learn to do so. If we are not doing this, our functional definition of life, and more importantly, the goodness of God, will be shaped by the nature of our circumstances. If we are experiencing good things, then we will tend to think that God is good and his grace is near, but if we are going through painful things, we will tend to conclude that God is distant and His grace absent.

Consider what Paul tells Titus that the goal of God's grace is, "a people that are his very own, eager to do what is good." You will never be able to recognize the grace of God in your life, let alone understand the struggles of midlife, without this goal as your interpretive lens. All that God is doing in your life has this one goal in view. His grace has been given so that he would have a people that are in every way eager to do what he says is good. This is the purpose behind all of the grace that daily operates in the life of each of his children. It is a subtle and subversive grace. It is designed once and for all to destroy the culture of self-absorption that seduces and controls us all and is tailored to produce a counterculture of zeal for divine good. It is grace that will take you where you would never have desired to go and produce in you what you could never achieve for yourself. It is grace that will finally take your eyes off your agenda for yourself and put them where they were designed to focus in the beginning—on God's kingdom and his glory. It is when I forsake all the other "goods" that would control me and live under the control of the zeal to be good in his eyes, that my life becomes the happiest and most satisfying. Why? Because I am finally living like I was originally designed to live.

A people who are eager to do what is good is grace's goal, but what is the process? Paul says that the process is purification. You see, my heart is corrupted by other goals. I am not pure in heart. I tend to give my heart to whatever appears will give me comfort, identity, pleasure, meaning, success, or station (all things which we are meant to find in God). So, God's goal is to produce in me perseverant singleness of heart. How does he do this? He does it by demonstrating that nothing outside of him can ever satisfy. So, he will allow my dreams to go sour, or success to sicken in my stomach, or friends to prove unfaithful, or my body to fail me, or my good efforts to show that they were not so good after all. All of this is very painful to go through, but it is not random pain. It is the painful grace of purification, and therefore, a very good thing to go through. Remember that things "are not always what they seem" in view of grace.

You are in the often-painful midlife years. You are beginning to have to deal with aging. You have had to face your regrets. You have had to deal with disappointment. Are you seeing God's grace? Or are you quite skilled at thinking that God is distant and unloving at the very moment when you are a recipient of powerful, heart-and-life-changing grace? It is time to correct your vision so that you would clearly see that your story is a story of grace. Let's consider what God's grace really looks like as it comes to us in the middle of our story. His grace is:

1. ***The grace of disappointment.*** If God is the God of grace, then he must be the author of disappointment as well. Since his grace calls us away from our bondage to ourselves and the resulting slavery to anything that we think will make us happy, it is necessary for God's grace to lead us to moments of intense personal disappointment. He must cause the things that we would put in his place to fail to produce, to fall through our fingers, or to prove unable to satisfy us. He is a jealous Redeemer. He cannot share the allegiance of our hearts. He knows that the things of this earth will not satisfy us. He understands that we were designed for relationship with him, and that this is where the highest of human joys will be found. So, he leads us through the pain of loss, disillusionment, discouragement, and failure, not because he is unable to rescue us from these experiences or because he is unattached and uncaring, but because he loves us so much and is providing a greater rescue.

The problem is that we tend to misunderstand and misinterpret what is happening to us, and we do it for two reasons. First, we all tend to have a comfort and ease agenda for our daily lives. We want life to be safe, predictable, successful, pain-free, and pleasurable. Now there is nothing wrong with the desire for these things, but as sinners, it is very hard for us to hold these in their proper place. Let me say it this way. Perhaps the thing that it is easiest for us to forget is that life in the here and now is a process. It is not designed to be a series of unfolding comfort events. I am somewhere other than where I should be, and God is in the daily process of taking me where I should be. Life with Christ is literally a journey of grace. The journey is a journey of rescue, restoration, and reconciliation. Our problem is that on Tuesday night or Thursday morning we would rather have a predictable day or a comfortable moment than an uncomfortable moment of rescuing grace. Ask yourself, as you stand in the middle of the realities of life, what do you really want from God? Is it grace you that you want, or do you honestly wish things would be a little easier and happier?

But there is another issue here. We often fail to recognize the power of misplaced zeal. We are all zealous for something. Maybe you have a zeal for being physically fit, or you have a zeal for being financially secure, or you have a zeal for making sure that you have good relationships with your grown children, or you are zealous that your house be a beautiful and comfortable place, or you have a zeal for dreams that are still unrealized. The point is that there is some zeal that commands your allegiance, shapes your responses, and controls the way you think about your daily life. Again, no zeal is evil in and of itself, if it does not compete with the one central zeal that God is working to produce in every situation and relationship of our lives. He is working so that everything we desire, think, say, and do would be shaped by a zeal for him and an eagerness always to do what is good in his eyes. This zeal always flows out of a recognition that our lives belong to him. Ask yourself, what zeal organizes your life and commands your allegiance right now?

God's grace is a disappointing grace. It must be because it is a zeal clarifying grace. It is grace that will take away your most precious possessions. It is grace that will take away your most prized accomplishments. It is grace that will take away your most loved relationships, not because God is uncaring and loves to watch you suffer but because he is so incredibly loving that he will not stand idly by and watch our hearts be wooed away by another lover. And what we do not realize is that it is in the middle of a life-controlling zeal for him that we will experience the best of accomplishments, the most beautiful of relationships, and finally find our possessions in their proper place. God's "taking-grace" is not really taking at all; it is giving us what is much, much better. In God's willingness for his grace to lead us to disappointment, he is recognizing how all of us tend not to demand too much from him but are willing to settle for far too little. Well, he is not willing to settle for less; he will unrelentingly work until we are zealous for the one thing for which we were created; him.

Much of the disappointment of midlife is the disappointment of grace. The problem is that, in the middle of all the carnage and the pain, it doesn't feel like you are being showered with love and bathed in grace.

2. ***The grace of regret.*** You do not want to live near a person who is incapable of feeling regret. Yet we tend to do anything we can to deny and avoid regret because it is such a painful thing to go through. We are all quite skilled at taking ourselves off the hook. We come up with creative excuses and logical rationalizations. We deftly shift the blame to another person. We quickly point to the difficulty of circumstances. We rename our failures as misunderstandings, or forgetfulness, or sickness. We are even good at blaming God, saying, "If only____ then we would have." It is so hard for us to see ourselves as we really are and to admit how much everything we do is tainted by sin. It is so hard to confess how much we want our own selfish way. It is hard to face how demanding and vengeful we can be. It is hard to face our laziness and our fickleness. It is difficult to admit that we really do like being served better than serving. It is hard to face that what we do is not forced on us by people and circumstances but rather is the expression of the true thoughts and desires of our own hearts.

We can be so incredibly blind to who we really are and to what we really have done. That is why one of the most important things grace does for us is to help us to see, and one of the things that is most important for us to see clearly is ourselves. Grace allows you to begin to look clearly in and around and back. Grace is an MRI that allows you to be able clearly to look inside of yourself and own what is there. Grace is a history book that allows you to look accurately at what you have done. Grace is a window through which you can look around you and see clearly what you are now doing. Because grace calls you to see, it will lead you to regret. Regret is the beginning of a new and better way. Regret is the first door to real personal change. Regret is a necessary ingredient in the ongoing process of spiritual growth to which God has called you. In a fallen world regret is a gracious and a good thing.

It is hard to stand in the middle of life and look back. It is hard to face the fact that you weren't what you thought you were. It is hard to hear what you said, to watch what you did, and to consider what you decided. It is tempting to wish that you could turn back the clock and be a better person. The clock is turning back, however, and the purpose of regret is not to lock you in your past but to welcome you to a new and better future, one characterized by a new humility, a new joy, and a new zeal. It is a fearful thing for a person to stand in the middle of his or her life with no ability to regret, and it is a sweet grace to see, to regret, and to run to the One who makes all things new.

3. ***The grace of weakness.*** We all tend to be seduced by thoughts of our own invincibility and sufficiency. We all like to think of ourselves as wise and able. We want to think that we understand the issues and are up to the task. We like to think that we have within ourselves the things that we need to do what we need to do. Sure, we can recognize weakness in other people. We can clearly see their deficiencies, and we can point out where they fail to measure up, but it is much harder to see the same things in ourselves. Grace calls us to own weakness and in owning weakness finally to be ready to find true strength. If you think you are strong and able you will never reach for help.

Perhaps this is what much of the struggle of midlife is about. God, in his grace, is ripping back the curtain of our personal delusion and showing us who we really are. He wants us to own up to our weaknesses of body, heart, and behavior, not so we will be paralyzed by our inability, but so that we will reach out to where real strength can be found. It is hard to face your own lack of wisdom. It is painful to see how weak you are in the face of difficulty and temptation. It is difficult to see how ready you are to give up or run away. It is hard to face how you cave in to pressure or quickly grow impatient, and how easy it is for you to get irritated and to be critical. It is difficult to realize how hard it is for you to reserve your opinion or hold your tongue. It is hard to face how quickly you can be gripped by envy and how much you can be motivated by greed. It is painful to recognize how many opportunities to love and to serve you have tended to miss. It is hard to accept how much you personalize what is not personal and turn a moment of ministry into a moment of irritation or anger. It is difficult to face your own tendencies toward materialism and pride and to accept your own weakness, but it is spiritually vital to do so.

Grace is for the needy. Grace is for the weak. Grace is for the foolish. Grace is for those who say, "I am not able and I am not wise." Grace will lead us to places where that is exactly what we have to admit. Grace will put our failure in our face, not as an unloving rebuke but as a welcome to ability and wisdom, free for the taking, purchased for us by the only One who was always able and never unwise. The humble recognition of weakness is not a curse or a condemnation. It is a call to run to the One who alone can make you able. Grace calls you to be weak because grace intends that you be strong. Grace calls you to be a fool in order to be wise. You are never closer to true strength than you are when grace has called you to own your weakness.

Have you been paralyzed by the weaknesses that midlife has revealed? Have you taken the exposure of your weakness as a sentence or as a call? Have you sought to fight weakness and marshal strength, or have you admitted your weakness and run, in new ways, to the Lord, the source and provider of all true strength?

4. *The grace of decay.* We all hate decay. You don't like the fact that the food in the refrigerator will all go bad very soon. You don't like the lines on your face or the gray in your hair. You hate to see the cracking of plaster and the peeling of paint. You are irritated when your appliances quit working and your furniture wears out. You hate the fact that your new car won't smell new for very long and will only properly function for a few years. It is hard to deal with the fact that everything around us is in the process of decay, yet it is very important that we do so.

The lie that physical things are permanent is very dangerous. We all tend to be more hooked by the physical than we are the spiritual, but the physical becomes even more seductive when we look at it as being permanent. So God's grace calls us to be eyewitnesses to the decay of the physical. It is a good thing that you have to witness the decay of your possessions. It is a good thing that you have to witness the decay of the world around you. It is important that you have to witness the decay of your own body. Because as you witness the physical world around you going bad, your values are being divinely clarified. In each of those moments of decay, God is graciously reminding you of what is really worth living for. The physical world is impermanent by its very nature. It is in the process of passing away. It is only God and his Word that will last forever. When you and I attach ourselves and our hope to him, we become part of the one thing that will never pass away.

One of the breathtaking and often discouraging insights of midlife is the recognition of decay. What are you doing with the decay that midlife has forced you to recognize? Are you in a panic? Are you discouraged and in despair? Are you frantically working to keep yourself young and the things around you new? Or have you gotten the point that God's grace focuses your eyes no longer on what is seen but on what is unseen, simply because you now clearly understand that what is seen is temporary but that what is unseen will last forever?

5. ***The grace of defeat.*** In a success and achievement-driven culture, it is hard to accept that success is not always a good thing. The Bible, moreover, does not give a summary endorsement of success, and because it doesn't, it calls us to look at our successes in a very different way. Listen to the words of warning that Moses speaks to the Israelites as they finally enter the land that God had promised them:

> *When you have eaten and are satisfied, praise the LORD your God for the good land he has given you. Be careful that you*

> *do not forget the* Lord *your God, failing to observe his commands, his laws and his decrees that I am giving you this day. Otherwise, when you eat and are satisfied, when you build fine houses and settle down, and when your herds and flocks grow large and your silver and gold increase and all you have is multiplied, then your heart will become proud and you will forget the* Lord *your God, who brought you out of Egypt, out of the land of slavery...You may say to yourself, "My power and the strength of my hands have produced this wealth for me." But remember the* Lord *your God, for it is he who gives you the ability to produce wealth, and so confirms his covenant, which he swore to your forefathers, as it is today.*
> *(Deuteronomy 8:10-14, 17, 18)*

Moses gives Israel one of those "says it all" warnings. Success can be a very dangerous thing because it can make us think that we are far better off than we really are and delude us into believing that what we have is the result of our personal achievement and nothing more. When you believe both of these things you are no longer holding onto the desperateness of your need for God, and that will surely result in no longer seeking him. The issue here is not just that we tend to replace spiritual satisfaction with the satisfaction of physical things, but that material success tends to distort the way we look at ourselves. Success tempts you to think that you are stronger and wiser than you actually are. Wealth tends to stand as a testimony that you have made good decisions and have taken the right action. Power tends to make you think that you are smart and wise. In short, the danger of success is that it tends to elevate our view of ourselves while at the same time tempting us to forget God, who is the real source of any successes we have had.

So, God will let us taste failure, not because he is mean and vengeful, but because he recognizes that we have fallen into success traps and need to be rescued. He will shock us with defeat, so that with a new clarity of personal insight and a newfound gratitude for the Lord, we begin to live with appropriate humility and obedience.

What have you done with your midlife defeats? Have they made you feel like God has ripped you off? Have they caused you to be depressed, playing and replaying what could have been? Have you fought even harder to achieve your dreams? Or have you begun to be more grateful than ever before, now recognizing in a new way that every good gift in your life, every moment of success, and every instance of abundance is a gift from the loving hand of your Lord? Has defeat caused you to once again remember who you are and who he is, and, in remembering, to worship all the more?

6. *The grace of restoration and reconciliation.* God showers his painful and uncomfortable grace on us simply because he is a God of forgiveness. Using the vehicle of circumstances to point out our sin and failure is not an act of condemnation, but the beginning of God's work of forgiveness. He calls us to confess how much we want our own way, how often we replace him, and how much we tend to set our own rules. He works so that we will recognize how uninterested we are in his kingdom and how thoroughly committed we are to the building of our own. He wants us to recognize the subtleties of our own selfishness and greed. He does all of this not to devastate us and walk away, but so that we would confess and recommit ourselves to him. And when we do, he welcomes us with open arms. The cross made forgiveness possible. God offers us more than forgiveness. He offers us reconciliation and restoration as well. It is amazing, but true, that, even in this broken world, relationships that have been horribly torn apart can be restored and things that have been terribly broken can be repaired. In God's forgiving us, he welcomes us to be reconciled to him, and when we are reconciled to him, we can then be reconciled to one another. Families, friendships, and marriages can be restored. People can once again be reconciled and live in loving relationship to one another. Institutions that have been damaged by our sin can be restored again. The painful realizations and confessions of midlife are not meant by God to be the end of the road for you, but rather a welcome to a new and better life. There is hope for you and your family. There is a new day possible for you and your children. You and your spouse can enjoy a new and better love.

God forgives and, in forgiving, he reconciles and restores! Embrace the new life that his grace offers you. See his forgiveness. Be reconciled to him and then look for places to be part of his work of restoration in your life and in relationship to those around you. What God has brought to an end he has done as a necessary step towards a new beginning. Let your sadness give way to excitement. Let your disappointment give way to expectancy. Let your shock at the devastation give way to a joy at the restoration that can follow.

7. ***The grace of sight.*** One of the things that all fallen human beings share is dramatically poor eyesight. We all tend to be blind. The problem is that because our blindness is spiritual and not physical, we all tend to be blind to our blindness. We think that we see quite well, when really we are blind to the things that really matter. We fail to see God even though he is near and active. We fail to see ourselves as we really are, being blind to matters of the heart. We fail to recognize the spiritual war that lies underneath our struggles with situations and relationships. We tend to be blind to God's agenda. We tend to be better at seeing difficulty than we are at recognizing redemption. All of this means that it is a gift of grace to be able to see clearly, because it is not something we are able to do on our own.

Midlife is all about God giving us eyes to see as we have never seen before. He removes the cataracts of our pride, our achievement, our possessions, our physical strength, our righteousness, and our power—all things that can keep us from seeing clearly. What he then gives us are the eyes of grace. With eyes wide open, we begin to see who we really are, who God truly is, and what life really is all about. It is a very good thing to move out into life and to have the eyes of your heart really able to see, because you will be able to live well only if first you are able to see well.

The Crescendo in the Middle

Is midlife, then, a valley of discouragement and disappointment? Is it a dark night of regret and remorse? Is it a crisis of confidence and faith? Is it a war for truth and hope? There is a way in which it is all of these things, for in this time of life I am faced with the fact that many of my dreams will never come true and that many of my efforts have been for naught. In this moment, as I do my personal archeology, I am faced with how far I have fallen below God's standards and my own. I am faced with how many things that I determined to do I never did, and how many things I determined not to do I did repeatedly. During this period I am faced with the loss of my youth, the growing weakness of my body, and the undeniable ticking clock of my aging. Yet, with all of this being true, I am deeply persuaded that midlife is not just a dark valley. No, it is rather a crescendo in the middle of the world's most beautiful piece of music.

I love the experience of sitting in one of the front rows in a great concert hall as the orchestra begins to crescendo. I love the beginning of the rolling of the timpani, the crashing of the cymbals, and the ever louder blare of the brass. It is exciting to hear the crescendo begin to build until it has built to the place where you can actually feel it in your chest. There is a moment when you cease to be audience, and you begin to be carried along with the music as it builds. There is a moment where you forget that you are sitting passively and taking in a performance, and at that moment the crescendo suddenly becomes yours.

Midlife is a crescendo. The music of redemption has been playing in your life for a long time, and even though you didn't know it, it was moving toward this passage. Perhaps you have been lulled to sleep a bit by its familiar themes, unaware that the music was beginning to build. Now you are in the middle of God's redemptive symphony, and the drums are beginning to roll, the cymbals are starting to crash, and the instruments are beginning to blare. This crescendo of redemption needs everything that has gone before it in order to build to this moment. You are in redemption's front row and you are experiencing its music at its most powerful. You are hearing the rolling timpani of God's love, the crashing cymbals of his grace, and the blaring trumpets of his rescue. The music isn't a dirge; it is alive and celebratory. You are in the middle of a crescendo of redemption, and all that has come before has been necessary to get you to this powerful moment of divine grace.

Don't shut your ears to the music. Stop and hear. Your life is not over. You are not imprisoned in your past. This moment of pain is actually a moment of redemptive crescendo, and it is meant to make you hunger for the final crescendo that will roll on for all of eternity. Let the music of redemption get your attention more than the sounds of your regret. Let the song of God's grace command your ears more than your cries of disappointment. Let the crescendo of God's love overwhelm the sad music of your fear. Stop and hear redemption's symphony as it comes to a powerful crescendo right in the middle of your own story.

No one captures this crescendo of God's grace better than Paul does in his letter to the Ephesians:

> *For this reason I kneel before the Father, from whom his whole family in heaven and on earth derives its name. I pray that out of his glorious riches he may strengthen you with power through his Spirit in your inner being, so that Christ may dwell in your hearts through faith. And I pray that you, being rooted and established in love, may have power, together with all the saints, to grasp how wide and long and high and deep is the love of Christ, and to know this love that surpasses knowledge—that you may be filled to the measure of all the fullness of God.*
>
> *Now to him who is able to do immeasurably more than all we ask or imagine, according to his power that is at work within*

us, to him be glory in the church and in Christ Jesus throughout all generations, for ever and ever! Amen (Ephesians 3:14-20).

What is midlife about? Yes, it is about painful regrets, crushing disappointments, and physical aging. It is about decisions, words, and actions you would like to take back. Furthermore, it is about dreams that seemed so good but that now seem like they will never come to be. It is about the loss of youth and the dread of old age. It *is* about these things, but it is about so much more. Midlife is about the glorious riches of God's grace that call me in my lostness to find something better. It is about learning in my weakness to find the inner strength that is mine because the Spirit of power lives inside of me. Midlife is not a time for weakening faith but a time of trial that is designed to leave my faith in Christ stronger than it has ever been. It is a time when I really begin to understand that no other glory (relationships, career, health and physical beauty, or material ease) can compete with the glory of being loved by Christ. Midlife is more than a time of assessment, it is a time of refinement, where the character of God's fullness dwells more and more in me. It is a time when I learn to celebrate the redemptive realities inside of me more than the physical, situational, and relational realities outside of me. The God who is able to do more than I could conceive or imagine in my most brilliant and creative moment actually lives inside of me in power and glory!

Require yourself to stand in the middle of your midlife struggle and listen for the music. Your struggles are the struggles of grace. Listen well, for even though it does not seem like it, you are in the first row of the concert hall of redemption. The timpani of God's love is rolling louder and louder. The cymbal crashes of his grace are growing more rapid. The strings, woodwinds, and brass of his rescue are growing stronger and stronger. It is not the music of defeat and loss. It is the music of victory and celebration. Yes, there are losses to face, but each loss welcomes something better, and each defeat is an invitation to real victory. For your whole life the music has been building to this inevitable crescendo. The redemptive symphony would not be complete without it.

The music will quiet once again but other crescendos will follow, each pointing to the final movement of the great redemptive symphony that will roll on for eternity.

As you stand at the center of this midlife moment, what do you see? What do you hear? If all you see is disappointment and loss, if all you hear are the sad songs of what once was or what could have been, then you need to listen again. Within your loss there is a God of amazing grace to see, and woven together with your sad songs you can hear the celebratory music of redemptive grace. The notes of disappointment, regret, weakness, decay, defeat, restoration, reconciliation, and sight are not parts of another song. They are each a part of God's symphony of grace and redemption.

Even though you are lost in the middle, stop for a moment and listen to the music, for it will inevitably change you.